Hard Times in Paradise
Coos Bay, Oregon, 1850–1986

Victor Mueller
uw

Hard Times in Paradise
Coos Bay, Oregon, 1850–1986

WILLIAM G. ROBBINS

University of Washington Press
Seattle and London

Library of Congress Cataloging-in-Publication Data

Robbins, William G., 1935–
  Hard times in paradise, Coos Bay, Oregon.
  Includes index.
  1. Lumber trade—Oregon—Coos Bay—History.
2. Logging—Oregon—Coos Bay—History. 3. Loggers—
Oregon—Coos Bay—History. 4. Coos Bay (Or.)—History.
I. Title.
HD9758.C6R63 1988   338.1'7498'0979523   87–37180
ISBN 0-295-96616-5
ISBN 0-295-96617-3 (pbk.)

For Karla Brewer Robbins

"We will sing one song."
Joe Hill

Contents

Illustrations

Preface

This is a story about a small cluster of timber-dependent settlements on the southern Oregon coast. It describes a people and the forest resource that served as the staple for their survival. The study uses documentary and oral sources to recreate the social atmosphere and economic conditions that shaped people's lives. These communities developed in concert with other timber-dependent enclaves on the North Pacific Coast and experienced most of the social, economic, and technological shifts in the lumber industry—from skid roads to steam donkeys and diesel-powered yarding machines, from logging camps to permanent communities, and from bustling centers of industrial activity to the stark and idle mills of the present.

The book will assess the circumstances that attracted people to Coos Bay and the extent to which their expectations were realized or denied. Because the economy was always heavily dependent on logging and lumbering, the study will examine the effects of market forces on work life in the logging camps and mills; it will inquire into the changing ethnic mix of the labor force; it will look at the influence of technological innovations (e.g., the introduction of the steam donkey, gasoline-powered vehicles, and the chain saw) on workers and the work environment; and finally it will outline the important industrial changes that took place in the size and scope of operation and capital outlay in the twentieth century. The first part of this account relies on documentary records: census and tax reports, personal reminiscences, local histories, biographies, and newspapers.

Documentary sources also provide structure for the remainder of the study. But the oral interview, wherever possible, is used in addition to traditional sources to explain the cultural and working world of those communities—their sense of shared experience and cohesiveness (or lack of it), and the influences that new technologies imposed on laboring people and their work place. The interviews embrace a broad spectrum of the community: loggers, mill hands, riverboatmen, and their families; plant owners and managers; small businessmen; a variety of public employees; restaurant workers, counselors; longshoremen; union leaders; and senior citizens.

Although personal experience is the focus of the book, the observations of the people who participated in this study are placed within the context of the national and international currents that deeply

influenced timber-dependent communities like those on the southern
Oregon coast. Those forest settlements shared much in common with
other centers of lumbering activity in North America and in other
parts of the world. A forester who has studied the Tasmanian wood-
products industry remarked about the introduction for this book: "I
could have changed a few names and called it an Australian study
writ large!"[1] That remark underscores the integrated nature of the
forest products world and its effect on the communities that evolved
around the centers of wood manufacturing.

Acknowledgments

This book marks the end of a literary odyssey that has taken me through two earlier inquiries into the broader meaning of the politics and economics of lumbering and forestry in the United States. Those studies provided the background for the present work, an investigation of the relationship between the once magnificent timber stands in southwestern Oregon and the people who have depended on those resources for their livelihood. I wrote most of the manuscript in the midst of an epidemic of plywood and sawmill closures in the Pacific Northwest, an industrial "shake-out" that extends to this writing. Friends and neighbors who have suffered the brunt of that hardship—and the people that I interviewed in the Coos Bay area—have contributed to the focus and direction of this study.

Fred Pfeil first suggested the idea for this undertaking. But that early cooperative venture ended when each of us took leave from Oregon State University and Fred eventually accepted a teaching position elsewhere. Although this would have been a much different book had we continued our association, it still bears the mark of Fred's imaginative and perceptive mind.

Stephen Dow Beckham, a native of Coos Bay, provided some of my earliest contacts for interviews. Nathan Douthit also suggested potential interviewees and guided me to valuable sources in the Southwest Oregon Community College Library. Both have written extensively about the southern Oregon coast, and hence I am grateful for their counsel and guidance. Elaine and George Case were generous in suggesting contacts and in offering their observations about life in the Coos country. Emigres from Arkansas and Texas, Elaine and George also offered the warmth of their home, good food and wine, and delightful story telling. The photo portraits in this book testify to George's skills with a camera.

Others who appear in the following pages taught me more than they realize. From them I learned about life in the logging camps; the extensive water-borne environment on the southern Oregon coast; technological change in the woods and its effect on workers; the realities of being a longshoreman, both before and after unionization; the social trauma of unemployment and poverty; and a myriad of events and details that shaped and directed daily life. Among the many people interviewed, I am especially indebted to Eleanor Anderson, Don Baldwin, Curt Beckham, Dow Beckham, Florence Berg, Bill Brainard, Shannon Chamness, Garnett Johnson, Pete Kromminga, Jerry Lantto, Paula Laurilla, R. J. "Chappie" McCarthy, Bill McKenna, Jeff Manley, David Mickelson, Jerry Phillips, Charles Reigard, Dorotha Richardson, Chris Short, Wylie Smith, Forrest Taylor, Valerie Taylor, Cliff Thorwald, Harold "Cardy" Walton, Eugene Wechter, and Lionel Youst.

Over the last four years I have presented some of the material in this book at professional meetings and select portions have also appeared in *Journal of the West, Pacific Northwest Quarterly,* and *Western Historical Quarterly.* In those forums I have benefited from the advice of Richard Maxwell Brown, Robert E. Burke, Joe Conlin, Tom Cox, Hugh Lovin, Charles Peterson, Al Runte, Carlos Schwantes, and Tom White. Others whose works have influenced this study include John Dargavel, a forester at Australian National University at Canberra, and Patricia Marchak, a sociologist at the University of British Columbia.

I express my gratitude to the National Endowment for the Humanities for a College Teaching Fellowship for 1983–84 and to the American Association of State and Local History for a grant-in-aid for the same period. As usual, the Oregon State University Library, the Department of History, and the university's Research Office provided generous support.

An ongoing dialogue with a few scholar-friends has continued to sharpen my perception and understanding of the workings of market capitalism in the American West. My special appreciation goes to Ivan Doig, David Horowitz, Mike Malone, Spencer Olin, Carlos Schwantes, William Appleman Williams, and Donald Worster.

Finally, I am grateful to Julidta Tarver, Managing Editor at the University of Washington Press, for her kind cooperation, and to Lane Morgan for her skilled editorial work.

Hard Times in Paradise
Coos Bay, Oregon, 1850–1986

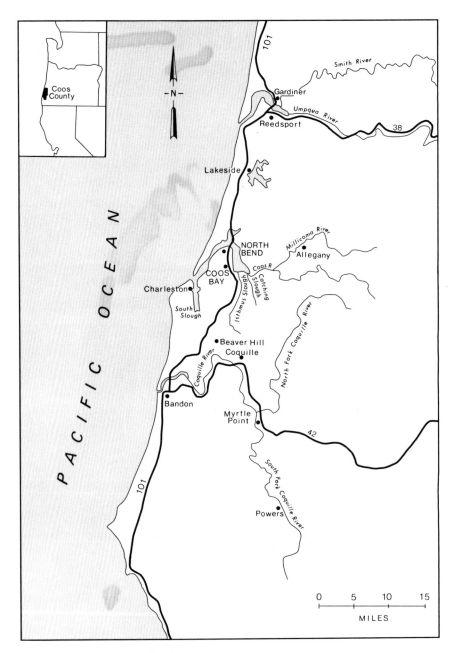

MAP 1. Coos County, Oregon

Introduction

To hell with love of country. I compete for myself. People say I should be running for a gold medal for the old red, white, and blue and all that bull, but it's not gonna be that way. I'm the one who has made all the sacrifices. Those are my American records.

Steve Prefontaine (1975)

The Coos Bay district on the southern Oregon coast is a unique geographic region in one significant respect—it represented the last frontier for a migrating logging and lumbering industry that had its beginnings in the great white pine forests of New England. Since the days of the colonial mast trade, the timbered wealth of the continent has provided the basic raw material for empire building, and it has served as the centerpiece for the commercial and industrial expansion of American capitalism. Products from the forest were as important to seventeenth-century New England shipbuilders as they were to the California home-construction industry after the Second World War.

Operating within a laissez-faire ideological framework, lumbermen were part of the dynamic of an American capitalism that produced a mercurial economic environment of overproduction and cutthroat business competition. Virtually unnoticed in the headlong quest for profits—at least at the time—were the social costs in eroded soils, cutover forestland, tax delinquency, and decaying and impoverished communities. Those insecurities and hardships have persisted, visiting every center of lumbering activity—the river-born mill towns of New England, the sawdust hamlets like Saginaw and Muskegon in the Great Lakes states, the longleaf pine manufacturing centers along the gulf plain, and finally the communities of the Douglas fir region on the North Pacific slope.

That volatile economic world bestowed short-range advantage and opportunity on a mobile work force and then exacted a heavy toll in human misery when the market failed or the investor moved on to new or more profitable sources of wealth. For more than 150 years, the lumber and forest products industry has provided a prime example of migrating capital, rapid liquidation of resources, and boom-and-bust cycles for towns dependent on the forest bounty. That story has a contemporary ring: when the long shadow of want and hardship settled on many of those communities in the 1980s, there were no virgin timber stands beckoning beyond the squeal of the yarding machine; to make matters more difficult, increasingly mechanized and capital-intensive operations are diminishing the size of the forest industry work force.

The lumber trade has left its mark on communities from the Atlantic to the Pacific shores of North America. Lumber entrepreneurs flourished in a culture that provided few restraints beyond the market. Theirs was a world that placed little value on forestry principles that would contribute to economically stable communities. With few exceptions, the industry pursued cut-and-run practices well into the twentieth century and on every successive logging frontier.

Coos Bay is a semi-enclosed body of water that offers meandering access to the ocean and is located midway between the Strait of Juan de Fuca and San Francisco Bay. The estuary is, in truth, an elongated series of sloughs and tidewater streams where salt and fresh water mix, with tidal action normally causing a slow drift to seaward. The drainage tributary to Coos Bay—approximately 825 square miles—embraces Oregon's rugged Coast Range, which runs north and south in a series of sharply defined valleys and narrow canyons.

A mild, marine climate, with 80 percent of the precipitation occurring between October and March, provides abundant moisture for one of the fastest-growing forest environments in the world. When Indian people dominated the area, Douglas fir, Port Orford white cedar, and Sitka spruce reached water's edge. Tributary rivers and creeks teemed with salmon and trout, and the estuary supported a large variety and an abundant quantity of shellfish and other marine life. To add to the area's attractive bounty for people who would come from another cultural world, quantities of low grade coal lay beneath the hills adjacent to the bay.

Until white fur trappers and traders began penetrating the southern Oregon coast in the early 1850s, the native people—the Coos, a Penutian-speaking group—inhabited the area around the bay and lived well and peacefully. Adjusting to the rhythms of the natural world and its changing seasons, they skillfully utilized both the estuarine and land resources to provide a rich variety of food and material goods. For centuries they lived in that relatively stable and productive environment, perpetuating certain species and discouraging others. The white newcomers, who first established homes on the bay in the 1850s, eventually altered those ecosystems, and destroyed much of the cultural complex of the native people.

For the past 130 years the Coos Bay area has been the scene of logging and lumber manufacturing, shipbuilding, coal mining, farming, and fishing. All of those activities have shaped the region, but the men and women who worked in the logging camps and mills have been the mainstay of the economy. Their labor made the Coos Bay region one of the leading forest-products manufacturing centers in the world by the middle of the twentieth century. The forested slopes tributary to the bay provided the principal resource and the economic base for the immigrant workers who came to the area. That 87 percent of the region is still forestland today emphasizes the significance of the resource to the southwestern Oregon economy.

The opening of the vast timber stands on the North Pacific slope—to speculation, the establishment of mill towns, and the liquidation of old growth forests—required a large work force to carry on the back-breaking and dangerous tasks of felling the giant trees, moving the logs to mills, sawing them into lumber, and finally shipping the finished product to market. Those men and women produced and delivered the goods, built the towns, established community institutions, and then suffered when the resource was liquidated and the investment capitalist had moved on to more lucrative fields.

A combination of factors attracted people to each new forest frontier, most of them values and attitudes associated with the economic culture of capitalism. Boosters for land companies, spokesmen for transcontinental railroads, and proponents of frontier expansion all described the land to the west as a New Eden, an environment lush with promise and offering the good life to those willing to pull up stakes and head toward the sunset. In the timbered region along the North Pacific Coast, the abundant stands of old growth forests attracted both capital and technical expertise—the two vital forces required to transform the resource into commodities to be shipped to distant markets. Whether they were lumber entrepreneurs, local businesspeople, mill workers, or loggers, they were part of a culture that sought to turn nature's bounty to advantage.

And there were few doubters in the lot. Most believed that those massive timber stands would last forever. In the days when the cedar, spruce, and Douglas fir grew to water's edge, logging operators harvested the forest with reckless abandon, using hurried and careless practices that wrought destruction on both humans and the environment. To magnify the problems of that wasteful and troubled world, periodically depressed lumber prices and cutthroat competition made it profitable to take only the best logs out of the woods. There was no consideration to logging selectively, no thought to the environmental consequences of logging practices, and very little attention to reforesting cutover areas. Lumbermen, bending to the will of an unstable

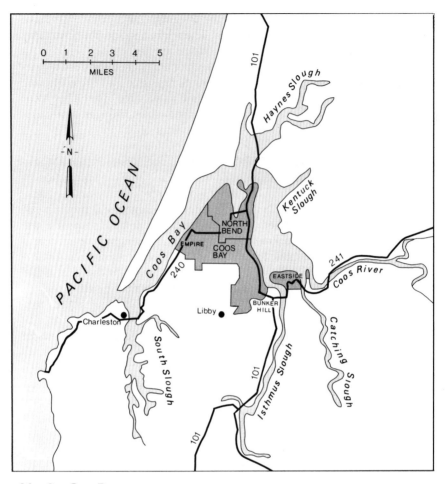

MAP 2.   Coos Bay area

market, carelessly exploited the region's timber abundance in their
quest for profits. Those practices were not conducive to a humane
social environment.

The pattern of exploitation was set before the lumbermen arrived.
From the time the first European venturers sought out the riches of
the Northwest Coast 200 years ago, the region has been a centerpiece
in the dreams of profit seekers. Its wealth of marine and land mam-
mals offered lucrative trade opportunities to ship captains who
plumbed the coastal bays and harbors to exchange trade goods with

native people for furs. Those sea otter pelts, bartered in Chinese ports for silks and spices and other goods of value to London and Boston buyers, reaped great rewards for the merchants who underwrote the voyages. More important, that pattern of exchange established a precedent for the future—the region's largely extractive economy would continue to attract outside capital, and much of the wealth gleaned through its exploitation would eventually make its way to metropolitan centers beyond the region.

Capital first created communities in the Pacific Northwest and then milked them of profits when the region's resources were sold in domestic and world markets. When the first white communities were established in the Northwest, local and San Francisco capital financed much of their commercial activity. By the turn of the century that regional autonomy began to erode as eastern and foreign banking interests invested in transportation and resource development.

The extension of transcontinental railroads to the Northwest represents one symbol of that change. Agents of foreign and eastern capital followed the rail lines to the region as entrepreneurs poured money into coastal and Columbia River canneries, and funded the heavy equipment shipped to Idaho mines. To add to that speculative frenzy, Chicago, Wisconsin, Minnesota, and southern lumber capitalists purchased timber and constructed milling facilities along the Pacific Coast.

The Pacific Northwest took on the aura of an investor's frontier as capitalists from far points of the continent sought to tap the region's abundant resources. And the culture that spurred them on offered few words of caution. In western Washington, Seattle, Tacoma, and Olympia mushroomed into metropolitan centers within two decades while the land beyond—adjacent to Puget Sound and the Grays Harbor area—was becoming a vast stump farm as lumbermen turned the forest bounty to profit.

The aspirations of an expansive market economy and its business institutions set those forces in motion and moved people to action. Because that cultural ethos defined all resources as commodities, waterways and estuaries, timbered slopes, and even the resident labor force were valued chiefly for their potential convertibility to market items. Most communities in the Pacific Northwest, however, were not beneficiaries of that process; large capital organizations located at centers of economic power have been able to dominate the less-populated areas where most of the natural wealth lies. Because financial houses and banking institutions—at first in San Francisco, later in St. Paul, and Chicago—provided the capital to exploit those resources, most of the profits were siphoned away. Nowhere is that more evident than in the towns of the timbered back country where residents reaped the social costs in cutover forestlands, eroded mountainsides, and debris-filled and silt-laden waterways.

The movement of capital has become more sophisticated in the last half of the twentieth century as the Pacific Northwest economy has become more closely integrated at the national and international level. The charge can no longer be made that the region's wealth is being drained to the corporate coffers in the East. Today multinational forest products firms, some of them with central offices in the Pacific Northwest, as a matter of common practice shift their investment money to those arenas with the potential for highest return—the logging of southern timberlands, the construction of condominiums and resorts, the building of ocean-ranching facilities, or establishing indoor hydroponic lettuce farms in the Northeast. Meanwhile, the communities creating that surplus capital suffer the consequences. Which is to say that resource capital in the United States (and worldwide) has become increasingly mobile, and investment decisions under those circumstances have been made without community health and stability as a consideration.

The old tale of eastern advantage in the exploitation of western resources and the calculated investments of the multinationals in our present age is only part of the story. More important from a human perspective is what that relation has meant to communities dependent on single industries. That question brings us to the settlements on Coos Bay—communities significantly influenced by investment decisions made beyond the isolated southern Oregon coast.

This book is about the people who made Coos Bay, who forged a culture and tradition not unlike that of other timber-dependent towns in the region. But the bay communities were different in one significant respect; they were the last of the Pacific coastal lumbering centers where old-growth timber provided the raw material for plywood, sawmill, and pulp manufacturing. While other forested areas in the Douglas fir region began to decline as early as the 1930s, the mills on Coos Bay operated three shifts a day into the 1970s.

The people who came to the southern Oregon coast to earn a living and make their homes were part of a broader economic network associated with the Pacific lumber trade. The health and success of that business largely determined the well-being of the south coast communities. In the early years coal mining, and later dairying and fishing, were important ways of making a living. But for most of the period, the logging and lumbering trade was the mainstay of the local economy. The men and women interviewed for this study recognize that fact, and for better or worse, most of them believe that forest products will continue to be the primary economic activity on the bay.

This study is framed in the presence of an area that is experiencing the social stresses associated with high unemployment—a declining population, increased alcoholism, spousal and child abuse, and foreclosures on homes and other personal belongings. The virtually closed housing market in the bay communities of the late 1970s has come full circle; vacant houses, real estate, and for sale signs abound and building construction is at a virtual standstill. Few people are optimistic that conditions will improve in the forseeable future. Increased automation in the mills and a drastically reduced supply of privately owned timber have cast gloom over the future.

U.S. Highway 101 passes through the manufacturing centers of Coos Bay and North Bend. For the tourist, the drive along the industrial waterfront presents a sharp contrast to the windswept vistas of the nearby ocean beaches. For travelers approaching from the California end, the graying, rusting, and silent plywood plants and sawmills stand as mute reminders that not all is well here.

The City of Coos Bay (population 15,000), once a bustling center of forest products manufacturing, does not have a fully operational mill at this writing. Only in North Bend (population 9,000), where the giant Weyerhaeuser plant sprawls along the bay front, is there a sign of industrial activity. Here one sees ships loaded with wood chips and unprocessed logs bound for Asian markets, symbols of the extractive character of the regional economy. The Coos Bay area, proclaimed as the lumber capital of the world following the Second World War, is still dependent on a single industry and, for much of its income, on a single company.

While the communities have brought certain advantages to residents when the lumber market was strong, they have exacted a heavy toll during periods of depression, when building activity was down, or on the occasion of protracted waterfront and sawmill labor disputes. Absentee ownership and management also have influenced the spirit of the settlements and contributed to an element of bitterness, particularly in the wake of the plant closures of recent years. But job instability was inherent to an industry where seasonal layoffs, periodic shutdowns, and business failures were regular occurrences.

When economic disaster struck lumber towns in the Pacific Northwest in the early 1980s, seven out of ten jobs on Coos Bay were timber related, a higher percentage than in any comparable area in Oregon. A Portland *Oregonian* writer observed in November 1981 that Coos Bay provided "a cautionary example" for the entire Douglas fir region. The Eugene *Register-Guard,* serving Oregon's depressed upper Willamette Valley, agreed: "Coos Bay's undiversified economy troops in lockstep with the timber industry. For the past two years, the march has been steadily downhill."[1]

Today the giant Weyerhaeuser complex, after forcing concessions in wages and benefits from its work force, operates with a sharply reduced crew; every other mill on the bay has either closed or has reorganized under a different corporate title. The new firms are nonunion and employ only a few people. Paula Laurilla, who still operates the tavern and rooming house her father established in 1913, worries about the future: "This is the worse since 1932 and '33. We've had strikes and shutdowns before. But you always knew things were going to be settled and that there would be an end to it. Now you wonder how it's going to turn out."[2]

Other people are asking similar questions while the newspaper and the local development agencies pursue new industries for the area. Although Laurilla and many of the older generation in the community still think in terms of the past, events of the last few years have largely destroyed that world.

But Oregon's south-coast residents are a tough, gritty, persistent people, unafraid of hard and dangerous work and always ready "to go down the road" when the boss became overbearing or there were rumors of a better job in the next camp. The late Steve Prefontaine, a graduate of Marshfield High School in Coos Bay and America's premier distance runner at the time of his death in 1975, typifies that tenacious spirit. "His racing style," a *Life* magazine article reported in 1972, "reflected the tough, elemental life of Coos Bay, Oregon, the logging town where he grew up." "Pre," as he was known worldwide, was a short, cocky maverick who bucked the Amateur Athletic Union establishment in the United States. "To hell with love of country," Pre told a sports writer two months before he died, "I compete for myself."[3]

Pre's spirit of toughness and sturdy independence lives on in the logging towns of the Coos country. The difficult times of the present mirror a historical tradition that has involved struggle, sacrifice, and a willingness to "stick it out." Shannon Chamness, who lost a good-paying job when Georgia-Pacific closed its mill in 1979, describes herself as a survivor and more fortunate than some of her neighbors—even though she holds two jobs, one of them a minimum-wage position in a local donut shop. But experience has taught her to be cautious about where she works: "I did not want to be back into woods products, because I did not want to be right back in the same vicious cycle again."[4]

CHAPTER 1

Poor Man's Paradise

"Coos Bay as the place is called, is shut out from the rest of the world, and forced more or less to rely on its own resources."

Marjory K. Cowan, 1913[1]

As the imperial center of a nineteenth-century western trading network that extended the length of the Pacific Coast, the city of San Francisco developed a voracious appetite for a great variety of goods and raw materials. Ships carrying New England textiles, British manufactures, and silks, spices, and fineries from the Orient entered the rapidly expanding commercial port. In many respects San Francisco was an entrepreneur's dream—at least for the capitalists who provided goods and services to the city and who outfitted and supplied the gold seekers who swarmed through the gullies and hills of the hinterland. To transform that community of tents into a permanent settlement and to provide structural materials for the camps and mines in the interior also required vast amounts of timber. In answer to that need, a thriving lumber trade developed in the 1850s.

Only the gamblers, the bold and venturesome—and those with capital—made the effort. Frederick Pope and William Talbot, whose families had been in the lumber business since the American Revolution, sailed a shipload of lumber from their native Maine to San Francisco to test the possibilities of establishing a regular trade. Although the long ocean voyage around Cape Horn was discouraging, the lush forests along the North Pacific Coast quickly suggested other possibilities to the enterprising Yankees. Sailing north in 1852, Pope and Talbot built a sawmill at Port Gamble on Hood Canal near Puget Sound and thereby established one of the first satellite lumbering towns to serve the California trade. Similar circumstances attracted the first entrepreneurs to the Coos Bay estuary on the southern Oregon coast.[2]

Ties of capital, trade, and culture linked communities like Port Gamble and the early Coos Bay settlements to the economic network extending outward from San Francisco. Coos Bay's geographic isolation from the main centers of population and commerce in Oregon enhanced its link with California's preeminent metropolis. Henry Heaton Luse and Asa Mead Simpson, early sawmillers on the bay, established a sea-oriented traffic in lumber by the late 1850s that set a pattern for regional trade that lasted into the 1960s.[3] And we should not be surprised by their attraction to the area.

The huge timber stands and other natural attributes along the southern Oregon coast impressed newcomers. A visitor to the bay observed in 1853 that the harbor was "certain and safe," and that the area abounded with coal and timber of the finest quality in Oregon. "As a commercial point and depot, it is second only to San Francisco on the Pacific coast." Another traveler that year reported "an abundance of the white cedar timber, well calculated for lumber." With its "extensive coal banks," the visitor reflected, "Koose Bay" was destined to be "a place of great importance."[4]

The first crude lumber manufacturing set up on Coos Bay was a two-man whip-saw mill in 1853. Daniel Giles, age seventeen and robust with energy, pulled one end of the saw: "Being young and stout, I stayed with it for a while and when I wanted to quit and go to mining, they insisted on me taking a third interest in the business. We sawed all winter." The same year, a water-powered Muley sash saw began operating on the Coquille River, a short distance to the south of Coos Bay. George B. Wasson, a native of New Brunswick who came to California to search for gold, was part owner of the operation and used oxen to haul logs to the mill.[5] But the productive capacity of those water- and human-powered operations was limited. It was left to others, especially the steam-powered Luse and Simpson operations on Coos Bay, to capitalize on the California lumber market.

For the first thirty years of white settlement, coal and lumber exports sustained the area's economy and established patterns of contact with the outside world. California entrepreneurs provided the capital for investments in mining ventures, and although a few local businessmen engaged in those activities in the early years, San Francisco capitalists dominated the Coos Bay economy by 1875.[6] From an early period, therefore, outside investors controlled the exploitation of resources on the south coast.

Asa Mead Simpson, a California lumberman and shipbuilder, set the tone for the colonial link between the Coos country and San Francisco Bay. During the 1850s Simpson established sawmills in several coastal estuaries, including the small operation on Coos Bay in 1856. That sawmill dominated the local economy for several decades and was part of a chain of mills that extended from Santa Cruz to Puget Sound. In addition to retail outlets in California, Simpson operated a shipyard on Coos Bay that turned out an impressive number of cargo ships. By the 1880s the Simpson plants along the coast employed about 500 workers, turning those isolated areas into extractive tributaries for the urban markets in California.[7]

Investment capital and marketing outlets spelled the difference between success or failure for those early sawmilling ventures on Coos Bay. The same could be said for the entrepreneurs who wanted to tap the rich veins of coal that underlay the surrounding hills. But for the most part speculation in coal proved to be a great chimera—even for investors from outside the region. The quality of the coal was poor (high moisture and low sulfur content), and exports provided an unsteady market at best. Although the industry attracted capital and laborers to the bay, the value of coal shipments ranked behind lumber by the early 1880s.[8]

Like the early sawmilling activities, the first coal-mining ventures were small operations and employed only a few people. Moreover, Coos Bay was only one of several places along the Pacific Coast where coal was discovered. Patrick Flanagan, an Irish immigrant with capital and credit, successfully mined coal in the Coos Bay area for thirty years. According to his son, who was born in one of the mining towns, "promoters would organize companies, sell stock, or induce men to 'jump into the venture' without adequate investigation." They spent money recklessly for buildings, bunkers, ships, tools, and equipment "only to find in too many cases and too late that the vein was broken, or the coal was of an inferior grade, or mining conditions were unfavorable."[9] Although a few investors profited, the freight charges to San Francisco ruined many of those who speculated in coal.

To establish the business on a regular basis an operator needed capital, transportation facilities, and marketing outlets. And luck and ingenuity! Patrick Flanagan lived at his Libby mine and kept a watchful eye on its activities; his partner operated the company store and took measures to assure that paychecks were recycled on the spot. The Libby operation had storage facilities on Coos Bay, marketing outlets in San Francisco, and at the peak of its operation in the 1880s, employed 350 workers.[10]

But that locally owned operation passed into the hands of nonresidents when Patrick Flanagan and his partner sold the Libby mine to San Francisco investors in the mid-1880s. Stephen Beckham, who has written extensively about his native Coos Bay, concludes that coal mining "by the 1870s was definitely in the control of men of means." Nor were the entrepreneurs permanent residents of the bay, "for the capital that moved into the region to develop new mining prospects

was almost exclusively an outgrowth of California's booming economic colonialism of the Pacific slope."[11]

But those mining and sawmilling ventures helped line the shores of
the Coos estuary with family dwellings and the makings of small
communities. Although the record is spare, the annual coal shipments across the Coos Bay bar fluctuated wildly from one year to the
next—a fact that did not bode well for the men and women who
depended on coal exports for their livelihood. The 44,857 short tons
exported in 1874 fell to 16,000 tons in 1883 and did not surpass the
1874 figure until 1886, when operators shipped 51,595 tons. Thereafter, outbound shipping statistics show the same dramatic annual
shifts until 1905, when coal exports from the bay began a steady
decline, a reflection of the increasing use of fuel oil in the larger
population centers.[12]

Even when the San Francisco market was strong, the demand for
coal was seasonal. The brisk fall and winter trade normally tapered off
when the warm, dry weather returned. The problem for workers on
the production end, therefore, was surviving the off seasons. Some
miners used the summer months to establish homesteads, to plant
gardens and subsistence crops, and to raise small herds of livestock.
One farmer-miner reported that he and his neighbor "worked at the
coal mines during the winter and improved our places in summer.
Our wives lived together during our absence, that being convenient,
as our farms joined."[13] Area sawmills and logging camps provided
employment for others, and for the single men who were always a
sizable percentage of frontier populations, there was the "freedom" to
move on.

Both natural and market-oriented disasters made life uncertain for
people who depended on the coal industry. A storm-tossed winter
ocean and the always risky crossing of the Coos Bay bar contributed to
numerous shipwrecks. But at times the market was even more treacherous. Foreign ships stopping in San Francisco and Oakland for
cargoes of wheat in 1885 unloaded several tons of ballast in the form
of coal. As a consequence, outward-bound coal from Coos Bay
dropped by more than 50 percent. On those occasions, small but well-
cultivated gardens, cattle and sheep, and chickens liberally supplemented with game animals and fish, meant the difference between
starvation and survival.[14]

Although lumber shipments regularly surpassed coal during the
nineteenth century, local newspapers showed an intense interest in
coal. That was particularly so when the lumber market was down. But
nothing could rescue the fledgling coal industry, not even the

rumored investments of the James J. Hill railroad interests in the Libby operation. In 1909 the Coos Bay *News* repeated an old refrain— that the coal market was dull and that the Libby mine was "generally closed between spring and fall." San Francisco, it warned, "is only a winter market at best, and since oil is being used so extensively the demand for coal, even in winter, has not increased" with the population.[15]

The Libby operation closed for a few years and then reopened in 1912. A local newspaper reported that the town of Libby, which was "quite a deserted place" after the mine closed, "is now gathering a new set of inhabitants." A few months later, according to the Coos Bay *Times*, "practically, every house in the place is occupied and the little settlement is taking on its old time activity." But the mine was open for only a short time before the manager ordered the operations closed while he fired "floaters" who were causing "labor troubles."[16] By that time coal mining was only a marginal undertaking, and workers were finding better-paying jobs in the woods and in the local mills.

On the eve of the European war, coal mining on the bay was strictly a local affair and the Libby operation employed only a few men. Other ventures were even less successful, and in at least two instances, workers had to file liens to recover back wages.[17] Although the mines supplied only a small amount of coal to local buyers, the romance with coal continued to provide an illusory dream for promoters, especially when times were difficult. During the Great Depression, the immediate aftermath of the Second World War, and in the wake of the mill closures in the early 1980s, the coal savior surfaced again.

Despite "the apparently exhaustless beds of coal" reported by a writer in 1884, the future of the Coos country was clearly linked to the massive virgin stands of fir, hemlock, spruce, and cedar. Although the writer wondered whether nature "ever concentrated upon so small a section so many and such varied sources of material prosperity," it was the dense coastal forests that gave flight to the imagination (and to outside capital).[18] As lumbermen worked their way toward the end of the pine forests in the Great Lakes states, the future for the North Pacific Coast seemed bright and assured. By the 1870s logging and lumbering in the Coos country was showing signs of expansion.

The Coos Bay *News* observed at the onset of the logging season in 1874 that the streets of Marshfield (the name was changed to Coos Bay in 1944) "were crowded with rough dressed, hearty looking fellows, who wear their pants in their boots." Those loggers, the paper reported, were falling timber and making the three mills on the bay "run to their utmost capacity," an activity that "makes business lively when the boys come to town." According to the *News*, there were about twenty-five logging camps, each employing between eight and a dozen men. Logging operators in search of good work oxen sent camp bosses as far as central Washington to purchase the animals.[19] Loggers used the oxen to haul the huge logs over "skid roads," usually to water's edge, a method unique to the Pacific Northwest.

E. B. Dean and Company, a firm of California-based investors, threatened the supremacy of the Luse and Simpson mills when it purchased a small mill and shipbuilding operation in the hamlet of Marshfield in 1873. The company constructed a new steam-powered plant capable of cutting 50,000 board feet a day, more than twice the combined capacity of the Luse and Simpson mills. E. B. Dean and Company operated nine logging camps by 1874 and began to turn out an impressive number of small ships. At the onset of the 1880s Coos Bay mills had a daily capacity of 100,000 board feet and by mid-decade, the area was an important center of cargo mill production.[20] Those water-oriented outfits produced rough, unfinished lumber that was shipped to finishing plants in established markets like San Francisco.

The cargo mills on Coos Bay gave added emphasis to the region's commercial tie to San Francisco and other California ports. The Portland *Oregonian*, perhaps with a bit of jealousy, referred to Coos Bay early in 1884 as "a part of California." Because its businesses and industries were "made and directed in San Francisco," the journal complained, "their profits with their products go out of state." The Coos Bay *News*, however, saw the matter differently; the problem was the lack of a railroad: "As it is now, all the wealth and trade of Coos Bay towns and people are falling into the hands of the Californians." Two years later the *Oregonian* pointed again to the southerly orientation of Coos County trade and culture. The social and business connections of Oregon's south coast, it noted, "are almost wholly with San Francisco, and carried on by way of the ocean."[21]

One Coos resident was blunt about the California link: "We do all our business and trade there. We don't know anything of Oregon except that our votes are returned and counted in Salem. Otherwise all of our affiliations are with California." Even at the turn of the century the *News* was wary about the pleas of Portland's commercial community. Southern Oregon's trade went to San Francisco, it proclaimed, "and why shouldn't it?" The California metropolis purchased "our lumber and coal, the output of our creameries, salmon, apples, potatoes, and other products." There was more to the San Francisco connection, the *News* pointed out, than ties of loyalty and kinship: "Where a community sells, it will naturally buy."[22] Those early commentaries about California ties became even more significant as the lumber economy of the Coos country expanded in the twentieth century.

Frontier newspapers were uninhibited in extolling the virtues of their communities, and the press in the Coos country was no exception. During one booming summer season, the *News* exulted about the amount of work for "ship and house carpenters, coal miners, sailors, and loggers." Prosperity was so evident in the area that "Coos Bay can be truthfully called the Poor Man's Paradise." The *News* applauded the arrival of new immigrants on the bay: "Coos County is the place for men with means and muscle to come."[23] But most south coast newspapers focused on the abundant resources, healthful climate, and economic potential of the region.

J. W. Bennett, a prominent editor and one of the more articulate (and unrestrained) of the early Coos County promoters, praised western settlement in general in an 1875 editorial:

> Here is a vast wilderness to be subdued, capable of furnishing food, clothing and homes to millions, with grand rivers leading to the sea. . . . Railroads will build and cities will spring up. Oregon commerce will, by the end of the next decade, be found on every sea. Emigration is tending thitherward and thousands will be added to our population yearly, and improvements will keep pace with population.

To encourage settlement, Bennett and others formed a county immigration society to publish brochures and advertise the Coos Bay region in "San Francisco and points east."[24]

Although most news columns emphasized the agricultural and industrial potential of the bay area, an occasional article cautioned readers to be wary of an overweening optimism. The *News* warned on one occasion: "People . . . imbued with the idea that they can pick greenbacks off the huckleberry bushes in Oregon, and that farms ready for the plow are waiting to be homesteaded, have been sadly imposed upon." As the century drew to a close, the *News* counseled newcomers not to expect "to find good agricultural land lying vacant"; if they did, they would be "sadly disappointed." In earlier years it was possible to find good farm land to homestead, "but those days have gone by." The present work force, the *News* remarked, was adequate to supply the demand, and the arrival of more "would only make matters worse."[25] The newspaper pointed to the obvious—that the newcomers of the 1870s and 1880s had taken up most of the valuable farmland in the lowlands adjacent to Coos Bay and in the nearby valley of the Coquille River.

The valleys of this section of Oregon are narrow, and while the rich bottomlands are capable of growing lush grasses, the limited acreage suitable for commercial agriculture was soon occupied. Although the county has supported a small but thriving dairy industry for much of the twentieth century, logging and lumbering has been the primary source of income for most people. Without question it was the immense stands of fir and cedar that drew capital and labor to the area. Or, as one resident put it, logging and mill work enabled a family to support a small farm.[26]

For the entrepreneurial minded, however, the Coos country needed more—prosperous and sturdy citizens of "means" and above all, capital. At the onset of the speculative boom in Northwest timberlands in the 1890s, the *News* offered an open invitation to outsiders with money: "For capitalists this country affords opportunities for investment, and for men with good muscle and good habits the inducements are good." The Coos Bay Board of Trade observed that the absence of a railroad had delayed "development of this favored section," but the promised construction of rail lines would remedy that situation, "and all who desire investment, whether in mining, lumbering, mercantile business or otherwise, will find this a good field."[27]

Meanwhile, rudimentary and crude transportation and competition from mills with easy access to timber limited production on the bay. Although the county's population doubled each decade, it was still only 10,000 by the turn of the century. Isolated from the main arterials of trade in Oregon and without a rail connection to the interior, Coos Bay looked to the sea and Pacific markets for its livelihood.[28] But when lumber and coal operators began to use short-line railroads to haul goods to water's edge—facilities that became increasingly important as loggers exhausted the timber along the estuary—the pace of change quickened.

The importance of oceanic routes of travel also linked mill operators and workers to market conditions and economic cycles of a wider world. From the very beginning, therefore, the health of the regional economy was closely tied to price fluctuations and business activities in far places. The high interest rates and the decline in construction activity of the early 1980s are merely the most recent of the destabilizing influences that have affected timber-dependent communities like those on Coos Bay. When lumber orders slowed along the Pacific Coast in 1879, mill owners laid off employees and curtailed operations. To counter those conditions, coastal lumbermen, including the two largest in the Coos Bay area, formed an association to fix prices and to cooperate in marketing.[29] Although that early cartel-like effort did not succeed, newspaper editors and workers on the southern Oregon coast reacted sharply.

San Francisco capitalists, an editor warned, were "evil birds of omen," perched "upon the manacled and prostrate industries of our country." The Simpson company was "denuding" the timber resources of the bay "to enrich a foreign city" and forcing "store pay" upon workers for "wages honestly earned." One letter writer accused an employer of "low, oppressive meanness" when the operator reduced wages and hours to counter a slumping California market. Because the company store charged high prices for its goods, the correspondent added, "the possibility of a man with a family earning anything more than a bare subsistence is out of the question."[30]

Activities and events far beyond western Oregon continued to influence the lumber economy on the Pacific Coast. The rapid growth of the Midwest and the construction of hundreds of miles of railroad had consumed huge quantities of timber from the Great Lakes pineries. The *Oregonian* reported in 1882 "that the lumber supply of the Lakes States . . . can hold out only a few years longer." Because southern timber was "of an inferior kind," lumbermen would turn to western Oregon and Washington, the "last great supply of first-rate timber." Two years later the Portland *Telegram* also observed that the timberlands in Michigan, Wisconsin, and Minnesota were showing "signs of exhaustion." Whereas lumbermen harvested only the choicest pines in the past "and left the remainder to be devastated by fire," now they were taking it all. The *Telegram* saw a parallel: At the present rate of production and "the unwarrantable waste in this country, how long will it be before we shall be making a similar report?"[31]

Those undoubtedly were two of the earliest publications on the Pacific edge of the continent to bring attention to the migratory nature of the lumber industry. Although George Perkins Marsh influenced a whole generation of scientific thinking when he published *Man and Nature* in 1864, the work of Franklin B. Hough, the federal government's first forestry officer who first became aware of the phenomenon of forest depletion when he assisted with the decennial census of 1870, was more significant to an understanding of forestry in the United States. Hough recognized both the decline in Northeastern lumber production and the finite nature of the nation's timber resource. In his famous address to the American Association for the Advancement of Science in 1873, "On the Duty of Governments in the Preservation of Forests," he emphasized the "economical value of timber" and "our absolute dependence on it."[32] Hough's antidote to overcutting was federal action to encourage better forest practices.

Published literature about forest conditions in the United States multiplied. Charles Sprague Sargent, a participant in forestry conferences and a member of several prestigious scientific societies, published his monumental *Report on the Forests of North America* in 1884. Sargent's study, the first significant survey of forestland in the United States, called attention to the rapidly diminishing white pine stands in the Great Lakes states.[33] His was also a reminder that the heedless liquidation of timberland was harmful to the environment and to the communities dependent on the resource.

A broad spectrum of the public was aware by the 1890s that the eastern forests were in trouble. National lumber production had nearly doubled the previous decade, and competition from substitute building materials still lay in the future. But that tremendous increase in lumber manufacture was taking its toll—the Great Lakes pineries were being cut over to the point that forecasters were predicting the region would no longer be a significant factor in the production of saw timber.

To satisfy the burgeoning industrial markets of the East, lumbermen moved south to the Gulf Plain forests and later westward to the cedar and fir country of the North Pacific slope. Bonanza speculation in southern and western timberland accompanied that shift. Operators backed by outside capital built hundreds of miles of logging railroads in the more accessible Douglas fir country of western Oregon and Washington; at the same time the development of the steam donkey and other technological devices speeded the movement of logs to mills and the finished lumber to market. The Coos Bay country was part of that process; the two largest locally owned plants were sold to outside operators, a move, according to one historian, that "embodied the economic colonialism that characterized so much of Coos Bay's economy."[34]

Speculative interest in the Coos country increased in the 1890s. A railroad line was completed in 1893 that reached twenty-seven miles from Marshfield to Myrtle Point, a small town on the Coquille River. The San Francisco capitalists who funded the railroad intended to build the line to the Umpqua Valley and a connection with one of the transcontinental routes. Although Myrtle Point remained the terminus for more than ten years, that short line penetrated some of the finest timber country on the Pacific Coast. Its principal function was to funnel the huge logs to the mills on Coos Bay. When the Southern Pacific Railroad Company purchased the line in 1905, it gave an added dimension to the colonial nature of the Coos economy.[35]

The health of the sawmilling and shipbuilding industry during those years, as usual, rested on the strength of the market. When the California-based E. B. Dean Company encountered problems with town officials in 1885, the firm simply ordered the construction of a new mill outside the Marshfield town limits. The local newspaper reported numerous "vacant houses . . . on the sawdust," a refrain that became more familiar in the twentieth century when the lumber market entered a long period of turbulence. When another California group, with George K. Porter as president, decided to build a new mill between the towns of North Bend and Marshfield in 1888, the Coos Bay *News* reminded its readers that the improvements were "based not upon a boom, but upon natural resources to justify them. Our timber, so far as our generation is concerned, is inexhaustible." As the spring season wore on, the paper observed increased activity "in logging circles and business on the bay."[36] The future would show that the health of the one depended on the other.

By the 1890s Californians dominated the Coos Bay lumber and shipbuilding industries. E. B. Dean and Company employed fifty men and sold its lumber exclusively on the Pacific Coast. San Francisco capitalists owned the California Lumber Company (the "Porter Mill") which employed 100 workers, and the Simpson operation in North Bend employed ninety men in its sawmill and shipbuilding enterprises. California money also backed the Oakland Box and Barrel Factory and its thirty employees.[37] Although those mills did not place Coos Bay in the front ranks as a producing district, the region enjoyed a solid position in the expanding Pacific Coast lumber trade.

When depression struck the American economy in the early 1890s, the Coos area probably did not suffer as badly as other sections of the country. During the hot summer of 1893, as labor unrest spread across the industrial heartland of the United States and the prospect of revolution loomed on the horizon, the *News* reported that the county was "enjoying more prosperous times." Of the twelve sawmills on the southern Oregon coast, all but one was operating and still more were under construction. To keep those plants supplied with logs required a large work force in the woods and on the waterways, the paper reported, an "army of laboring men" that provided a ready market for farm produce.[38]

The West Coast lumber market behaved erratically even when the national economy was expansive. Depressed lumber prices in California in the mid-1890s prompted the Simpson Lumber Company, Pope and Talbot, and other operators to organize a selling agency (the Central Lumber Company) to which all the member companies would consign their output. A committee of lumbermen deliberated but never reached a formal agreement. An advance in prices in late 1895 may have stalled the "combine." But, the "dull" market persisted and the efforts to put together an effective lumber cartel continued into 1896.[39] Like other efforts of its kind, the attempt failed because competitors were always willing to undersell the opposition to rid themselves of an excessive inventory of lumber.

What one newspaper dubbed the "War Among Lumber Men," subsided in 1898 when the market recovered. The *News* told its readers that local sawmills expected to operate two shifts to satisfy orders for the California and Alaskan markets—the latter a consequence of the thousands of treasure seekers who flocked to the Klondike gold fields.[40] The greatest problem for the Pacific Coast lumber industry during those years was its excessive sawmilling capacity. Except when demand was brisk, as in the case of the Alaska gold rush of 1897, the California earthquake of 1906, or construction booms elsewhere, lumber producers often faced glutted markets.

As the century drew to a close, information from the north—Astoria, Grays Harbor, and Puget Sound—indicated that the lumber trade had recovered from the depressed conditions of the preceding years. Astoria mill owners reported that logs were in short supply, a problem they attributed to the small number of logging camps in the vicinity. Grays Harbor mills were operating twelve hours a day, and logging companies supposedly had purchased several new donkey engines in anticipation of the "good times." Although shipments to the Orient, Australia, and South Africa had quickened, the busiest market for West Coast lumber was California. The *News* announced in the late spring of 1899 that "the prospects of the lumber trade never were brighter in California than at the present time." It credited the state's healthy agricultural economy and the "surplus capital awaiting investment" in the cities for the returning prosperity.[41]

Despite the improved market, Coos Bay mill owners complained that they were operating at a competitive disadvantage; manufacturers further north along the coast, they charged, shipped their best lumber east by rail and then dumped the lower grades on the California market at reduced prices. Coos-area producers grumbled that the high-quality wood products shipped out of southern Oregon—which had no eastern market—had to compete with that "poor class of lumber." To make matters worse, a recent price increase had stimulated the northern mills to an even larger output, a move that promised to dump more culled lumber on the San Francisco market. Although those circumstances were "detrimental to lumber interests on the southern Oregon coast," a rail connection to the interior would solve the problem.[42] That cutthroat competitive atmosphere persisted well into the twentieth century.

Fifty years after its first substantial white settlements, the Coos Bay landscape had a decidedly different cast. Settlers had cut and burned the thick stands of myrtle trees that grew in the bottomlands to clear land for agricultural use. Occasionally someone criticized the clearing of those unique trees and regretted the waste, because the "beautiful wood should be utilized and made a source of profit." Other critics pointed out that cutting the myrtle trees had quickened bank erosion; still others argued that leaving trees along the Coos River impeded the flow of water during spring freshets and caused large sections of the bank to be washed away.[43]

Those same settlers also purposefully put the torch to the woods even when the fire danger was high. During the summer and fall smoke lay heavy over the bay, restricted visibility, and even prevented ships from crossing the bar. Many long-time residents recalled the summer of 1867 when "smoke was so thick you could handle it with a shovel"; forest fires raging along the coast obscured light to the point that mill whistles on the bay sounded periodically to "guide parties who were forced to leave home."[44] But logging activity brought the greatest change to the Coos country, especially to the waterways that served as the principal means for transporting logs to mill sites.

And the increased volume of timber in the Coos estuary was apparent to all. Newspapers mentioned logs loose and adrift in the bay, a hazard both to humans and the estuarine environment. Several hundred logs which were being run down the river on the high freshet blocked boat traffic on the Coos River in 1884. Later that year, Henry Luse went "beech [sic] logging" at the mouth of the bay to capture logs set adrift by early fall rains. Handloggers, working without the aid of oxen or steam donkeys, added to the disruption of the Coos waterways; in the late 1880s they began constructing chutes and splash dams to transport logs to tidewater, thereby establishing precedents that lasted into the 1950s.[45] As a result of those practices, the Coos estuary developed one of the greatest wood-sediment problems on the North Pacific Coast.

And yet industrial activity on the bay was only beginning at the turn of the century. The volume of lumber shipped out of the Columbia River and Grays Harbor and Puget Sound in Washington far surpassed the production on Coos Bay. Although the Simpson company mills, shipbuilding plants, and retail yards were well-integrated operations, the capacity of Simpson's Coos Bay mill was limited. But bolder and more expansive ventures were in the offing, developments that would permanently alter the face of the Coos country. Those changes, for better or worse, were associated with the dramatic expansion of the logging and lumbering industry in the Pacific Northwest at the turn of the century.

Because of sharp increases in lumber prices and fears of an impending timber famine, speculation in western timberland reached its peak shortly after 1900. Lumbermen from the Great Lakes states and investors from centers of eastern capital descended on the Pacific Northwest in search of cheap forestland. Their agents subverted federal and state land laws in their efforts to "block up" huge acreages of valuable timberland, especially in western Oregon.[46] That scenario was played out in the Coos country as well.

CHAPTER 2

An Empire Itself

If the largest sawmill in the northwest undertook to convert into merchantable lumber
the standing timber in Coos county, it would have a 270 years' job on its hands. . . .
The ninth generation of those who might undertake this gigantic task, would be in their
graves before the work could be completed.

Coos Bay *Harbor*[1]

The frenzied speculation in Northwest timberland at the turn of the
century took place in the midst of a sharp rise in lumber prices,
suspicions of a pending timber "famine," and the establishment of the
federal forest reserves. Lumber capitalists who had made fortunes
elsewhere swarmed to the lower Columbia River country, to Puget
Sound and the Grays Harbor district in Washington, to the forests of
British Columbia, and to the Douglas fir slopes in western Oregon.
Operating through federal and state land offices and the real estate
departments of the great railroad companies, agents for Great Lakes
lumbermen and other eastern investors blocked up huge acreages of
virgin forestland.

Rumors about timber locators and buyers—pockets reportedly
flush with greenbacks—filled the pages of Northwest newspapers.
The speculators and their friends in the public land offices played fast
and loose with state and federal land laws to transfer thousands of
square miles of timber to private ownership. Those were activities that
made fortunes and created problems. Before the orgy had run its
course, several elected officials—including a United States senator
and congressman—and their counterparts in the private sector were
found guilty of defrauding the public. Those events touched Oregon's
south coast.

The timber locators who prowled the estuaries and forested slopes
of the Coos hinterland stirred the imaginations of local promoters.
Railroad rumors abounded and local newspapers called for "more
capital" and the building of additional manufacturing industries in
the area. If those developments materialized, one editor predicted,
Coos Bay would be "second to no city on the entire Pacific coast." Its
vast timber resources and "natural short route to the Orient" pointed
the "finger of destiny" to Coos Bay.[2] But southwestern Oregon was
only a small part of speculative activity that was general throughout
the region.

26

The timber buyers who flocked to the coastal rain forests of British Columbia were of a kind with those south of the border. The race to gain access to timberland peaked in 1903 when the provincial government, in an effort to increase revenue, made Crown lands available to Canadian and foreign interests. The government sold timber licenses for twenty-one-year periods, with the licensees required to pay only the annual interest on the value of the timber when it was harvested. To whet the appetite of potential buyers, the license could be transferred after only two years. The result of the provincial government's decision was an inrush of rascals and land agents and rampant speculation until authorities discontinued the practice in 1907.[3]

One of the more colorful accounts of the speculation in British Columbia forests argues that it was easy to stake out a square mile of timberland at that time:

> There had arisen a fierce rush to stake timber. Hundreds and hundreds of men—experienced loggers, inexperienced youth from town—blossomed as "timber cruisers." The woods were furrowed with their trails. Men in rowboats and sail boats, and small, decrepit steamboats, and gasoline motorboats had pervaded the waters of every channel and fiord.

According to a prominent lumber journal, many of the investors were "Great Lakes capitalists" who already had exhausted the pine forests of that region. One of them, Frederick Weyerhaeuser, was amassing even greater acreages in Washington, Oregon, and Idaho.[4] The most striking consequence of the speculative mania—and the one that has had the greatest impact on the Pacific Northwest—was the concentration of timberland into large ownerships. In that sense, the Weyerhaeuser interests led the way when they purchased 900,000 acres of magnificent timber from the Northern Pacific Railroad in 1900; that transaction, involving the original congressional land grant to the railroad, was one of the largest single land transfers in American history. While Frederick Weyerhaeuser was pioneering the way in acquiring thousands of square miles of Northwest timber, his firm also changed the emphasis for leaders in the industry from manufacturing to land holding. Ownership and control of timberland, not the operation of sawmills, was the wave of the future.[5] Those circumstances also lend credibility to the old loggers' saying that "only speculators make good profits."

Fraud, deception, and cajolery were part of the speculation process. In a classic understatement, one writer noted that organizing private holdings into large units "was not infrequently obtained . . . through fraudulent claims and political machinations."[6] Courts of law con-

_ew scoundrels for their misdeeds, but most of them escaped
legal scrutiny—with their landholdings intact.

Because of the frantic speculation in the state's timberlands, Oregon
newspapers began to worry about the future. The Portland *Oregonian*
estimated in 1902 that eastern capitalists had invested $30 million in
the Northwest, "a careful and complete exploitation of this country by
men from Michigan and Wisconsin." Although the Coos Bay *News*
argued that it was natural for Great Lakes lumbermen "to seek other
worlds to conquer," it worried about the "Eastern men" who were
holding land for speculation. Such activities were detrimental to a
community because they prevent development, the paper said.[7] But
most local boosters, especially those along the Coos estuary, wanted
the building of plant and manufacturing facilities.

Jobs were abundant during those years, and newspaper advertisements carried frequent references to the need for labor. A construction operator, promising "good wages," wanted "40 men for
railroad work" along with "10 or 12 teams." Just as common were
rumors about outside investors who were interested in the area; a
case in point is a news item that speculated about the sale of the Porter
mill to "eastern capitalists."[8] For their part, local developers were
more interested in the prospects for real estate on the bay than they
were about speculation in timberland. That is, unless the latter would
aid and abet the former.

The Coos Bay *Harbor* joined the chorus promoting the south coast
when it began publication in 1905. The Coos country, it boasted, was
"on the eve of the most important development in its history"; real
estate was brisk, and the "gambling and sporting element" looked
forward to a good year. As well they should! In early summer, the E.
B. Dean and Simpson mills were operating extra shifts, the sure signs
of prosperity according to the *Harbor,* and an indication that "the
capacity of our plants will have to be increased."[9] That plea for the
expansion of sawmilling facilities was not new, because for several
years the logging camps had little difficulty providing the Dean and
Simpson mills with an adequate supply of timber. In truth, there had
been a revolution of sorts in the technology of moving the huge logs
to mill sites.

Since the 1880s loggers on the North Pacific slope had been adapting steam power to their woods operations. The widespread use of
steam donkeys by the turn of the century had dramatically speeded
the process of yarding logs to water's edge or a railroad siding. With

the introduction of the high-lead system (hauling logs in the air with cable suspended from a topped-off tree) by 1910, a technology was in place that would change very little until the introduction of gasoline-powered engines in the 1930s. By replacing "bull teams" with the powerful donkey machines, loggers were able to work through the rainy winter months, thereby providing a steady supply of logs to the mills. Under conditions where oxen would become mired in mud, the "bull donkeys" now hauled logs clear of mud, underbrush, and other obstructions.

In the midst of that revolution in logging technology, the Southern Pacific Railroad announced that it would build a rail connection to Coos Bay. Booster spirits soared to new heights. Give us "40 feet of water on the bar," the *Harbor* declared, because "it is the foundation stone of our future greatness." A rail connection and a deeper harbor would make the bay country "one of the best places on the coast for manufactories." Its industrial successes would invite other developments, perhaps even the establishment of a university ("the climate is ideal for the scholar").[10] A flurry of timberland and real estate purchases soon added a sense of urgency to the call for a deeper harbor.

One of the trademarks of timber speculation at the turn of the century was secrecy. To successfully block up large acreages under a single ownership, according to the *Oregonian*, meant "no one knowing" what the buyers were up to.[11] Between 1890 and 1910 the activities of the shadowy agents of eastern capitalists filled the columns of Northwest newspapers. And in few places did the speculators work with greater skill and secrecy than they did in southwestern Oregon. When their mission was accomplished, the agents had amassed thousands of acres of timberland into a few large holdings, a move that has significantly influenced the area's economy in the twentieth century.

Coos Bay newspapers hinted frequently early in 1906 that important developments were in the making. The *Harbor* reported "a large party of wealthy capitalists" visiting the bay whose "presence here may be fraught with great importance to this section." David Eccles, the Utah Construction Company "millionaire," employed an agent who was "frequently in the bay negotiating purchases for buyers." By midsummer, "a large number of strangers" were in the area, "nearly all of whom represent considerable capital." The *Times* reported "a famine in sleeping accommodations in the city" with local hotels turning away customers nearly every night. Speculators from Los Angeles, Boise, and elsewhere were investing in Coos Bay real estate because of "their confidence in this country."[12] But the most important transactions—and the ones with the most lasting significance—involved the transfer of thousands of acres of timberland in southwestern Oregon.

Agents for Great Lakes lumber capitalists were the most significant of the interested parties. O. E. Sether, representing the Menasha Wooden Ware Company from Wisconsin, had put together more than 10,000 acres of fir and cedar by the summer of 1906. Sether told a *Times* correspondent that he had been traveling about the Coos country for five years "on the same errand." Menasha had assembled nearly 100,000 acres of timberland by 1908, most of it still in the company's possession today. And, as part of its financial stake in southwestern Oregon, agents for the Weyerhaeuser Timber Company purchased approximately 30,000 acres.[13] The buyers had merely established a legal (or illegal) base for the hard work that had already been done in the field by the surveyors or "timber cruisers."

Surveyors and timber estimators were much in demand during those years. Federal, state, and county governments, timber companies, claim locators, and real estate firms all sought the services of people trained in the art of cruising timber. Dennis McCarthy, a native of New Brunswick who followed the logging frontier to Minnesota and eventually to Oregon, kept a series of work diaries that describe his timber cruising activities in Minnesota, Montana, Washington, and by 1905, in Coos County.[14] Although the entries mention only the technical details of timber cruising, the fact that McCarthy lived for a time in Minneapolis indicates that some of the Great Lakes lumbermen sought his services cruising timber in the Pacific Northwest.

Although it was not a certain route to financial success, timber cruising could benefit a man with little capital. After a stint at timber surveying for Coos County, McCarthy switched to logging. His diaries show that he worked at that trade from 1916 to 1936 and operated several camps. Eventually, several of his New Brunswick relatives, including brothers Richard and John, emigrated to southwestern Oregon to work in the woods.[15] There undoubtedly were many other self-trained men who used their technical skills to carve a niche for themselves in the lumberman's world. But the real advantages went to individuals with significant wealth whose access to capital enabled them to make large purchases of old-growth forest.

Good timberland in the Pacific Northwest soon became more difficult to find. Although agents for "eastern capitalists" were still active and locators still prowled the hills, "even in stormy times," the best timber had already been taken. A Portland newspaper commented that the "rush of the past three years" had involved forestland all across the state. But, more stringent enforcement of federal land laws was making it more difficult to obtain timber for third parties. One speculator told a reporter in late 1906, "the law must now be very closely complied with in order to obtain title."[16] The "stringent" application of the land laws, however, came after the horse had been stolen. The land office machinations of the first few years of the twentieth century witnessed the transfer of thousands of acres of valuable timber in Oregon and Washington to the private sector.

One of the largest of those transactions involved a prominent Minnesota lumberman—C. A. Smith—and his was the most secretive of operations. On December 22, 1906, the Coos Bay *Harbor* carried the banner headline: "Coos Bay Gets Sawmill Employing 1,200 Men." The article reported that C. A. Smith had purchased the E. B. Dean Lumber Company holdings—30,000 acres of timber, logging railroads, and mill facilities. According to the *Harbor,* by virtue of the Dean purchase, the Smith interests controlled more than 100,000 acres of timber in the Coos region. The negotiations to amass the properties, the newspaper said, "were made with the greatest secrecy," even to the extent that "Smith traveled incognito and did not register at hotels." The report called the purchases "by far the most important deal ever consummated in Coos County"; they meant "big things" for the region.[17] And indeed they did. The C. A. Smith Company and its successors—the Coos Bay Lumber Company and the Georgia-Pacific Corporation—dominated lumber production in the region until the 1950s when the new Weyerhaeuser complex began operation.

The three large holdings put together between 1900 and 1910—Menasha, Weyerhaeuser, and C. A. Smith—have had a significant influence on the course of events on Coos Bay. The concentration of Coos timberlands into a few large ownerships has affected the lives of thousands of people. In the best of times, when the mills operated to capacity, the community prospered. But just as often, when glutted markets and periodic depressions in the construction industry on the Pacific Coast brought hard times to the bay, people looked for other ways to survive. There is another and darker side to those purchases; they assured that management and harvesting decisions would be made far from Coos Bay and that the "economic colonialism" of the nineteenth century would continue. But, in the best of all possible worlds, local ownership and control would only partially have alleviated the strains of colonialism. Those arrangements still would have been subject to the grip of the market system and large capital institutions.

The Smith, Weyerhaeuser, and Menasha timberlands included some of the original Oregon and California railroad land grant. In the case of the Smith holdings, the evidence shows that his agents used dummy entrymen under the federal Timber and Stone Act of 1878 to fraudulently block up large acreages of timber into single units. According to Stephen Puter, who exposed much of that corruption in the sensational Oregon land fraud trials, C. A. Smith began acquiring land through dummy entrymen at the turn of the century. Puter had the timber cruised and hired "locators" to file claim on 160-acre blocks, and then Smith's financial agent, Frederick Kribs, paid everyone off. In the Coos country Smith and his agents worked through officials in the U.S. Land Office in Roseburg to get the inside track on land deals.[18] The thieves, however, had a falling out.

When Secretary of the Interior Ethan Hitchcock initiated an investigation into the possibility of land fraud, Puter and several others were indicted and found guilty. During his seventeen-month stint in Portland's Rocky Butte prison, Puter wrote an exposé of his work as a "real estate" broker for the timber barons. He described C. A. Smith as "one of the greatest criminals that ever went unwhipped of justice" and a man who seemed "to be imbued with shoplifting instincts whenever the public lands or timber are concerned." For his part, Smith referred to Puter as "a shrewd business man—but apparently absolutely unscrupulous."[19] Despite the scandal the C. A. Smith properties remained intact, as did most timberland blocked up in this fashion.

Shortly after Coos Bay newspapers broke the news about the C. A. Smith purchases, the *Oregonian* reported that the sale of the E. B. Dean waterfront property to Smith was the "largest transfer of water frontage in Marshfield ever." The Portland newspaper also hinted that the Minnesota lumberman had acquired his timberlands under dubious circumstances: "It was learned that many of the Smith holdings of timber lands in this section are in other names, but when it is known that the many big deals made by F. A. Kribs during the last 10 years were for none other than the Smith Company, the extent of the timber land owned by that concern reaches about 300,000." The holdings included property in Lincoln, Linn, Lane, Douglas, and Curry counties in Oregon and a sizable acreage of redwood in northern California. The *Oregonian* predicted that Smith's coming to Coos Bay "means a city of 50,000 within a few years at Marshfield" and the "death" of Minnesota's lumber industry.[20] Though exaggerated, the claim was not far from the truth.

Charles Axel Smith and the Minnesota influence loom large in the rough sawmilling towns on Coos Bay. A native of the province of Ostergöttland, Sweden, Smith gained the financial support of Governor John S. Pilsbury of Minnesota and became one of the leading lumbermen in the state. As Minnesota's pine stands diminished, Smith began piecing together several huge holdings of virgin timber in the Pacific Northwest and eventually announced plans to build a large modern sawmill on Coos Bay. The transplanted Swede was no dawdler. In February 1907 he sent seven millwrights to Marshfield to lay plans for the "Big Mill."[21] That was only the beginning of the Minnesota exodus to Coos Bay.

As C. A. Smith personnel prepared the way for the operation in southwestern Oregon, a swarm of Minnesotans descended on the bay—some to build the new mill, others to set up logging camps and begin the task of readying a supply of timber. Many of them, like Cliff Thorwald, who came to the bay with his parents in 1907, were Scandinavians. His father had been foreman at the Diamond Iron Works in Minneapolis, and because of his skills as a blacksmith and machinist, Smith convinced the elder Thorwald to make the move to Oregon. But he was only one of "the original people," the son recalls, who followed similar routes. Another was Axel Anderson, a native of Sweden, who left Minneapolis in 1908 to work as a blacksmith's helper on the new mill. His Finnish-born wife, Eleanor (née Elna Maria Junttila), recalls that her husband "knew lots of people here who came from one province in Sweden." When she arrived on Marshfield's docks in 1914, Eleanor remembers there were "three families from Minneapolis that had their own boarding house."[22]

Smith persuaded others, many of them company supervisors, to make the trek to Oregon. A. D. Adelsperger, a compassman and cruiser, left Minnesota in 1905 to carry on similar work for the C. A. Smith interests in Oregon; he was soon placed in charge of company timberlands. But the most influential of the Minnesota immigrants was the Canadian-born head of the company's logging operations, Albert Powers. Unlike Smith, Powers moved to Marshfield in 1907 and made the bay community his home until his death in 1930. He was vice president and general manager of the Smith-Powers Logging Company, a subsidiary of the parent firm.[23] "Uncle Al," as he is remembered by old-timers, "rode herd" over the C. A. Smith (later Coos Bay Lumber Company) logging operations.

The *American Lumberman,* the nation's most prominent lumber journal, described Al Powers as "the personification of energy." His rise in the logging industry of the late nineteenth century reads like an American success story—employment as a water boy in the Michigan

woods at the age of thirteen, to Minnesota with his family where he
worked on logging booms in the summer and in the woods during
winter, and finally success in Hibbing, Minnesota, where he directed
some of the largest logging operations on the nearby upper Mis-
sissippi River. Along the way Al Powers developed an intimate business and personal acquaintance with C. A. Smith, an association that
eventually landed the Minnesota logger in southwestern Oregon in
1907.[24]

But Al Powers did more than move his family and two prize horses
to Coos Bay. His daughter, Florence Berg, estimates that "about half
the men in the woods knew my dad in Minnesota and were anxious
to come out to this new country." In a special edition on the C. A.
Smith operations in 1911, the *American Lumberman* pointed to the
Minnesota connection—of the more than 400 men employed by the
Smith-Powers Logging Company, "probably one-half or more of them
have at some time worked for Mr. Powers in Minnesota." Mike Summers, who had been a restaurateur in Hibbing, came to the bay
country to oversee cookhouse operations in the Smith-Powers logging
camps; George E. Dix, educated at the University of Minnesota Medical School, hired on as the company doctor.[25] And there were many
others, the men (and an increasing number of women) who worked
in the logging camps and in the mills, but who left no recorded
account of their experiences.

Those influences gave a decided Minnesotan (and Scandinavian
and Finnish) cast to Coos Bay and the area logging camps. Raymond
McKeown, a retired physician whose father ran the Chandler Hotel in
Marshfield, remembers the unofficial "MinniWisc" club, comprised of
people from Minnesota and Wisconsin "who practically ran the town
for years." Al Powers, who served as a Marshfield city councilman,
school director, and on the commercially important Coos Bay Port
Commission, is the best example.[26] Through the Minnesota-Scan-
dinavian connection, relatives and friends continued to flock to the
Coos country, many of them from the Old World.

The construction of the C. A. Smith mill and the boom in the Pacific
Coast lumber industry in 1907 brought an aura of prosperity to the
bay communities. And a shortage of labor. When local carpenters,
some of them from the Simpson-controlled sash and door factory in
North Bend, struck for higher wages and a shorter workday, the
action threatened to stop all building construction. The strikers
claimed a "moral victory" when Simpson raised the wages of his mill
workers. A few weeks later the *Harbor* reported that nearly all the men

who were on strike had "found employment in other lines and there are few idle men in town." As the summer wore on, the newspaper noted that factories and mills on the bay "are utterly unable to secure adequate help." Because of the shortage, managers were "considering importing immigrants from New York or Chicago." In October another *Harbor* headline proclaimed: "Laborers Still Lacking on the Bay."[27]

Those were banner times for the Coos country. Probably not until the great boom period following the Second World War was labor in such demand. The isolation of the south coast and its tight labor market played to the advantage of working people when the lumber economy was strong. C. A. Smith, who visited the area to examine progress on the mill, praised "the wonderful commercial expansion" and the "excellent wages now being paid on the Bay." Those conditions, he told a reporter, made it possible for a young man to amass "a little fortune" in a short period of time.[28] Coos Bay newspapers were bursting with optimism, extolling the virtues of opportunity and the bright prospects for the future.

But that economic environment was also a risky one, subject to fluctuating and often depressed lumber prices—factors that induced owners to curtail or suspend operations when the market slowed. In short, it provided little security for working people. As Norman Clark has stated so well in his study of Everett, Washington, that "was not and could not be a humane system." Between the peak years of lumber production in the United States (1906–7) and American entry into the European war, frequently glutted markets drove stumpage values down. To avoid business failure, many firms had to continue operating to meet their carrying charges—timberland taxes, bonded indebtedness, and mill investments.[29] Those circumstances forced prices down further and made it worthwhile to remove only the best logs from the woods. Such a system encouraged plunder both of humans and the environment.

As coal shipments from Coos Bay diminished, the forest resource assumed increasing importance to the area's economy. Because the speculation of the early twentieth century had appreciated the value of timberland in the Pacific Northwest, landowners—including the likes of C. A. Smith and the Weyerhaeuser Timber Company—began to form forest protection associations to guard their investments from being consumed in fire. They also pressured state legislatures to establish public forestry agencies to assume those responsibilities. And, in the midst of the glowing optimism over the "inexhaustibility" of the region's forests, there were occasional words of caution.

Coos Bay newspapers reported on broader forestry concerns, an indication of the importance of those issues to bay readers. One article, warning about the excessive timber harvests in California and Washington, predicted that southwestern Oregon would "not 'miss the water 'til the well runs dry.'" It urged the United States to pursue a forestry program similar to that practiced in Germany in order to avoid becoming "a forestless nation." A related news item described the "thoughtless slaughter" of white pine in the Great Lakes states and demanded that federal and state governments adopt stringent measures to prevent fire and to stop wasteful methods of cutting.[30] Those matters would soon loom larger as timber became even more important to the Coos economy.

The Coos Bay *News* quoted a California lumberman, W. B. Mills, who warned in 1900 that the demand for timber in the United States "now exceeds the capacity of the forests to reproduce it." In phraseology that has characterized the industry for most of the twentieth century, Mills urged that the forests "be looked upon as a big timber orchard, and care should be taken to gather its crop as we gather others." Like other crops, he remarked, timber should be harvested when "the ripening process is complete and before it is 'doted' by age." Eighty years later, Jerry Phillips, head of the Oregon Department of Forestry office in Coos Bay, would agree. All forested areas in the world go through a "conversion" stage from old growth to second growth; therefore, he argues, it is necessary "to remove the old growth from the forest so you may have growing stock."[31] But, in Coos Bay at the turn of the century, there were few interested in regeneration; timber exhaustion was a phenomenon that happened elsewhere, not in the lush forests of the Pacific slope.

The timber resources in southwestern Oregon, the *Harbor* proclaimed in 1907, made Coos Bay "AN EMPIRE ITSELF"; its forests were perpetual and would never be "denuded." The *News* disputed an "expert" who claimed that timberlands required reforestation: "In Coos County reforesting was unnecessary, as nature attends to that herself"; only the cultivation of the soil would "kill off the Oregon timber permanently." When C. A. Smith announced that his company employed two foresters "for the sole purpose of attending to reforestation," the future seemed bright and certain. In an early version of "sustained yield" management, Smith urged timberland owners to plant new growth "as fast as the old growth has been cut and removed from the land."[32]

Like other large timber holders in the United States, Smith thought forest fires and timberland taxes were the greatest barriers to reforestation. Greater public assistance for fire protection and low land taxes, he argued, would encourage private holders to practice conservation. In similar fashion, George S. Long, superintendent of the vast Weyerhaeuser operations in the Northwest, asked states to assume a greater share of the costs of fire protection; that, he said, was one of "the state's duties to its citizens." Long added that reforestation was unlikely until taxes were low enough to assure a profit to the landowner.[33] Others with large investments in forestland held similar sentiments.

Despite the complaints about excessive taxes in southwestern Oregon, the large timber holders continued to add to their land base. In truth, the forests loomed large both to outside investors and to the communities that depended on the timber for their welfare. "Lumbering cuts a big figure with Coos County prosperity," the *Times* reported at the height of the boom, "and everybody is interested in seeing the lumber business in a healthy condition." But there also were persisting complaints about absentee investors who held land for speculation. Those individuals, the *Harbor* charged, were "a dead weight to the community." Keep profits and capital at home, it admonished. On another occasion, the *Harbor* suggested higher taxes to punish "those who are not here working for the country."[34]

The issue of a railroad, of course, continued to be of great interest. When Southern Pacific announced in 1906 that it planned to construct a spur line to Coos Bay, the reality of a rail connection to the Willamette or Umpqua Valley seemed assured. As proof of its intentions, Southern Pacific purchased right-of-way property on Coos Bay and the twenty-eight-mile railroad link to Myrtle Point. Real estate brokers on the bay were ecstatic, although some citizens protested when the new owners increased the rates on the existing line. Still others worried about Southern Pacific's potential monopoly of the waterfront. One writer observed that the idea of making Coos Bay "a Southern Pacific preserve should arouse a feeling of the liveliest antagonism."[35] For reasons of its own, Southern Pacific delayed construction until 1911.

Not everyone favored the rail connection. "That ruthless invader of paradise," the Coos Bay *Monthly* charged, "will blow its trumpet of fate" and set this "seaport gem . . . in its own commercial crown." A writer from Oakland, California, a former resident of Coos Bay, predicted that the railroad would help a few "get richer and more uncomfortable, while the bulk will get poorer." The Coos area had done well without a railroad, he argued. It had good educational facilities, and its clergy "know just as much about God and the devil as they do here, and very likely are much more sincere." When the Southern Pacific resumed construction in 1911, the *News* cautioned that it had printed items about the "railroad to Roseburg" as early as the 1870s. But there was consolation: "we are 40 years nearer a railroad now than we were then."[36]

Unforeseen difficulties delayed the completion of the railroad from Eugene to Coos Bay until 1916. In the interim, the waterfront communities had undergone a metamorphosis of sorts. The new faces passing through the towns gave an aura of restlessness to the area, for this was a population on the move—to the logging camps when the "bull donkeys" were in full swing, from mills to shipyard (or vice versa), or away from the region altogether when the lumber market was dull. That "floating population" sought out the restaurants, the lodging houses, and the drinking establishments for food, rest, and play. For the miners, loggers, millhands, and sailors who traveled Marshfield's Front Street, those establishments provided the vital stuff of working life—where one learned about jobs, conditions in the camps, pay scales and hours of labor, "highball" foremen, and a host of other matters of importance.

Although Johannah Powers protected her children from the colorful life on Front Street, her daughter, Florence Berg, remembers her mother telling the children: "When we came here, there were 13 saloons." Even though she was "kept at home," Florence grew up with the notion that Marshfield was a rugged town. Raymond McKeown, who played along the Marshfield waterfront as a boy and occasionally begged nickels from loggers, remembers "unbelievable brawls," even an occasional death in the vicinity of Front Street—an area he describes as a "mass of saloons interposed with houses of ill-fame." The rest of the community, he says, was little different: "They just worked and raised hell." When an interviewer asked diminutive, silver-haired Eleanor Anderson about logger brawls on Front Street, she replied with a twinkle in her eye: "No, I haven't heard that. I think you are misinformed."[37]

The landscape of those rough mill towns was changing as well. The most heavily traveled streets had been planked, and the town of Marshfield began replacing rotting planks with asphalt, signs of modernity and the automobile. Developers were filling low-lying areas adjacent to the waterfront to make room for commercial expansion. And the new entertainment technology, motion pictures—came to the area before the completion of the rail link to the Willamette Valley. But the outlet to "real culture" and the refinements of urban life, at least as defined by the small middle class, was the three-day trip to San Francisco. When people made money, one resident recalls, they went to San Francisco, "the shopping center of Coos Bay."[38] Even the railroad did not alter that relationship.

The water route to Pacific markets pointed the way to success for the Coos economy. That had been true in the nineteenth century when the Luse, Simpson, and E. B. Dean mills dominated production on the bay; when the Big Mill began sawing lumber in 1908, the C. A. Smith Company followed the same pattern. The Port of Coos Bay (established in 1912) led most other ports in shipments of lumber to San Francisco. For its part, the Big Mill produced more lumber than all other Coos Bay producers combined. The C. A. Smith manufacturing and logging operations had become the single most important element in the Coos economy.

CHAPTER 3

The "Big Mill" and Its World

The most extensive holdings of the C. A. Smith Timber Company are tributary to Coos Bay by water and rail, including the timber in Coos, Curry and Douglas counties, of which the company owns about 180,000 acres, containing perhaps 18,000,000,000 feet.[1]

When fire destroyed an old sawmilling facility belonging to the Georgia-Pacific Corporation in the spring of 1984, it marked the end of an era in the history of lumber manufacturing on Coos Bay. For that building complex, in the process of being dismantled for scrap metal, was at one time the envy of lumber manufacturers worldwide. Known as the Big Mill, the plant was the center of the fully integrated C. A. Smith operations, a facility once reputed to be a "sensation and a revolution in the manufacture of lumber."[2] But the Big Mill was even more; it was the bay country's largest employer from the time it began sawing lumber on February 29, 1908, until the new Weyerhaeuser mill opened in 1951

As such, the Big Mill was the center of industrial activity for an area that extended to neighboring Douglas and Curry counties. Its network of production included miles of logging railroad, several logging camps, extensive booming and rafting facilities, waterfront docks for loading lumber, and company ships to transport the rough-cut lumber to the C. A. Smith finishing mill at Bay Point, California. Although the antiquated Simpson operation at North Bend limped on for a few years and other plants opened on the bay, they all paled beside the Big Mill and its supply and transportation system. The C. A. Smith work force also gave a particular cast to the population on the bay; by 1910 there was a greater percentage of Scandinavians, especially Swedes, living in Marshfield than any other town in the county. The bloodlines of those early comers still linger.

Helene Stack Bower's father came from Minnesota to direct the construction of the Big Mill. Her father, like others, came from north Minneapolis and lived in a boarding house until he sent for his family in 1914. Helen's nephew, Chappie McCarthy (one of the last independent loggers operating in southwestern Oregon), remembers proudly that his Minnesota grandfather had built mills for C. A. Smith and others "all over the damn country." The Big Mill was the grandest and for several years "the largest single head rig mill in the world." Canadian-born William E. Major came to Coos Bay in 1906 with his father who worked as millwright for C. A. Smith. He remembers that the new plant "was so big that it had its own construction crew." Cliff Thorwald points out that his father and other Minnesotans did "all the big, heavy iron work for the Big Mill." That was a considerable feat with a steam-powered flywheel twenty feet in diameter, huge shafts running the length of the building, and "many, many big leather belts."[3]

The construction of the Big Mill was a large and well-planned operation. The old E. B. Dean sawmill cut lumber for the new buildings and experienced Minnesota millwrights directed the construction of the most modern and efficient lumber manufacturing plant of its time. When it began sawing in 1908, the C. A. Smith operation employed 250 workers in the plant on Coos Bay and another 350 in seven large logging camps. Before the year was out, Smith added a second shift of "experienced mill men . . . brought out from Minnesota." That pushed total production for the two ten-hour shifts to an average of 500,000 board feet a day; and more new machinery was on the way.[4] As long as the marketing end of the operation held up, economic conditions on the bay held steady.

To increase the capacity of the Coos Bay operation, Smith ordered the remodeling of the old E. B. Dean mill. It was designed to cut spruce, cedar, and the finer grades of fir, and newspapers reported that the plant would be able to saw 150,000 feet a day and employ about 100 men, which would of course "add to the volume of business here." The Smith company also announced "improvements" in the Big Mill with the installation of a new waste burner; hitherto, wood wastes had been ground up and used to fill mudflats in the vicinity of the plant.[5] That innovation would haunt the community in later years when cinders and ashes from the burner created a severe pollution problem in the upper bay.

The C. A. Smith Company further expanded its Coos Bay manufacturing facilities in 1912 when it announced plans to build a modern paper mill to employ seventy-five to 100 workmen. Two Finnish nationals with broad experience in pulp and paper manufacturing supervised the construction of the plant. At the same time the firm expanded the Eastside mill (the former E. B. Dean facility) to bring the combined capacity of its two plants to 600,000 feet daily. The company also installed a modern electric generator to power the huge cranes used to load the great slings of lumber aboard ships; it planned to market the surplus electricity commercially. The introduction of electrical power, an expanded shingle plant, and the completion of the pulp mill, according to the Coos Bay *Times*, would make the C. A.

Smith operations "one of the biggest shippers of lumber products in the country."[6] But, as the future would show, the vagaries and cut-throat atmosphere of early twentieth-century capitalism could destroy seemingly well-integrated, modern business worlds like those of C. A. Smith.

Logging the rugged slopes of the Coast Range required a heavy capital investment, a large labor force, and access to sizable stands of timber. The Smith-Powers Logging Company had all three. When the Big Mill and the Eastside plant operated to full capacity, they con-sumed a tremendous volume of logs, timber that had to be hauled to water's edge or a railhead for shipment to the manufacturing facilities on the bay. That process required the use of heavy, steam-powered machinery and dangerous, back-breaking work from the crews. For reasons having to do with danger, injury, and death, it was the woods more than the mills that inspired the rich logging folklore of the Northwest. That all-male work force (except for the "flunkies" who assisted in the cookhouses) endured summer heat and the cold winter rains to turn out an incredible volume of logs each year.

Although the production figures for the Smith-Powers operation obscure as much as they reveal about the company's logging network, the volume for the first five years shows a remarkable increase in the board feet of timber delivered to the mills (see Table 1). When the mills were going full steam, Smith-Powers' seven logging camps used more than forty donkey engines to haul the huge logs out of the woods.[7] Those activities were the stuff of story-telling, and tragedy when human error or an equipment breakdown occurred in the woods, and unemployment when the market was down. To make matters worse, because of the overweening emphasis on production, many camps—including Smith-Powers'—had a reputation for being "highball," production-at-all-cost operations. Such outfits were notori-ous for their high rates of turnover.

When Al Powers arrived on Coos Bay in 1907, he "went right into the woods," according to his daughter, Florence. His task was to organize the logging camps and transportation facilities to supply the new mill with logs. The company's production records underscore "Uncle Al's" success as a logging superintendent, and local news-paper items testify to the human costs of speed-up operations in the Smith-Powers camps. Henry Haefner, who began working on the Siskiyou National Forest in 1909, recalled Powers as "the biggest logger on the Pacific Coast, . . . and the best-known man in Coos County." He was short and heavyset, with a thick neck, red hair and

TABLE 1.   Board Feet of Timber
Delivered to Smith-Powers Mills

1907	25,000,000
1908	65,000,000
1909	85,000,000
1910	100,000,000
1911	150,000,000

red eyebrows.[8] Because of his position and energy, he was a man to be reckoned with.

The passing years have blurred the person of Al Powers. Although Henry Haefner described him as "a friend of the workingman" who "gave hundreds of free meals at his camp to men out of work," it should be remembered that he was also the boss logger for one of the largest operations on the Pacific Coast.[9] To the timber fallers, choker setters, donkey punchers, and others who worked out of the camps, people like "Uncle Al" usually were not known for their humanity. The game was production, and the logging superintendent was the person chiefly responsible for maximizing the efficiency and volume of work.

But Al Powers was more than the administrative head of the C. A. Smith log supply network. Unlike today's college-educated forest products executives, Powers grew up with the industry; practical working experience in the pine forests of Minnesota tempered his decisions, and if Henry Haefner is correct, he "never high-hatted his men." The large number of loggers who followed him to the West Coast suggests that he was more than a heartless ramrod of logging shows. He also ran a tight ship; he prohibited booze in the camps and in the company town of Powers and would summarily dismiss an employee who breached that rule. Florence Berg traveled with her father to the camps where she "knew so many of the men," and she recalls her parents' sadness and concern when logging accidents occurred.[10] But, "Uncle Al" was always the logging boss, fighting union organizers, especially the efforts of the Industrial Workers of the World (IWW). His was and remained a paternalistic world.

The Smith-Powers Company established most of its early logging camps along the sloughs and rivers. As a youth, Frank Younker delivered supplies by boat to operations like Camp Four, located on South Slough. On his return trip he remembers giving crew members a ride out; occasionally that meant a logger who "got kicked out of camp." Camp Four was set up to log the Sitka spruce and cedar that grew in abundance on the steep slopes adjacent to the slough. Steam donkeys hauled the logs to a railroad siding, and from there they went by rail to the head of the slough where they were dumped into the water and readied for rafting to the mills. Bud Metcalf, whose logging experiences began with bull teams and skid roads, recalls that donkey logging was practiced widely by the First World War.[11] But moving the logs to water's edge was only part of that transportation system.

The Weyerhaeuser Company still uses the Coos estuary as its principal vehicle for moving logs. That practice, which predated the introduction of gasoline-powered logging trucks and the use of the railroad, provided the only means for transporting the huge timber to the mills on the bay. During the first half of the twentieth century, one of the most frequently mentioned items in local newspapers concerned the movement of logs, both intentional and unintentional, on Coos waterways. Seasonal storms pounded rafts asunder and left the logs adrift in the bay. Hauling Camp Four rafts from South Slough during the winter months was a precarious undertaking. As the rafts left the slough and entered the bay proper, they had to pass the pounding surf at the entrance to the harbor. On one occasion, Smith-Powers logs went adrift and were swept to sea on the ebb tide. Dave Holden, who rafted for Simpson and others, described the situation near the entrance of the bay as "too strenuous even for a Wisconsin man."[12]

Transporting logs on the rivers created similar problems. In the days before the construction of hydraulically operated splash dams, loggers used the snow melt and heavy winter rains to "run out" their season's cut. Their task was to control the timbers and place them in "booms" near the mouths of the rivers.[13] That effort was not always successful: winter storms often wreaked havoc on rafts and booms, and unusually heavy rains and the sudden melting of snow turned the rivers into raging torrents that tore logs loose and sent them pounding into the bay. Until recent years when there was an organized move to clear the bay of debris, graying and rotting hulks dotted the mudflats and shorelines of the Coos estuary.

The volume of traffic on the bay increased sharply when the Big Mill began sawing logs. In 1911 the Smith-Powers camps alone dumped 223 million board feet of timber into the water; the Smith mills sawed about 150 million feet, and the Simpson Lumber Company purchased the rest.[14] Those large harvests also began to take their toll, especially on forests with easy access to the waterways. Railroads pressed further into the steep-sided and winding valleys and loggers rigged steam donkeys capable of relaying timber as far as one mile. But the demand for logs, especially for the Big Mill and its auxiliaries, required access to still more timber.

Because the Smith-Powers camps on South Slough and elsewhere were beginning to run short of timber, the company began to move deeper into its holdings, especially the great stands in the drainage of the Coquille River southeast of Coos Bay. The *Times* headlined that shift early in 1913: "Last of the Operations on Tidewater on Coos Bay is in Sight." Henceforth, it pointed out, "logging will have to be done by railroad." The Smith-Powers Company already had commenced surveying the route and purchasing the right of way for a major railroad from the Southern Pacific terminus at Myrtle Point up the South Fork of the Coquille River. Victor Stevens, who spent much of his adult life in the area, remembers the project as the largest of its kind in the state up to that time.[15] Construction of the railroad also meant that the Smith timber on the tributaries of the Coquille would be milled on Coos Bay.

Although small cargo mills shipped lumber over the bar of the Coquille River, the lumber manufacturing plants on Coos Bay consumed a far greater volume of timber. The C. A. Smith Company's domination of timberland ownership in the region, its efficient milling facilities on the bay, and the small and treacherous entrance to the Coquille River meant that Coos Bay would remain the major manufacturing and shipping point for wood products. All roads seemed to lead to Coos waters. At one point mill owners on the bay even asked Congress to appropriate funds to build a canal from the Coquille River across the low divide to the head of Isthmus Slough, part of the Coos estuary.

The stands of timber on the South Fork of the Coquille were enormous. One source estimated that the completion of the railroad would provide access to enough timber to run the Smith mills "at their present capacity for fifty years." The construction project itself was immense, involving hundreds of men, mules and horses, a large steam shovel, and a pile driver. From his classroom in the Myrtle Point High School, Victor Stevens could hear the exhaust of the steam from the pile driver "as the heavy one-ton hammer was raised, a second's silence, then the thud of the hammer as it hit the piling." The crew completed approximately nineteen miles of railroad in the fall of 1914 to the site of an old ranch where Smith-Powers constructed a company town.[16] For the next several decades, Powers was the center of logging activity and the principal source of timber for the C. A. Smith mills and their successors.

Clare Lehmonosky spent all of his adult life working in the woods for C. A. Smith, the Coos Bay Lumber Company, and finally, the Georgia-Pacific Corporation. When he first visited Powers in 1915, construction crews were still building the houses and the facilities to service the needs of the company and the community. He remembers that the company-owned grocery store, the maintenance shop, the roundhouse, and the schoolhouse were built at about the same time. The town grew rapidly, private businesses established themselves, and Smith-Powers finally got out of the housing business and sold the residences to workers. But the company held onto the grocery, the maintenance buildings, and the lodging house. As in other company towns, the employer issued scrip that, Lehmonosky recalls, was "drawn against a man's payroll."[17]

As a career Forest Service officer, Henry Haefner lived in Powers between 1916 and 1918 and then spent "many days at a time" in the community until 1924. During those years, according to Haefner, Powers was the center of one of the largest logging operations in the United States. The company built three spur railroads, the first one extending southeast toward Eden Ridge, the location of the main body of timber. It was a tortuous line largely built on trestles in a series of long switchbacks with steep grades to the high ridge two or three miles from Powers. From an elevation of about 2,900 feet, the rail bed passed through "heavy cuts and fills" and across more sharp ridges and deep creeks.[18] Needless to say, Pacific Northwest newspapers were filled with stories about the train wrecks that occurred on such lines.

Although it is isolated from major routes of travel, Powers has been the home for hundreds of loggers and trainmen over the years. It has long since lost its cast as a company town, but the influence of its years as a busy center of logging activity weighs heavily. It suffers, like many rural communities in America, from the forces of modern capitalism that have concentrated wealth in the larger urban centers. From a bustling center of lumbering activity in the second decade of this century, Powers has become the home of retired people and a few logging families who survive on uncertain employment. The trains that traveled regularly between Myrtle Point and Powers stopped running years ago; today the log trucks that rumble down the South Fork of the Coquille pass by the small town and its graying buildings on their way to the mills on the lower Coquille or on Coos Bay.

The Smith-Powers Logging Company introduced several innovations to cut costs and to improve its self-sufficiency. The company purchased a large ranch on the South Fork of the Coquille River in

1912 with the intention of raising its own cattle. The costs of providing beef to its camps, boarding houses, and ships forced the move. The cookhouses required about two head of cattle each day, and the company expected the ranching effort to save money. Because the firm owned nearly six townships of timber in the vicinity, the ranch would be adjacent to some of its bigger logging operations.[19]

The C. A. Smith Company also invested heavily in steam locomotives and ocean-going vessels to enhance its ability to deliver logs to the mills and lumber to its finishing plant on San Francisco Bay. For a time the company operated the largest steam engine in Coos County, a seventy-two-ton Baldwin locomotive, to haul timber over the rail line to Coos Bay.[20] But the lumber ships, specially designed to navigate the shallow bar at the mouth of the harbor, attracted the most attention. For years those vessels were the vital lifeline for the large volume of lumber shipped out of Coos Bay. When foul weather or longshore strikes tied up its steamers, the lumber piled high on the dock at the Big Mill.

The *Nann Smith* and the *Redondo* were the first company ships to haul lumber to San Francisco; in 1913 the firm added a third vessel, the *Adeline Smith*. The new steel ship, fitted for burning oil or coal and capable of hauling two million board feet of lumber, was one of the largest carriers of its kind. The company's ships hauled lumber from Coos Bay and on the return trip brought supplies and equipment for the mills and logging camps. C. A. Smith and other company personnel used cabin accommodations aboard the vessels to travel to and from San Francisco. Florence Berg regularly made the trip to California aboard the Smith lumber steamers and recalls that her father occasionally would take his car to San Francisco to provide transportation for the family.[21]

The C. A. Smith Company also added its powerful influence to those calling for harbor improvements. While local politicians lobbied in Washington, D. C., for federal appropriations, the Smith and Simpson interests funded a private effort to deepen the harbor channel to eighteen feet. The project, completed in December 1908, had an element of urgency because the Big Mill had come on the line earlier that year. The increased shipments across the bar reflect, in part, the improved channel conditions in the harbor.[22] The volume continued to grow as the Smith mills expanded production in the next few years.

The Coos Bay business community also set about organizing a port authority with taxing power to direct development on the bay. After fits and starts and a legal wrangle over a state law authorizing the formation of such governing bodies, the Port of Coos Bay was established in 1912.[23] The new port commissioners, Albert Powers and Asa Mead Simpson's son, Louis, immediately began a campaign to deepen the interior channel. Their representation on the port commission established another precedent; that body has always included prominent shippers on the bay, especially officials of the major forest products firms.

With the formation of the port authority, the future for C. A. Smith and the Big Mill appeared certain. Its modern manufacturing facilities, its expanding system of logging railroads and camps in the Coos hinterland, and its finishing plant and marketing network on San Francisco Bay were the talk of the West Coast lumber industry. The C. A. Smith seedling nursery was a model of progressive forestry. Lumber trade journals praised the efficiency of its mills, and writers marvelled at the ingenuity of its logging engineers. The company also was pioneering an irregular trade in large timbers with the coastal ports of China.[24] But, at that point the firm entered a period of protracted difficulties, problems that were endemic throughout the industry.

Beginning in 1907 the lumber trade entered a prolonged period of depressed prices and overproduction. E. T. Allen, a widely respected forest economist in the Northwest, attributed the problems to "relentless" competition. In 1914 George Cornwall, the veteran editor of the Portland-based *Timberman*, reported that lumber prices were the lowest ever recorded; he urged lumbermen on the Pacific Coast to curtail production as "an economic necessity." E. B. Hazen, a Portland trade leader with ties to large financial institutions, advised bankers to assist lumbermen "to amalgamate their properties" into larger units.[25] Operating in that cutthroat competitive environment, the C. A. Smith Company soon found itself in a financial bind.

Although the firm was a force in the San Francisco lumber market, low prices, the company's heavy capital expenditures for expansion, the indebtedness on its timberlands, and the annual taxes on its properties began to take their toll. Like many of his peers in the lumber industry, Charles Axel Smith was overextended. For that was a speculative and unstable world, subject to the warp and woof of business cycles, seasonal fluctuations in the demand for lumber, and the intrusion of the government in times of national emergency. But the root cause of that instability was in the social system itself. Market forces far beyond Coos Bay exerted an increasing influence over Oregon's south coast. Similar conditions prevailed on Puget Sound and in British Columbia; decisions made in eastern financial houses increasingly dominated those isolated, back-country forest communities as well.[26]

Because the C. A. Smith Company operated out of offices in Minneapolis and San Francisco, most Coos Bay residents knew little about the firm's difficulties. Florence Berg vaguely remembers that "it was kind of a disastrous time" and that the building of the pulp mill had something to do with it. Of her father's involvement, she recalls only that "a telephone call would come through" once in a while. Victor Stevens, who worked as a logger out of the community of Powers, blames the fall of the company on federal intervention in railroad and shipping matters during the First World War. A brief account of the C. A. Smith financial empire in a history of Coos County attributes the company's problems to disrupted markets during the war and investments "financed by bond issues bearing interest as high as eight percent."[27] Lumbermen referred to the latter predicament as "excessive carrying charges."

Because the firm was deeply in debt and faced what it termed heavy carrying charges in taxes and fire protection, the C. A. Smith Company required a healthy lumber market to remain financially stable. In a remarkable bit of candor, Smith told a local reporter in 1913 that industrial conditions were discouraging. With the exception of the previous year, he doubted "if there was a single mill on the Pacific Coast that earned interest on the investment regardless of profit. Even last year I think 50 percent of the mills did not make a penny of profit and barely earned interest without dividends."[28] The timber empire that Smith had pieced together—through the help of Governor Pilsbury's money, by manipulating state and federal land laws, and financed with a high-interest bank loan—was coming apart. The shrewd Swedish immigrant had misjudged the market.

The Coos Bay *Times* made public the company's financial problems in 1916 when it reported the firm's decision to sell all of its timber holdings that were not essential to the Coos Bay mills. The objective was to "reduce the overhead expenses of the company in carrying the immense holdings." But there was a silver lining in the Smith company sales; it "MEANS BIG DEVELOPMENT" because it would bring more mills to western Oregon. According to H. F. Chaney of the company's sales department, the move was "not a forced sale but purely a business arrangement." After selling its timberland in Linn and Lane counties, a tract in the Alsea Bay area, and another one on the redwood coast, he told a reporter that the firm was in "better condition than it has been in a long time."[29]

As for C. A. Smith, the *Times* described him as "a good friend of

Coos Bay." Although the "creditors committee of the Smith properties" had forced the sale, the newspaper estimated that the company had an adequate supply of timber to operate "the two big mills" for nearly a century. Timberland in the Coos country, the *Times* reminded its readers, "is closely held and combined in a few large interests." Before the Smith sales, an independent mill had difficulty obtaining a dependable source of supply for logs. The "new plan," therefore, would attract eastern and southern operators who had already cut out.[30] The ownership of both a sizable volume of timber and manufacturing facilities usually has meant the difference between success and failure.

The creditors' committee changed the title of the reorganized properties to the Coos Bay Lumber Company. Although C. A. Smith stayed on in an advisory capacity, active management of the firm had passed to the investment capitalists who had financed the company's expanded operations. The *Times* put the matter kindly—the new management believed that Smith "was entitled to a rest." But, the financial problems of the revamped Coos Bay Lumber Company persisted, and in 1919 it went into receivership. Although the business continued to operate under its old trade name, the Pacific States Lumber Company emerged as the new corporate unit.[31] Banking interests in San Francisco and Chicago now controlled the operations on Coos Bay.

Both international events and the precarious financial underpinnings of the forest products trade shaped the southwestern Oregon economy. When the patriarch of the West Coast lumber industry, Asa Meade Simpson, died in 1915, the Portland-based Buehner Lumber Company purchased most of the Simpson estate, including its waterfront properties and extensive timber holdings. The outbreak of the European war altered normal trading channels and brought further hardship to the Pacific Coast lumber trade. For Oregon's south coast, the reorganization of the Coos Bay Lumber Company and the sale of the Simpson estate added to those difficulties.[32] Although war orders eventually quickened the demand for lumber, in the early summer of 1917 workers in the Big Mill went on strike to gain their share of the profits.

The Coos Bay Lumber Company strike was part of a wider protest for better wages and a shorter work day in the West Coast lumber industry. The strikes in the logging camps and mills in the summer of 1917 were the most spectacular up to that time. By August only 15 percent of the mills in the Pacific Northwest were operating. Ship carpenters in places like Grays Harbor refused to handle lumber from "ten-hour mills." Although some employees returned to work, once back on the job they practiced "conscientious withdrawal of efficiency" to slow production.[33] At that point, officials from Washington, D. C., intervened and worked in collusion with industrial and commercial groups to get the lumber mills operating.

Federal government agents and leading lumbermen formed a quasi-company union, the Loyal Legion of Loggers and Lumbermen (4-L), to enforce the eight-hour day, better living conditions in the camps, and higher wages. But that achievement was a victory for the militant unionism of the iww and progressives in the American Federation of Labor locals, not the 4-L. According to Al Martin, who worked for the Coos Bay Lumber Company, the aggressiveness of the iww and others was responsible for the improved conditions in the camps: "Up until that time, we carried our bedding on our backs, our bed rolls. Soon after that they started furnishing blankets and sheets." Victor Stevens, who logged in the Powers area, agrees: The outcome of the "iww scare" was clean bed sheets, deloused and warmer bunkhouses, and more attention to men who were injured.[34]

The strike against the Coos Bay Lumber Company was brief. Because of a shortage of labor and fears that loggers would join the walkout, the company raised wages in the mill to comply with the strikers' demands. During the next few months war-related orders for cedar and other lumber products and a thriving shipbuilding industry boosted the Coos Bay economy. The eight-hour day became a regular feature of employment in the mills and logging camps, and local newspapers were unstinting in their praise for workers who joined the 4-L.[35] But those conditions were quickly reversed once the war ended.

The local shipbuilding industry was even more unpredictable than the lumber trade. The Kruse and Banks operation, the largest shipyard on the bay and the successor to the Simpson plant in North Bend, provides a good example. The firm began producing "steam schooners," a hybrid sail and steam coasting vessel soon after it opened in 1905. Over the next few years the company built a freight-car ferry to be used on San Francisco Bay, a tug, several barges, and a few gasoline-powered vessels. Although Kruse and Banks closed its doors when the United States economy slowed in 1913, the war put the shipyards back into production, and by 1916 the company's North Bend plant housed 200 employees. When the United States entered the fighting in Europe, the Kruse and Banks yards employed nearly 500 workers building ships for the Emergency Fleet Corporation.[36] As with other shipyards on the Pacific Coast, Kruse and Banks' brief

boom in shipbuilding ended when the government cancelled all orders at the end of the war.

But when the shipyards were busy, they dominated construction
activity in North Bend and Marshfield. Mary Banks Granger, the
daughter of shipbuilder Robert Banks, remembers that "everybody
was involved in one way or another on the waterfront." The shipyards
employed skilled carpenters and shipwrights who prepared the
"ways," laid the keel, built the frames and shaped them to conform
with the curvature of the hull, and finally placed the shoring timbers
and guy wires to hold everything together while workers fastened the
frame and keel. During the last stages of construction, shipwrights
laid the planking, caulked it with "oakum" to make it watertight,
braced the hold, and added the decks, spars, and machinery.[37]

Those were exciting and busy years for the Coos Bay communities.
James H. Polhemus, who headed the short-lived Coos Bay Shipbuilding Company, complained about the shortage of skilled labor. According to Jack McNab, an Irish immigrant who hired on with Kruse and
Banks during the war, jobs were abundant: "When a guy came into
town, there was ten men in the street wanting to hire him." Another
resident remembers the smell of wood and caulk and the incessant
sound of hammering that filled the air on the bay fronts in Marshfield
and North Bend. Most of that demanding manual labor was done
outdoors.[38]

But that hectic pace of activity ended with the war. Shortly thereafter, financial difficulties forced the Coos Bay Lumber Company to
suspend operations, putting nearly 1,200 men out of work. Although
the Big Mill started up again in the summer of 1919, that pattern of
layoffs and suspended operations continued for the next two decades.

At the beginning of the 1920s, the Coos Bay country still had one of
the most extensive stands of old-growth timber on the Pacific slope. A
few large concerns controlled most of it—the Coos Bay Lumber Company, the Southern Oregon Company (a subsidiary of Menasha), the
Weyerhaeuser Timber Company, and the Buehner Company. The
original Oregon and California railroad grant, lands formerly in the
private sector, had been revested to the federal government in 1916.
The concentrated ownership of timberland—in both the public and
private sector—made it difficult for new sawmill operations to obtain a
dependable source of logs and undoubtedly limited the number of
manufacturing units on the bay.

Although the Coos Bay area was becoming a settlement of family
residences by the 1920s, in addition to the all-male lumber camps, its

citizens were increasingly at risk to decisions made in the boardrooms of distant centers of capital. The profit ledgers of the corporate owners who controlled the resources, not the stability and welfare of the working people on the Coos estuary, shaped their decisions. The organization and control of capital also assured that labor would bear the brunt of the industry's problems. The volatile nature of the lumber trade, therefore, contributed to a highly mobile work force that was quick to move on when the steam donkeys and mills ceased operations.

The most popular lumberman's journal in the Pacific Northwest, the *Timberman*, published a lengthy article in 1922 extolling the future for the industry on the Pacific Coast. The journal pointed out that the South, like earlier logging frontiers, was nearing the end of its timber resources. To illustrate that shift, it listed the annual harvest for each of the major forested regions in the United States (see Table 2).

The Pacific Coast states held more than half the remaining timber supplies in the country. And Portland, the *Timberman* predicted, would be "the coming lumber center" in the country.[39]

During the 1920s Grays Harbor, the Puget Sound districts, Portland, and the Columbia River area shipped more lumber than any other timber-producing center in the United States. By the end of the decade, however, those areas were beginning to show the strains of the heavy rate of harvesting. At the onset of the 1930s it was generally acknowledged that the Coos Bay region held the largest remaining stand of old-growth timber on the Pacific slope. But a collapsing American and world economy meant that the heyday for sawmilling on Coos Bay still lay in the future.

TABLE 2.   Percentage of Annual Harvest

Year	Northeast	Lakes States	South	Pacific Coast
1919	7.5	7.8	46.6	25.5
1914	9.5	10.5	47.6	18.7
1909	11.7	12.3	44.9	15.5
1899	16.3	24.9	31.7	8.2
1889	19.8	34.6	20.3	8.5
1879	25.8	34.7	13.8	3.6
1869	35.7	28.2	10.1	4.1

Logging the Coos Timber

Most of the camps you lived in a bunkhouse with four people in it, and a barrel stove, that is, a stove made out of an oil barrel. And, of course, you came in wet and cold, and you took off your clothes and dried them off as much as you could during the night. And you lay there and breathed all that stinking, sweaty clothes, but you thought nothing of it. It's just the way you lived in those days.

Dow Beckham[1]

When Paul Bunyan made the long trek from the Great Lakes pineries to the forests of the Pacific slope, he brought with him a rich tradition of folklore and ballad that loggers had passed along for generations, some of it dating to the heyday of river drives in the Maine woods. But on this last great timber stand there was a new twist to the stories that glorified the strenuous work and the danger involved in the logging and lumbering enterprise. In the Pacific Northwest, beginning in the 1930s, lumber trade organizations began hiring skilled writers like Stewart Holbrook and James Stevens to add a luster of authenticity to the old romantic tales. The fact that the Bunyanesque version dominates popular thinking about the industry suggests that the public relations effort has succeeded.

In the last two decades folklorists and writers of fiction have embellished that vision—of life in the lumber camps, the epic stories of the logging drives down western rivers, and the legendary accounts of free-wheeling hedonism when loggers entered the skidroad districts of far-western towns. In that view, the dawn-to-dusk work in the woods and the sweat and blood of the speedups in the mills are described as a composite of patriotism, apple pie, and duty to family and motherhood. Anything, that is, but the daily reckoning with death and crippling injury and the protracted periods of unemployment that have characterized the industry. Ken Kesey's *Sometimes a Great Notion*, especially the movie version, fits the former prescription. It portrays a logging family of heroic proportions—Hank Stamper, the family strongman, can work harder, swim farther, and fight better than any of the logging and mill-working fraternity on the Wakonda Auga River.

In truth, those who have worked in the woods, often with a twinkle in their eye, helped to perpetuate some of the tales. Barre Toelken, a gifted folklorist, relates the story of an interviewer who once asked an old logger if there was any substance to the rumor that men in the woods were superstitious about getting killed during their last day on the job:

> Did I ever hear of getting killed on the last day of work? Well, I guess if you got killed it *would* be your last day of work, wouldn't it? Anyhow, you know, no matter whether you're killed or injured, they leave you there by the cold deck and take you in with the last load of the day, so you won't lose out on a day's pay. And no matter what, a day's pay is a day's pay.[2]

The man's response has elements both of polite teasing and recognition about the reality of work with an arbitrary employer.

The daily experiences of loggers and mill workers from the Humboldt redwoods north to British Columbia differ from the romantic version. While popular lore depicts a tradition of larger-than-life hemen, Charlotte Todes and Vernon Jensen, two of the earliest historians to write realistically about the industry, argue that the story was also one of working people struggling to make a living in a difficult and demanding environment.[3] The far-western timber industry and the frontier were one in the early twentieth century. To make matters worse for those who lived in the lumber towns and the logging camps, chaotic and unstable business conditions and uncompromising and individualistic operators were daily points of reckoning. Those circumstances influenced life in southwestern Oregon as they did elsewhere on the Pacific Coast.

There were other features that made North America's last forest frontier unique. It was widely believed that logging and lumbering in the Douglas fir region would be permanent sources of employment. By contrast, in the South loggers normally were farmers as well. There were more people employed in the industry in California, Oregon, Washington, and Idaho by the 1920s than in any other single activity. Lumbering provided more than half the wages earned in Oregon and Washington. The federal census returns in the early twentieth century also show that the vast majority of workers in the timber trade were unmarried men. The estimate for 1910 of 90 percent single males emphasizes the itinerate and unstable nature of the work, especially in the logging camps.[4] Although conditions changed over the years, single males dominated the work force well into the automobile age.

It was in that world of adverse working conditions, swashbuckling bosses, frequent job changes, and always unstable employment that men—and by the Second World War a growing number of women—sought to make a living. In their struggle, they had to cope with a variety of industrial innovations—new technological devices, shifting market strategies, the introduction of substitute building materials, and the company's efforts to increase efficiency and cut production costs. Speed was of the essence, and the widespread use of steam power in the woods early in the century meant that lumbermen had cut the technological gap between their logging and milling operations.

The use of steam donkeys to yard and load logs vastly stepped up the pace of activity in the woods and increased the incidence of injury and death. "Steam was fast and required fast work," according to one contemporary, "and then there was always ten men sitting around waiting for a job." Another veteran Coos logger who admired the adaptation of steam power to the woods, points out that "steam engines didn't get tired." And, he might have added, they forced workers to conform to the rhythms of the machine and made them vulnerable when a "wire rope" mainline or choker (a wire cable attached to a log) snapped while hauling in timber. The development of the high-lead system, with cables suspended in the air, increased the accident rate even more. Logging bosses worsened those mechanical hazards when they offered "yarding bonuses" to crews that exceeded a predetermined volume of timber.[5]

Although Coos loggers probably were slower in adapting steam power to the woods because of the great timber stands close to the extensive waterways, the C. A. Smith camps used steam donkeys from the beginning. But there is also evidence that bull teams, the manual rafting of logs on the rivers, and older forms of "handlogging" lasted well into the twentieth century. The use of older, less capital-intensive technologies allowed farmers to log through the winter months and ride their cut to market on the spring freshets.

Many south coast loggers bridged the transition from animal to steam power. Roy Rozell, whose parents came to Coos Bay from Minnesota, began logging on South Slough at the age of fourteen in 1896. He lived in camp, where he did chores and helped the "bull puncher" yoke oxen. The bulls, he recalls, were half wild, but when the punch struck the animals with his goad stick, "by God them bulls learned to mind pretty quick." According to Rozell, the slow moving beasts could haul three to five logs per turn. Bud Metcalf also grew up in the bull-team era on South Slough; he was a skid greaser—one who walked behind the oxen but in front of the logs, applying thick oil to the small trees felled across the skid road so that the animals could haul the huge timbers with less friction. Metcalf remembers that a five-yoke team could pull up to ten logs at a time. On longer trips, the oxen sometimes made only two "turns" a day.[6]

Both Rozell and Metcalf witnessed the end of bull-team and skid-road logging in the Coos country. By 1910 the sounds of the steam engine and the squeal of the yarding machine had replaced the profanity of the bull puncher and the grating of the oxbows. Shortly after the turn of the century, Rozell hired on with a "ground logging" operation where a steam donkey was used to haul logs to a railroad siding. In some instances, as many as three donkeys were used to relay logs to a landing. Metcalf worked in high-lead camps during the First World War, occasionally doing the high-climbing duties. Later in life he became a saw filer, one of the most respected skills in a logging camp.[7]

Despite "daylight-to-dark" workdays, Bud Metcalf stayed with logging for the rest of his life. "That's all I ever did," he recalled at the age of eighty-three, except for a bit of moonshining. For Rozell logging meant being in the woods at daylight and working until dark. Although the change to steam power meant little difference in the length of the workday for Rozell and Metcalf, it dramatically altered the pace of activity. Men who had walked behind the slow moving oxen now ran and scrambled to get out of the way of the wire rope when the "donkey puncher" threw the lever that set the steam-powered capstan in motion.[8]

Turn-of-the-century loggers were both innovative and capable. As the Smith-Powers Company was extending its heavily capitalized transportation system into its vast holdings, Louis David Root carried on small-scale logging on the Coquille River using a variety of ingenious methods. Operating with little capital, Root used bull teams to haul logs to the river; when that proved too slow, he used a team of six horses to pull the timber over rails on a tram car. He moved the logs into a boom with a rowboat and rafted them to Coquille on the tidal current.[9]

Dow Beckham, with forty years experience in the woods, speaks convincingly about "the brilliant men during those years [who] worked in the logging camps out in the woods." Although they "never were around towns much" and lacked formal education, they were intelligent and "knew how to do their job."[10] The "dumb logger," the butt of so much humor in the region, was in reality an innovative and highly skilled technician. The difficult terrain on the Pacific slope encouraged workers to look for easier ways to get the job done and placed a premium on people with a wide range of experiences. Old-timers insist vehemently that loggers were more skilled before the introduction of gasoline-powered equipment to the woods.

Until motorized vehicles and chain saws were used, it took more men to fall, yard, and transport logs to mills than it did to cut the same volume of timber into lumber. Logging with steam, therefore, required a large work force regardless of the size of the operation. Even a small camp might employ forty or more men, depending on the number of "sides" it operated (a side included a complete crew to run the steam donkey and yard the logs to a landing). A camp also included timber fallers and buckers, saw filers and other maintenance personnel, men to operate the logging railroad, and finally the camp cook and the flunkies who helped in the kitchen and waited on tables. Curt Beckham's uncle employed between twenty and twenty-five men for his small family operation in the 1920s. In addition to his woods crew, the uncle employed about ten men to run a small sawmill. The "Beckham camp," according to Curt, "was a relative operation, because the relatives would come out from Arkansas and Texas to work for the relatives out here."[11] Most camps, even the smaller ones, lacked the intimate atmosphere of the Beckham outfit.

Life was more arbitrary in large operations like the Coos Bay Lumber Company, where hirings and firings were everyday occurrences. Jack Dashney, one of the company's boss loggers, had a reputation for being particularly ruthless. Another Minnesota import, Dashney was said to have three crews, "one coming, one going, and one working." When he sent his timekeeper to town for a crew, Dashney reputedly told him on one occasion: "Just send me half a dozen men. If they don't wear suspenders, send twelve." Chappie McCarthy argues that bosses like Dashney cultivated "being a mean old son-of-a-gun. They always try to." Victor Stevens puts a different twist to the story that Dashney was a hard man to work for: "The truth is that he was a hard man to not work for. If you weren't a good worker, you didn't stay long."[12]

To the camp bosses, however, there was a certain production-oriented logic to arbitrary firings; fresh men worked harder than those who had been on the job longer. Camp superintendents "had no regard for whether a man had his own plans or had family responsibilities," according to Dow Beckham. "Men were just like tools, and you used them and threw them away if you didn't need them anymore." Those circumstances made the Coos Bay Lumber Company "a ruthless highball outfit" in the early days. Curt Beckham holds a different view: the Coos Bay Lumber Company, he believes, was a good, stable outfit to work for; the most notorious highball operations were the big camps on the Columbia River. "They killed men and they waited until evening before they'd bring them in."[13] Although stories about the Columbia River outfits are widespread among loggers on the south coast, those tales applied equally well to the Coos Bay country where the volume of production was the measure of a company's success.

From a company's point of view, Dow Beckham points out, leaving a dead man behind a stump for the remainder of the day was not altogether a ruthless decision. Cost and distance were important factors. Some of the men might be cutting timber a mile down in the canyon, he says, and it would take the rest of the day to get the crew to the landing where they could ride the speeder out.[14] The incidence of fatality and injury did not lessen until the 1940s, when unions forced most logging bosses to observe specific safety procedures. By that time crews also could get medical attention to an injured man much more quickly.

Most of the men who worked in the woods between 1920 and 1940 agree that the smaller camps did not tend to be highball operations. That might be attributed to the daily intimacy of working with one's boss or the fact that many were "relative" operations like the Beckham camp. But it did not mean that small camps were safer; in fact, the opposite was more likely. The small outfits or gyppos, Curt Beckham believes, probably had as many "fatals" as the larger units; most "used poor equipment and poor lines," and there were no safety inspectors. The combination of worn machinery and cables and the need to meet production quotas often was disastrous.[15] Like the more heavily capitalized companies, gyppos had to turn out a large volume of logs as cheaply and efficiently as possible.

Living and working conditions in British Columbia were similar to those south of the border. Turnover in the camps was high—foremen fired men indiscriminately and workers frequently left camp because of arbitrary bosses. Charles Hemstrom, who came to the Lake Cowichan area from Sweden in 1906, described the living quarters in the camps as poor. But, he added, "we were not used to anything anyway, so bad conditions didn't matter too much." If a worker was "union-minded," he remembers, you kept it quiet or "you went down the road if they found out."[16] Like workers elsewhere in the days before union organization, the British Columbia logger's main weapon was to pack his bedroll and move on.

Whether they were attached to large or small camps, loggers worked in isolated areas away from the comforts of hearth and home, and the cultural distractions of urban life. Even the sizable company town of Powers fits that description. The bunkhouses in the early years of the century were little more than temporary shacks thrown together to provide cheap housing for as many men as possible. Damp and often filled with fleas, those rough, unventilated bunkhouses usually were dirty and overcrowded. The occupants slept in double bunks one above the other. A special trademark of living quarters in the Douglas fir region was wet and steamy clothing hanging to dry.[17]

Wet clothing was conventional on the North Pacific slope where the rainy season often lasted from September until June. "You liked to have them warm the next morning," Dow Beckham indicates, but "they weren't dry as a rule." Besides, if your job kept you dry, "you'd sweat so much you'd be wet on the inside anyway." The solution was woolen underwear: "It didn't make any difference how wet or cold you got," Beckham explains, "you were always warm or dry; it's the expression we used." That also meant short lunch breaks during the winter weather—"if you stopped for a little while, then you'd begin to get cold."[18]

From most accounts—both by boss loggers and the single men who ate in the cookhouse—the food in the camps was fairly good by the time of the First World War. Although we might quibble today about the amount of fatty and starchy food in the logger's diet, men who worked from dawn to dusk complained little about meat, potatoes, and biscuits topped with gravy—as long as the meal was prepared well. One of the sure ways to lose a top logger was poor food.

The "fine" kitchens impressed Florence Berg when she traveled to the camps as a child with her father, Al Powers. "The men needed good food," she says, "and I think my father was particularly conscious of that." Henry Haefner, who ate in many of the Smith-Powers cookhouses during his travels for the Forest Service, remembers that the food "was good and plentiful." Another Powers-area logger recalls that in the later camps, "you couldn't afford to set your table at home the way they did."[19] But it was the loggers protest and their willingness to quit if the food was bad, not the goodwill and generosity of camp bosses, that brought quality meals to the cookhouses.

The bunkhouses were another issue—crude and roughly furnished at best. Before electricity came to the larger camps in the 1940s, kerosene lanterns and oil barrel stoves were standard equipment. Although many of the larger operations provided bedrolls by the 1920s, the smaller outfits still expected men to pack their "own balloon." In the small camps loggers sometimes lived in tents, or as one did, in a hollow stump during the summer months. The big companies stationed many of the bunkhouses at railroad sidings so that they could easily be moved to the next logging site.[20] Fixed residences were out of the question, because logging superintendents wanted the camps as close to the timber as possible to eliminate travel time.

Rexford Tugwell, who later gained prominence as one of Franklin D. Roosevelt's "brain trusters," captured the spirit of those small, isolated communities in an article published in 1920. The lumber camp, he wrote, was "a sad travesty," made up of "a half dozen box-car-like shacks of weathered wood." They included two or three bunkhouses for seventy-five or a hundred men, a cook shack, the foreman's office, and the commissary. Located along a railroad spur, the sites were usually "a dozen, perhaps twenty or more miles" from the nearest town.[21] Although he was far removed from the Coos country, the urbane Tugwell provided a good description of the crude and makeshift housing arrangements.

Loggers improvised to make themselves as comfortable as possible in the confined quarters of the bunkhouse. One innovation was the widespread use of empty dynamite, or "powder boxes," for a variety of purposes. Armed with his bedroll and a company lantern, a logger could fashion some makeshift comforts for himself. The powder boxes, or "Dupont furniture" as the loggers referred to them, served as chairs, lamp tables, and, nailed to the wall, a storage area for sundries—tobacco, snoose, and cigarettes. Theolo Steckel, who lived in Coos Bay Lumber Company camps in the 1920s, recalls that "a good many of the loggers had them in their homes too."[22]

That was the world of the bachelor logger. For married men accommodations were more limited. In his travels to the Coos Bay Lumber Company camps between 1915 and 1925, Henry Haefner noted that there was no family housing, except at Powers. Bill McKenna, who grew up near his uncle's railroad logging operation between 1918 and 1928, remembers that housing arrangements were separated into a "family camp" and a "single camp." Fifty-five to sixty single men lived in the upper camp and fifteen to twenty families in the lower or family camp. Although the McKennas had a "reasonably nice house" with inside plumbing, most of the dwellings were "shacks." Wandering around the family camp, he remembers, was a child's delight—the maintenance shops for the entire logging operation, including the railroad cars and locomotives, were located in the lower camp.[23]

The McKenna camp included a one-room school that housed about thirty students through the sixth grade. But beyond the family camp was a world of mystery, that is, until a child grew older. "Just over the hill," the dying coal mining town of Beaver Hill still offered "a real four-room school" for seventh and eighth graders, a motion picture house, and other "things that coal mining towns had." Like Bill McKenna, Garnett Johnson was raised in a series of small logging camps. Garnett played near her mother around the cookhouse, and "most of my life," she recalls, "I was alone as far as other children were concerned." When she was old enough to attend school, Garnett began boarding with relatives in town. She says with some bitterness, "I hardly knew what a home was."[24] Except for moving more frequently, her experiences were similar to those of other young people who grew up in isolated places.

As a child, Garnett Johnson lacked the advantage of socializing with childhood peers that Bill McKenna enjoyed. Although the McKenna business was family operated, it was much larger than the gyppo outfits. McKenna's uncle ran the logging end and his father did the scaling and took care of the payroll. Travel to and from the camp, other than the short trek to Beaver Hill, was by rail. Because the community was relatively self-contained, trips to "real" towns like Marshfield were limited to Christmas and the Fourth of July. Still, "there was a constant coming and going all the time," especially among the single men.[25] And the quickest way to another job was over the hill to the next camp.

Although males dominated the logging camps, women held important positions in some of them. In the Powers area men ran the cookhouses at first, but eventually the company began hiring women. Henry Haefner remembers the first woman head cook in one of the Powers camps. In an occupation still reserved for men, "she was an excellent manager and cook and knew her job." Garnett Johnson's mother worked in various logging camps, first as a "flunky," and later as a cook. Although women made up a sizable portion of the work force in some of the mills on Coos Bay during the First World War, they did not begin working in the woods until the 1940s, and then mostly for gyppo operators who hired them as whistle punks (a person who signaled to the donkey operator to haul in a log). According to Dow Beckham whose work experiences spanned those decades, "we didn't have any women in the woods except as hashers in the camps."[26]

Logging outfits varied in size from the huge Coos Bay Lumber Company operation of 400 men on Eden Ridge to the small family undertaking of fifteen men that Chappie McCarthy remembers. The

McCarthy camp included two bunkhouses, a cookhouse, an old forge, a saw-filing shed, and "a place that my dad called his office. It was just the same as the bunkhouse only it had sleeping quarters in the back." Although McCarthy left the camp when he began school, he returned every summer when he was old enough to work.[27]

Living conditions in the isolated camps improved with each passing decade. Militant union activity at the onset of American entry into the First World War, especially on the part of the iww, brought better food, higher pay, cleaner bunkhouses, and for a time the adoption of the eight-hour day. By the 1940s most of the bigger outfits provided bath and shower facilities, reading and recreation rooms, and even washing machines. But highballing remained a fact of life in all camps until unions forced the companies to establish safety procedures that eventually cut down the accident rate. In Dow Beckham's words: "The unions helped stop some of that highball logging and killing and maiming of men."[28] But the strong market and the dramatic expansion of logging activity after 1945, especially by gyppo operators, kept the accident rate high.

There was more to logging than simply hauling timber to a railroad siding. Because of the extensive waterways in the Douglas fir country, most of the larger companies also had sizable booming and rafting crews. Until the widespread use of gasoline-powered equipment, therefore, operators usually employed many more men at the logging end than they did in manufacturing. And many men spent more of their working life on water than they did in the woods. Transporting logs via water required a large crew—Ivan Laird once employed seventy-five men to drive logs on the Coquille River during the rainy season.[29]

The Coos Bay Lumber Company used both rail and water transportation to deliver logs from Powers to its mills. Locomotives hauled the long trainloads to the head of Isthmus Slough on the Coos estuary where the logs were dumped into the water. A "booming crew" sorted the timber by species into separate rafts, and from that point, the men rafted the logs to the mills. During the peak years of sawmilling, the estuary literally was jammed with log rafts. According to William E. Major, who spent most of his life with the Coos Bay Lumber Company booming crews, there were so many logs in the slough at times that "a boat could hardly get through."[30] Like their fellow workers in the woods or on the railroads, the booming and rafting crews faced constant danger from rolling logs and could be crushed or drowned if they fell into the water in the vicinity of the rafts.

Until the 1930s when companies began using log trucks on a wide scale, loggers also "splashed" millions of board feet of timber down the rivers each year. Although short-line logging railroads laced the Coos country at one time, splashing logs was an efficient and economical way to move a large volume of timber when the rivers were high. Environmental considerations aside, Dow Beckham considers the splash dam "the most efficient tool that a logger ever developed if you place it against the background of the time in which it was used." The problem was to move the timber to tidewater, where it could be placed in booms and towed to the mills. In the absence of logging railroads, Beckham observes, splashing was the answer. A logger could take "a small crew, and go back in the hills for thirty-five miles, build a dam, log all summer, and run several million feet of logs on the winter freshets."[31] Although fishermen complained about the destruction of spawning grounds and the gouging of the river bed associated with splashing, they lacked the political clout to end the practice.

Many operators who used splash dams worked on a contractual basis. Charles McGeorge subcontracted with a boom company to splash logs down river from a logging camp at Allegany. He and a partner would "turn everything loose at the head of the river during a freshet," and then try to beat the logs downstream with a boat to a point where they would place "a set of boom sticks across the river and stow those logs as they came down." Although it was difficult and dangerous work and required long hours, McGeorge says "it was a paying deal."[32] That crude but effective technique—with many refinements—lasted until the late 1950s when state regulations finally ended the practice.

The first splash dams built in the Coos country bore a striking similarity to those in the Great Lakes states and in eastern North America. That is not surprising, because of men like Chappie McCarthy's father, who had worked on splash dams in New Brunswick before he came to the West Coast. As time passed and the volume of logs on the rivers increased, splash dams became larger, more intricate, and costly. Dow Beckham worked on the river for nearly twenty years and was known as one of the most knowledgeable and innovative splash-dam operators. Before the construction of large splash dams in the 1940s, river men used "peavies and dynamite to break log jams" and other obstructions such as fish racks. That, he points out, made for "very harrowing times as far as your life or your danger were concerned."[33] Eventually, the construction of a second large splash dam on the South Fork of the Coos River provided sufficient water to move logs to tidewater safely.

Tidal action always played an important part in rafting logs on the Coos estuary. According to Richard Anderson, a tugboat operator since his teens, the tides dictated when people worked. For Bill Brainard, who "went on the water" because he disliked logging, a job on a tugboat meant from "daylight to dark and from dark to daylight, just whenever the tide was in, you was working." Although rafting activity was heaviest during the summer, by the 1940s some companies worked the year around.[34] Hauling the large cedar, spruce, and fir log rafts completed the journey for timber that had been cut many miles from the Coos waterways. And with the task accomplished and an extended period of leisure on their hands, loggers, railroad crews, and river men headed for the towns on the bay or the lower Coquille River.

Nothing is more celebrated in logging lore than the raucous behavior of workmen when they visited the famous "skidroad" districts. Towns like Bangor, Maine, Saginaw, Michigan, and Portland, Oregon, gained reputations as centers of loud and boisterous activity during holiday seasons like Christmas and the Fourth of July. Portland's Burnside district, Seattle's Yesler Way, and the Front Street area in Marshfield provided relaxation and pleasure for men who lacked the amenities of normal social life. Prolonged periods of isolation made it easy for business establishments to take advantage of men starved for entertainment and human company.

Although it was smaller than the better-known skidroad districts in the Northwest, Marshfield's Front Street was a point of rendezvous for loggers, railroad crews, riverboat men, mill workers, longshoremen, and sailors from the ships which came to haul lumber to distant markets. The waterfront, in truth, was a vital center of social activity for homeless workers—with a few days of leisure and money to spend—before they returned to the monotony of the logging camp or a lumber ship leaving port. Whether they got drunk, fought, or visited the houses of prostitution, men found the skidroad districts a place to relax and "blow off steam."

Before the automobile became common in the region, most loggers traveled to Coos Bay by boat. On special occasions like the Fourth of July, they came in droves down the waterways on the rivers and sloughs, by far the most convenient route to town. And, at least through the First World War, the Independence Day celebration was

the big event of the year for Marshfield and the men who poured into
town from the logging camps. On those occasions, young boys like
Raymond McKeown followed the loggers around town begging nickels. He added, perhaps with some exaggeration: "Everybody who had
money got drunk."[35]

One Fourth of July, to the surprise of his daughter Florence, Al
Powers participated in the log birling contests, an activity in which
participants "turned" a log floating in the water with the intention of
upsetting an opponent. After those festivities, Raymond McKeown
remembers, "unbelieveable brawls" took place. And there is copious
evidence to support that view. Logging required the unleashing of
tremendous mechanical and human energy, and loggers themselves
were part of a cultural system steeped in violence. Their personal
world was regularly punctuated with physical injury and disrupted
family life. On the special occasions when they escaped the long
hours of labor in the woods and the boredom of camp, they would, as
one man put it, "get a few drinks under their belt and start cuttin-
up."[36]

Technological change came slowly to the Coos country. The use of
crosscut saws (hand briars) and steam donkeys remained standard
through the 1930s. During the depression years, however, a few
loggers began using bulldozers (cats) to build roads and to yard logs,
and a few of the larger operators purchased gasoline-powered donkey
engines. But more than anything else, it was the manpower shortages
of the Second World War that revolutionized work in the woods. The
construction of all-weather roads and the use of pickup trucks and
van-type vehicles called "crummies" to transport loggers to the woods
enabled men to live in town and travel to work on a daily basis.

The introduction of gasoline power to the woods, especially the
chain saw, made it possible for a small number of workers to increase
production dramatically. Once again, mechanization had narrowed
the technological gap between logging and sawmilling. The changes
that took place in the woods in the late 1930s and 1940s meant that
logging operators required fewer men to cut and yard a given volume
of logs. Although the work force was still an itinerate one, there was a
difference by the 1940s—most of the sawmills and larger lumber
camps were unionized. That gave workers a degree of influence in
determining the conditions and circumstances of work, although it
had little effect on the stability of the industry.

One of the constant facts of life for the Douglas fir region between
1920 and 1940 was the volatile nature of its basic industry. Although

loggers and mill workers on Oregon's south coast experienced the same problems, newcomers, especially Scandinavians and Finns, still flocked to places like Coos Bay to seek jobs in mills that specialized in cedar products or to hire on with the Big Mill. The waterfront and its dock and shipping facilities remained—in good times and bad—the lifeblood of the community. And the timber reserves in the surrounding mountains were still impressive, perhaps the largest volume adjacent to any major shipping port on the Pacific Coast.

CHAPTER 5

Getting By

We came to Coos Bay and nobody was there to meet me. I was all by myself. I was seventeen years old. You can just figure the rest. I couldn't speak a word of English. Not one word. But it didn't take long till I learned. When I got off the boat, the pursor put my suitcase off. I had one suitcase only, clear from Finland and there wasn't much in that. The pursor put my suitcase on the wharf, and I said, well, that means I'm here. It was a hot July day and I started to walk up towards Front Street.

Eleanor Anderson, née Elna Maria Junttila[1]

By the 1920s the lumber economy on the Pacific slope was part of a financial and trading network that extended from Tokyo to New York and London. The commercial health of that increasingly integrated system influenced peripheral areas that produced the foodstuffs, minerals, and construction materials required in the great urban centers. Because of its access to large stands of timber and its heavy dependence on logging and lumbering, Coos Bay prospered and suffered within those worldwide arrangements. And because entrepreneurs distant from the bay controlled most of its resources and processing facilities, their decisions directly affected the welfare of the bay communities. But those conditions had existed in some form since San Francisco capitalists first became interested in the region in the 1850s.

The Big Mill, its auxiliary plants, its vast network of rail and water arterials, and its logging camps continued to be the largest employer in the area. Operating at full production, the Coos Bay Lumber Company's camps, mills, and transportation crews employed about 1,500 people in the early 1920s. The firm enjoyed natural advantages over some of its competitors, especially in the foreign market, because it owned nearly half of the Port Orford cedar in the United States.[2] But the increasing quantity and variety of substitute building materials made those favorable circumstances uncertain, and the company's fortunes continued to fluctuate in the decade before the depression.

The Buehner Lumber Company, successor to the Simpson firm in North Bend and the second largest employer, entered the foreign trade on a big scale in the 1920s. Buehner employed 210 people at its manufacturing plant and another 230 men in three logging camps by 1922. From its headquarters in Portland, the company operated a steamer that regularly plied the ocean waters between Coos Bay and

San Pedro, California. The Buehner firm also shipped regular consignments of lumber to Australia, China, Japan, and the Atlantic Coast.[3] But virtually every large operation on the Pacific Coast was doing the same thing, and that meant trouble for financially unstable enterprises like Buehner.

Eventually the Stout Lumber Company bought out Buehner, and in the process added to its timber holdings by purchasing the remaining Simpson lands from Louis J. Simpson. The larger of Stout's two mills burned in 1926, but the effect on local lumber production was negligible because of poor market conditions.

The market was the kicker. One source estimates that Coos Bay firms operated at about 65 percent of capacity during the 1920s. Although new specialty mills broadened the region's industrial base and provided a semblance of stability, they did not appreciably influence the value of the wood products shipped over the bar.[4] The large producers, particularly the Big Mill, were the mainstays of the area's economy and the combined output of the Coos Bay Lumber Company mills dwarfed all other production on the bay.

The C. A. Smith Lumber Company had pioneered in making battery separators from Port Orford cedar, and by the 1920s there were several mills in southwestern Oregon specializing in separators and other cedar products. Benjamin Ostlind, a former official with the Coos Bay Lumber Company, established the Coos Veneer and Box Company. The great stands of Port Orford cedar also attracted distant investors—the Evans Products Company to Marshfield in 1928 and Smith Wood Products to nearby Coquille the following year. The Evans plant manufactured battery separators and Venetian blinds, and the Smith operation dealt exclusively in cedar products.[5] The specialty mills hired women like Eleanor Anderson and Marguerette Therrien. Although wages were low, the take-home pay that women earned in the battery separator plants during the depression provided the only income for some hard-pressed families.

But the production statistics of the Big Mill and its lesser competitors, the monthly lumber shipments over the bar, and the opening of new plants reveal little about the condition of people's lives. Although prominent figures in the industry (and on Coos Bay) complained about market conditions, government tariff policies, county taxes, and a myriad of other matters, few of those people lost their jobs or were forced to move on when the lumber market was down. Others—the men and women who worked in the mills and woods— suffered the seasonal layoffs, endured reduced wages, and were left without any form of security when the plant closed. Those were the social and human costs of a system built upon the lumbermen's need to satisfy creditors and the investors' requirements for profits.

Eleanor Anderson spent seventy years in southwestern Oregon, and she enjoyed the love and companionship of three surviving sisters. "It's kind of a miracle the way our lives have gone," she mused in 1984, "we've all done good." Like other young Scandinavian and Finnish women, Eleanor worked as a housemaid when she first arrived on the bay. In those days washing had to be done by hand, she remembered, and "ladies didn't do that." After her marriage to Axel Anderson in 1918, she worked "with a big, big crowd" of other women in a veneer mill for "awfully small wages." Because her husband did not want her to continue in the mill, she quit after three years to work at home and raise her daughter. Still, her experiences on Coos Bay were positive: "I never felt the badness of it, because my husband always had good work, and he bought a home already before we were married."[6] But there were others who lacked the good fortune and modest success of the Andersons.

The majority of the people who drifted in and out of the area during those years appear only in the statistical ledgers of the county tax files or the decennial census reports. A local newspaper drew attention to the large number of people passing through in late 1921:

> Coos Bay seems to be a place for missing men to be found, or at least to be sought. . . . This is probably due to the fact that there is a big floating population in the locality. Men come here and work in the camps and go somewhere else, and the fact that it is a seaport adds to these conditions.[7]

For many working people that transiency and anonymity lasted into the 1950s and beyond. But there also were elements of community cooperation and stability.

That sense of mutual welfare and sharing was most evident among the Scandinavian and Finnish population on the bay. Those immigrant groups formed organizations to offer members a vehicle for socializing with fellow countrymen and to provide security against personal tragedy. Social clubs like Suomi Lodge, Knights of Finland, Sons of Norway, Martha Lodge, Finnish Brotherhood, Ladies Finnish Society, and the International Order of Runeberg held picnics, assisted the needy, and provided news about job openings, and information about working conditions in the mills and logging camps.[8] The organizations also sponsored a wide range of social activities.

Wedding receptions, dances, and national cultural celebrations were held at the two major meeting places for the foreign born in Marshfield—Finnish Hall and Suomi Hall. Although the Finnish organization "built a real cheap hall," Eleanor Anderson remembered it as a place where "we had lots of fun." When the loggers came to town on Saturday night, small crowds of Swedish-Finns would gather for socializing, dancing, and "a good time." The "Bunker Hill crowd," according to Eleanor, made up the majority of those attending the events. Men shared the expenses of hiring "cheap music" that usually included an accordion, drums, and occasionally a piano.[9] The experiences of Scandinavian and Finnish loggers who took part in those gatherings provides a striking contrast to American-born loggers, who were at the mercy of the entertainment establishments on the bay.

The foreign born gathered on other occasions to share music, to drink beer, or to dig a basement or roof a house. As a child, Cliff Thorwald saw his father hold a roofing party and provide his Scandinavian friends with a keg of beer while they worked. To an impressionable boy, his father's peers seemingly "could erect a structure of any kind." The same crew, most of whom lived in the lodging houses in the Bunker Hill area near the Big Mill, built a beer garden complete with rustic benches and tables in a small clearing in the woods. On Sunday afternoons they entertained all comers with their violins, accordians, and beer. Heady stuff for boys like Cliff Thorwald and his childhood friends, who hid in the bushes and watched the frivolity.[10]

But many Swedes and Finns had less fortunate experiences. Jean Sandine Monsebroten, the grandaughter of immigrants, checked through church, newspaper, and court records and learned that many of her people became part of the "working 'labor' force of North Bend and Coos Bay." While some prospered on a modest scale as dairy farmers, skilled craftsmen, or small business operators, others failed. The church records list an occasional murder or suicide; some minds broke under the pressure of poverty, and still others returned to Finland. Newspapers frequently mentioned the injury to or death of immigrants in gruesome logging accidents. Two items in the Coos Bay *News* make the point: Wilhelm Westerbeck, killed when a log rolled over him, crushing him to death, "leaves a wife and two children in Finland"; Albert Wickstrom, who lost his right forearm in a mill accident, "was about 18 years old, arrived here six months ago from Finland."[11]

Of her maternal grandfather who raised a family of eleven children, Jean Monsebroten concludes: "Andrew Sandine came to the United States hoping to make a better way of life. To the extent that he was regularly employed and his family enjoyed the benefits of a farm-country environment, he was successful. As for himself, Andrew had a life of constant hard work and made only one trip away from the area—to San Francisco in 1921."

Monsebroten's paternal grandfather, J. Ed Johnson (né Kotka), came to the United States in 1903 to avoid being drafted into the Russian army. He first worked as a logger for C. A. Smith; then he did a stretch in the coal mines; and finally he worked as a molder with the North Bend Iron Works until he retired in 1954. Johnson opposed anything having to do with the military; he refused to allow his daughter to join the Girl Scouts and was opposed to his son joining the Navy during the Second World War.[12] During their American experience, both Sandine and Johnson enjoyed social contacts with their ethnic peers and kept in touch with the old country through letters and immigrant newspapers. But their Scandinavian and Finnish brethren who lived in isolated logging camps were less fortunate.

Families, especially those in the outlying areas, resorted to a variety of subsistence strategies well into the twentieth century. According to Roy Rozell, several families on isolated South Slough, including his own, "hunted for market" until the state outlawed the practice. Residents of the area killed waterfowl to sell to passing ships for the "plume trade." In an age when it was fashionable for women to wear exotic feathers in their hats, the plume trade was a lucrative business. For Rose Younker Liberti's and other families on the South Slough, survival meant growing garden vegetables, raising chickens, beef, and pigs, and supplementing those with wild game. Although the people who lived along the water highway had "very little money crop," Rose Liberti says that they lived well and helped and trusted each other.[13] As elsewhere on the southern Oregon coast, permanent residents worked in the logging camps to earn a cash income.

Stories still popular in the Coos country tell with special pride of more exotic ways of surviving, especially on the South Slough. When the state of Oregon adopted prohibition in 1912 before the ratification of the national amendment, a flourishing bootleg liquor trade developed in virtually every corner of the state. South Slough soon gained a reputation as the center of "moonshiner" activity on the south coast. With a ready market in the thirsty lumber towns up the bay, selling moonshine provided South Slough families with money to purchase goods they otherwise could not afford. And the local moonshine was quality brew; residents point out that the manufacture and sale of moonshine continued into the 1950s, long after

Congress had repealed the prohibition amendment. Why that illegal practice persisted is no mystery to bay residents—it was cheaper and better than the liquor sold in the state-operated stores.

But mostly, moonshining, bootlegging, and selling illegal venison provided support for hard-pressed families during the 1920s and 1930s. Frank Younker, who had several "still houses" on South Slough, sold moonshine to merchants in town who displayed the bottles openly in their store windows. Although the "big cop boys" occasionally raided a still, Younker always had another one in operation. Bud Metcalf, one of Younker's neighbors, also moonshined because "everybody wanted it." Without a demand, he reflected late in life, "there wouldn't be any moonshining."[14] Younker, Metcalf, and their moonshining peers also devised skillful ruses to keep law enforcement officials guessing.

One of the sharpest and most notorious of all the South Slough bootleggers was Ruth Marie Wolfe, a young mother of two who used moonshine money to support her family. She and her neighbors on the slough could not make a living farming so they moonshined. During prohibition, she points out, there were "two classes of people—those who drank and those who furnished it." Ruth Marie began moonshining at the age of nineteen and continued the practice for ten years until 1928, selling to fishermen, doctors, lawyers, everybody that is, "except Christians." Frank Younker worked for her and remembers that Ruth Marie's house was on the water so that "moonshine could be brought right to her back door by boat." Ruth's first husband, she said, "was a total loss as a moonshiner" because he was too frightened.[15] That she was a modest success in what some have described as a cutthroat business is testimony both to her courage and daring.

Because of her extensive contacts, law enforcement officials offered Ruth Marie money to "squeal on neighbors," and on another occasion the "Dry Dicks" wanted to send her to Portland to work as an informer. As any true-blooded moonshiner would, she told them "nothing doing." Despite occasional hassles with the law, she made a good living and invested her income in property. Although "nobody got rich," there was evidently enough business to keep all the still houses on South Slough in operation. Describing herself as "just a small-time bootlegger," Ruth Marie sold moonshine to speakeasies and madams, the latter providing one of the main outlets for her sales. Looking back on those activities, she says with conviction, it was a good way "to make a living for my family," and it was fun: "We sure enjoyed ourselves. We had more thrills and spills than you could dream of. Anytime you evade the law, keep one step ahead, or try to, you have moments of thrills, and for some reason or another, I needed that."[16]

For most people in the bay communities, however, the mill whistles, the steamers, and the river boats docking at the wharves dominated daily life. And when the plants closed their doors, as they frequently did, families relied on garden vegetables, salmon from the rivers, shellfish from the bay, and poached venison to tide them over. Although the new cedar speciality firms provided some employment, primarily for women who worked in the battery separator operations, a chaotic lumber market and new people moving into the community kept good jobs at a premium.

Oregon's south-coast settlements gained some of the amenities of modern life in the 1920s—public water and sewage service, electricity and telephones, a hospital, and an expanding coastal highway system. But life still revolved around the waterfront mills and the logging camps. As young adolescents in the early 1920s, Marguerette Therrien and her brother occasionally brought lunch to their father at the Big Mill. Those experiences impressed the brother, who said, "I'll never make a living like my father." For her part, Marguerette ignored the brother's advice, hired on with the Coos Veneer and Box Company in 1928 at the age of sixteen, then showed her real independence by getting married.[17] But, as the next few years would show, that was no insurance against adversity.

Following in the footsteps of his father, Cliff Thorwald worked part-time at the Big Mill before he was fourteen years old. From his vantage point, the 1920s were good years: "You couldn't go down on the sawdust and play around the big mill yards without a foreman coming along and asking if you wanted a job."

Thorwald and a high school classmate worked at Coos Veneer "every night and we could work Saturdays and Sundays if we wanted to." He left the bay area to attend college, but returned and eventually hired on in the machine room at Coos Veneer. That job ended when the plant closed early in 1930, and the easy employment that he experienced in the 1920s "sure did change in the depression."[18]

Henry Brainard's childhood experiences were different from those of most people who grew to adulthood in the 1920s. Born to a Coos Indian mother and an Irish father, Henry attended the Chemawa Indian school at Salem, Oregon, and later an Indian school in California. His first job was on a Simpson family ranch in California. After that he returned to Oregon to work in the woods, signed on with the

Coast Guard for a time, and then went back to work for a logging company on South Slough at the onset of the depression. Henry married Marguerette Therrien in 1928, but their bout with unemployment and poverty was typical of others who struggled through the 1930s.[19]

Like many young men, Curt Beckham and his younger brother Dow were constantly on the move during the latter part of the "jazz decade." While he was finishing high school, Dow worked in his uncle's sawmill during the summers. Although the uncle "went broke" before the stock market collapse, he was soon back in business through a series of logging partnerships. For his part, Dow remembers topping his first tree as a "high climber" at the age of eighteen. He eventually learned to do the job well, but he recalls "gnawing the top off" on his first attempt. When he ran out of money in college, he returned to the woods and learned another facet of the logging business—running logs on the river for the Coos Bay Lumber Company and the hard-nosed Jack Dashney.[20] Until the depths of the depression he had little difficulty finding a job.

Curt, two years older than Dow, followed the "Beckham camp" to its seasonal locations, hired on with other outfits, and spent part of the time in college. He went to southern California in 1929 and worked on a construction crew. Even then jobs were tight: "You almost had to keep a shovel of sand in the air, because out at the gate there was a group of men waiting for your job." Curt returned to Oregon, completed a second year in college and earned a teaching certificate in 1930.[21] Armed with that impressive credential and the ability to fall and buck timber, he faced the uncertainties of the 1930s and the responsibilities of supporting a young family.

Clare Lehmonosky spent the prohibition years working his way up through the Coos Bay Lumber Company's logging hierarchy. Beginning as a whistle punk on the great Eden Ridge timber stand in 1919, he worked at other logging jobs and eventually switched to the construction end, operating a pile driver for several months, turning to surveying, and finally taking a correspondence course in engineering. When the company reshuffled its line of command in 1926, Lehmonosky had the opportunity to "pick up know-how" in railroad construction. In the late 1920s he went on extended trips into the timbered back country south of Coos Bay surveying for logging railroads. Then, in 1930, the company promoted Lehmonosky to superintendent of construction, assuring him a secure position in the firm's woods operation.[22] Which points to the obvious—men like Lehmonosky with special skills and knowledge had advantages that others lacked; that was especially so in times of great hardship like the depression of the 1930s.

Itinerancy in the work force was not confined to single males who were so conspicuously mobile during those years. Although it was more difficult and inconvenient to move a family, that did not stop married men from changing jobs or shifting to different sections of the country if the employment prospects appeared brighter. Loggers, as usual, were more prone to move on than mill workers. The seasonal work in the camps, the frequent moving of operations when the timber was cut out, and the frequency of market-induced layoffs made employment in the woods less secure. For married loggers, that meant the constant disruption of family life, new schools and new friends for children, and the likely prospect of doing it all over again. Garnett Johnson's plaintive cry—"I hardly knew what a home was"— strikes at the essence of the experiences of the men, women, and children who were on the move.[23] There were many more.

Forrest Taylor arrived on Coos Bay after traveling widely throughout the Rocky Mountain west. Born in Grants Pass, Oregon, Taylor moved with his family to Montana, Colorado, Idaho, and finally to Powers where his father hired on as a logger. While the elder Taylor shifted from one logging camp to the next, the son went to high school, spending summers in the hop yards and prune orchards around Salem. At the onset of the depression he went to work in the woods falling and bucking for small operators.[24] Forrest Taylor's employment resume for the next few years reads like a kaleidoscope. During the 1930s he shifted between sawmills, logging camps, and federally funded construction projects.

His future wife, Valerie Wyatt, was born in Morton, Washington, where her father was a "stump rancher" and worked in logging camps. After several moves, the Wyatts settled in North Bend in the late 1920s where Valerie's parents struggled to raise their family. But she remembers that home environment as being unique because the family was always talking politics. Her father, at one time a member of the iww, believed in the Wobbly slogan, "An injury to one is an injury to all."[25] Family influences, especially those of her father, molded the political commitments that Valerie would make as an adult. The searing experiences of the Great Depression would nurture those convictions still further.

Like the Taylors and Wyatts, Pete Kromminga's family moved often during his childhood. His father came to Coos Bay from Portland in 1912 to work as a dairyman, and eventually took a job as a dock worker for the Coos Bay Lumber Company. After a one-hour walk to the docks, his father worked a ten-hour shift, and if a lumber ship docked at the end of the day, he stayed on to load the vessel. Two years later the family moved twenty-five miles north to Reedsport, where the father milked cows and worked on cutting crews. The next stop was Roseburg, where Pete graduated from high school and then ventured back to the coast and a job in a logging camp—and the onset of the depression.[26] Pete Kromminga's journey to the coast was only the first move in a twenty-year career as a "camp inspector" (the term for those who changed jobs frequently).

Cal Thompson, who walked from Roseburg to Coos Bay in three and a half days in 1914, shifted from one job to another and finally went to work pulling green chain at the Big Mill in 1924. One year later the company transferred Thompson to the boiler room, where he helped maintain the eight large units that generated electricity for the Coos Bay Lumber Company mills and the city of Marshfield.[27] That job, like Clare Lehmonosky's, required special technical skills and knowledge—attributes that kept Thompson employed when others were out of work.

The Eickworth family led a relatively sedentary existence compared to the Taylors, Wyatts, and Krommingas. Settling on the Coos River in 1879, the Eickworths eked out a living as subsistence farmers, occasionally delivering strawberries and apples to bay-area markets by boat. At the age of twelve, Lorance Eickworth moved with his family to Empire where they sold crab meat and made a good living. When the Coos Bay Lumber Company ship, *C. A. Smith,* wrecked on the north jetty of the entrance to the harbor on December 16, 1923, the Eickworth family continued its tradition of self-sufficiency and used the salvaged lumber to build a modest home. After high school, Lorance went away to Oregon State College, where he graduated with a degree in lumber manufacturing in 1929. He returned to Coos Bay in time to get hired and laid off at the onset of the depression.[28]

Both Garnett Johnson and Paula Laurilla (née Lindblad) were born during the First World War. While Garnett's family traveled from one logging camp to the next, Paula's Finnish parents operated a boarding house that still stands on U. S. Highway 101. Those were relatively good times for the Lindblads; with a house full of Scandinavian and Finnish boarders who worked in the nearby Coos Bay Lumber Company mill, Paula's father built an addition to provide more space for boarding rooms, a grocery store, and a small dance hall. Paula waited on tables as a child, but most of all, she remembers the boarders who worked in the Big Mill, and the Sunday afternoon festivities when the families gathered at the Lindblads for music and dancing. What she describes as "a pleasant affair" in the 1920s became "a diversion" when market conditions forced the mills to close in the 1930s.[29]

When Bill McKenna was twelve years old, his father, two uncles, and another partner purchased the Coos Bay Lumber Company's Eastside mill and began sawing spruce and cedar logs. That was 1928 when white cedar "was a pretty good thing." When McKenna entered high school in 1930, the economic collapse "still had not affected the Coos Bay area." The mills were operating, and the high school of 500 students had a full band, competed in several sports, and sponsored a swimming program. But within the year, the smokestacks on the bay grew cold, including those at the McKenna plant, and high school activities were cut.[30] The McKenna partners had entered the sawmilling business at the very moment the bottom dropped out of the lumber market.

The Great Depression came early to most timber-dependent communities. Lumber manufacture in the United States had been declining steadily since the mid-1920s when home building and commercial construction began to lag. Coos Bay mills, so dependent on California as a market for their products, experienced the same difficulties. The statistics for Coos County reveal a gradual decline in production beginning in 1925, a brief recovery in 1929, then a precipitous drop in 1931 and 1932. The county's sawmills did not pass their 1925 production level until 1937—and that despite a population increase of 14 percent during the 1930s.[31]

White cedar products and log exports helped sustain the south coast economy in the early years of the depression. In June 1929, the *Timberman* reported that white cedar shipments made up two thirds of all forest products exported from Coos Bay. The veneer manufacturers—makers of battery separators—kept operating during the worst years of the depression. Because their markets pointed to the industrial centers of the East, most of the plants shipped their products by rail.[32] But the California construction industry still provided the greatest market for bay-area lumber, and when that market was down, the Coos economy suffered. The statistics for log and lumber production in Coos County offer graphic evidence of the impact of the depression (see Table 3).[33]

Although the raw figures show the sharp drop in production, they obscure the despair and suffering that had settled on the bay country and elsewhere. We can only make intelligent guesses about the percentage of unemployment, but one source estimates that more than half of the people in Coos County may have been out of work in 1933.

The logging department of the Coos Bay Lumber Company, which prided itself in being one of the highest-paying outfits on the Pacific Coast, closed its camps periodically in the early 1930s. And the steam boilers that powered the Big Mill lay dormant for extended periods.[34] In the face of those bleak conditions, a few business people on the bay attempted to mirror President Herbert Hoover's public optimism and to proclaim far and wide every rosy hue on the horizon.

A decade of opportunity and progress? At least one lumber company executive thought so. Coos Bay's excellent harbor gave the region advantages that "other great lumber centers no longer have"; moreover, its resources, "greater by far to begin with, are comparatively untouched." A *Times* editorial added to that false euphoria and pointed out that the area was fortunate in its "continued prosperity." The depression, it hinted, "may never be felt to any great degree on Coos Bay."[35] A rapidly contracting market and frequent mill shutdowns soon put the lie to such optimism.

For Marguerette Therrien and Henry Brainard, recently married and struggling to raise a family, public references to prosperity had an empty ring. With the help of Marguerette's father, the young couple built a one-room house near the White Cedar Logging Company camp where Henry worked on the South Slough. After the Brainards spent one season in the rough new home, the camp closed and Henry joined the growing ranks of the unemployed. Before the Brainards left the South Slough in 1931 to move back to Marshfield, Marguerette gave birth to a dark-haired boy. Back in town the family peeled chittum, (the bark was sold for medicinal purposes), and picked blackberries, ferns, huckleberry brush, and cedar boughs for small change. As a youngster, Bill Brainard's first recollections were meals of "peas, potatoes, and fish."[36] His experiences were common to many people during the depression.

TABLE 3. Log and Lumber Production for Coos County, 1928–1935 (in thousand board feet)

Year	Logs	Lumber
1928	468,320	287,465
1929	585,175	342,122
1930	293,062	312,330
1931	177,476	169,348
1932	105,992	98,809
1933	205,972	147,935
1934	517,890	187,189
1935	421,601	287,591

Surviving the Great Depression

Most of the people would work for a few weeks and they'd be off for a while. And then also at that time there was a lot of work without pay, sort of on the promise that eventually you would get paid. In our particular sawmill, this happened a couple of times. We'd get an order, open up and cut the order, and then close down.

Bill McKenna[1]

The deteriorating American economy convinced many business executives, including those in the forest products sector, that such drastic conditions required immediate attention. Postwar lumber production in the United States peaked at 41 billion board feet in 1925, declined to 26 billion feet in 1930, and then plummeted to just over 10 billion feet in 1932. John B. Woods, an industrial forester with close ties to the Pacific Northwest, remarked that the timber business had descended to the "slough of despond."[2] Lumber executives, who were normally suspicious of any form of government interference, began to look to Washington, D.C., for relief. As the economic crisis worsened, their proposals became more drastic, taking on overtones of the business syndicalism that eventually appeared in the form of the short-lived National Recovery Administration (NRA) in the 1930s.

The effects of the collapsing national economy reverberated from coast to coast and deeply influenced conditions in the Pacific Northwest. Everywhere production outstripped demand, even in the face of curtailed operations and periodic shutdowns. Some of the largest West Coast producers attempted to limit production voluntarily, but to no avail. The Coos Bay Lumber Company stockpiled large inventories of lumber at its finishing plants in California and waited for the market to improve.[3] But patience and optimism went out the window when prices and demand dropped even further. Even moderately brisk foreign sales could not sustain the sharp contraction in the lumber market.

Eventually, the collapse began to take its toll in business failure and backruptcy. Idle workers were becoming more noticeable on the bay by early 1931. But this form of unemployment was different from the seasonal meanderings of men who were on the move between logging camps. Even when the local mills resumed production after the holiday layoff, the *Times* reported that at least 400 men were still unemployed. Because there was "little prospect of putting them to work," industry representatives urged outsiders to stay away from the Coos district.[4] Business and civic leaders would give those sentiments added emphasis in the coming months.

As the armies of the unemployed increased, it became obvious—even to the Coos Bay *Times*—that not all was well. Declining lumber orders and heavy inventories, the editor contended, were "the barnacle on the ship of progress" in timber-dependent communities. Yet the editor saw signs of hope in an expanded trade with the Orient and with South Africa, and he praised the West Coast Lumbermen's Association for inaugurating its "Build Your Own Home Campaign." The *Times* urged residents to join the "Trade at Home" effort to sustain local business. "Think twice," it cautioned, "before you let your money leave town in search of bargains."[5] But those admonitions were lost as the tide of economic collapse continued.

As in other American communities, service clubs and civic groups organized a central clearinghouse to find jobs for the unemployed, to collect donations of food and clothing, and to investigate requests for assistance. Individuals seeking relief were required to work if they were able. The Marshfield Welfare Association, as the local organization was called, advertised for more jobs, distributed meal tickets to single men, and coordinated work projects for residents who were paid in scrip redeemable for food and clothing.[6] The dramatic increase in unemployment soon overwhelmed voluntary relief efforts in virtually every section of the country. Coos Bay was no exception.

The largest employer on the bay, the Coos Bay Lumber Company, adopted a sliding scale of wages based on monthly sales in June 1931, and shortly thereafter the firm suspended operations. The company's several logging camps already had been closed for several months. Although work resumed on a limited basis in the fall, market conditions forced the plant to close periodically during the next few years. Elsewhere, the industry fared no better. The West Coast Lumbermen's Association announced in August 1931 that its member mills were operating at 38 percent of capacity.[7] For the bay area, the full force of the depression arrived with the closing of the Big Mill and its network of logging camps.

Even when the Big Mill resumed work, it used only one side of its two head rigs and that on a limited production schedule. The firm hired only "old employees," and it activated only one logging camp. To assure that everyone shared in the "operating hours," the company rotated the work among the employees who had been laid off. When newspapers reported that the mill was reopening, the items usually stated that the plant would run for an "indefinite period." Another bit of depression psychology—the *Times* made only brief mention when mills closed, but it printed banner headlines when they resumed production.[8] Those conditions persisted well into 1934, when the Big Mill began to receive larger and more regular orders.

When Congress established the NRA in 1933, the Coos Bay Lumber Company was required to limit its hours of operation each month. The NRA encouraged production restrictions to reduce lumber inventories and to set minimum prices. Coos Bay Lumber Company head Homer Bunker, one of the chief critics of the NRA, appealed the restrictions to regional authorities. Like many of its competitors, the firm continued to operate its plants when the NRA denied the appeal.[9] The Supreme Court eventually found the NRA unconstitutional, and the market once again reigned supreme in the West Coast lumber industry.

Smaller companies with less extensive marketing facilities faced even greater difficulties. Bill McKenna remembers that his family's sawmill operation was "on and off for five years." Much of that time the family-run business merely sold logs to Japan—"old growth spruce and cedar logs. No cutting at all, or if you did cut it, you just cut it in cants [logs that were roughly slabbed into huge beams] and then shipped it out." When the McKenna mill received an order, the employees would be called back to fill the request and then immediately laid off. Other mills on the bay went through similar experiences. "There wasn't any sawmills that were steady at all," McKenna points out. "Most of the people would work for a few weeks and they'd be off for a while."[10] And when the mills were running, employees sometimes went without pay for weeks at a time or, as happened in several instances, lost their wages altogether.

Getting one's paycheck was often a difficult problem. James A. "Jimmy" Lyons, a young lumber entrepreneur who began a shoestring sawmilling business in the 1930s, was notorious for his inability to pay regular wages. With other investors, including Howard Irwin of Portland, Lyons ran a small mill in Empire and reopened the Stout Lumber Company's "Mill B" in North Bend. Until the Second World War when Lyons established a solid financial footing, he frequently had trouble meeting his payrolls. When Victor West's father worked at Mill B, the son recalls that his paychecks were "bouncing all over the place." But West admired Lyons, although he describes him as one would a fox: "He was running the mill down at Empire the same way. The crew down there put a lien on the mill in order to get their wages. But old Jimmy Lyons was too smart for them. He didn't own the mill so they couldn't attach the mill. All they could attach was the lumber

Douglas fir logs, C. A. Smith Lumber and Manufacturing Company (*American Lumberman*, 1911)

Al Powers, general manager, Smith-Powers Logging Company
(*American Lumberman, 1911*)

Al Powers in his motor boat. To make the circuit of all the camps required a
120-mile trip by water (*American Lumberman, 1911*)

Inside the Big Mill *(American Lumberman, 1911)*

Bird's eye view of the great sawmill plant for the C. A. Smith Lumber
Company *(American Lumberman, 1911)*

Eastside Mill, C. A. Smith Lumber Company *(American Lumberman, 1911)*

Yarding machines, Coos Bay Lumber Company, Powers, Oregon *(photo by C. K. Kinsey, courtesy Gerald Williams)*

Log train on its way to Isthmus Inlet, a distance of six miles (*American Lumberman, 1911*)

Coos Bay Lumber Company work crew, ca. 1920 (*photo by C. K. Kinsey, courtesy Gerald Williams*)

The ship *Redondo* unloading at Bay Point, California (*American Lumberman, 1911*)

Steam-powered piledriver, Coos Bay Lumber Company, ca. 1920 (*photo by C. K. Kinsey, courtesy Gerald Williams*)

on the dock. He never kept any lumber on the dock. So the crew didn't get hardly anything; the lawyers got everything."[11]

Curt and Dow Beckham worked for a gyppo logger and sawmill operator, John Aasen, who also was "notorious as bad pay." The Beckhams spent most of one summer cutting crossties for Aasen on a contract for the Southern Pacific railroad. When the crew went several weeks without getting paid, they placed a lien on the ties that had already been cut. "That stopped the whole operation," according to Curt; sometime later he received a small check for his summer's work. There were other problems with the Aasen business. Many of the workers in the camp broke out with boils from drinking bad water. That prompted Curt to refer to the experience as "the summer of short pay, bad water, and boils."[12] But there were instances in virtually every logging camp where the arrival of a paycheck was in doubt.

Nearly every lumber firm on the south coast went through financial difficulties during the 1930s. The Coos Bay Lumber Company experienced the throes of yet another "reorganization"; the Port Orford Cedar Products Company went bankrupt; thousands of acres of timberland went tax delinquent; the Sitka Spruce, Pulp and Paper mill went into receivership; and both county and local governments made drastic cuts in their budgets because of declining tax revenues. School districts made equally sharp budget reductions and the payment of teachers in "school warrants" became common practice. The warrants drew 6 percent interest and employees were paid when the school district had enough revenue to meet its bills. The business failures and declining fortunes of local taxing bodies touched nearly everyone in the Coos region.

The foreclosures and bankruptcies brought changes in management and the emergence of powerful new financial interests on the bay. When the Baker-Fentress Company of Chicago foreclosed on the Port Orford Cedar Products Company in 1932, it marked the entrance of another influential lumber investment firm into the Coos economy. Baker-Fentress, a leading proponent of consolidating ownerships in the lumber industry, foreclosed on several delinquent securities in the Pacific Northwest during the depression.[13] Other bondholders exercised foreclosures when firms were unable to make payments on their debts.

The fortunes of the Sitka Spruce, Pulp and Paper plant in Empire were typical. When orders for lumber and pulp lagged in the spring of 1932, the mill closed and left nearly 500 workers unemployed. In July a mortgage company brought a foreclosure suit against the firm and a receiver subsequently ordered the property sold. At that point, the hard-pressed owners appealed the sale and the matter eventually went to the Oregon Supreme Court, which upheld the receiver's order. The successful bidder, the International Wood Sulfite Company of Seattle, paid off claims against the company, including back wages, "reconditioned" the mill, and reopened the plant as the Coos Bay Pulp Corporation in the summer of 1935.[14] As far as the community's welfare was concerned, control of the company had merely shifted from San Francisco to Seattle capitalists. The change also brought to the bay a new resident manager, C. Wylie Smith, who would play an important part in the business life of the area.

Delinquent taxes proved to be a double-edged sword for residents of Coos County. On the one hand, they indicated business failure, the inability of employers to meet their payrolls, and economic demoralization. They also meant sharp cuts in school district revenue and drastic reductions in county services. County officials took voluntary pay cuts early in 1931, and when financial difficulties worsened, they reduced expenditures even more. But that marked only the beginning of budget axing. When the county court attempted to pay its employees in warrants, the workers objected and petitioned for money payments.[15]

Before Franklin Roosevelt inaugurated a vast array of emergency relief and public work projects in the summer of 1933, voluntary organizations provided the only assistance available in Oregon to people who were in need of help. In Marshfield the Community Chest assumed responsibility for filling grocery orders, issuing meal tickets, providing prescriptions, and giving fuel wood to those in need. Both Marshfield and North Bend also promoted home and business repair projects to provide short-term work for the unemployed. The Coos Bay *Times* applauded the success of similar efforts in other cities: "Men who were rapidly assuming the shuffling gait of a defeated person are now striding the street, dinner pail in hand, ready to look the world in the face once again."[16] Preaching the virtues of the work ethic, however, had limited utility in an economy that offered little more than sporadic, temporary employment.

Although voluntary relief measures offered assistance to families and individuals in distress, the *Times* repeatedly emphasized that authorities made those awards in exchange for labor. Marshfield relief officials provided transients with one meal ticket in exchange for two hours of work on city projects. Once fed, the individual was told to move on because there were no jobs in the area. Despite criticism of those policies from transients who "refused to work," the *Times* ar-

gued that "nothing could be more fair than the methods us
community chest officials in their disbursement of their lim
get."[17] When the ranks of the unemployed swelled even ᵐᵒʳᵉ ____
local unemployed councils became a force in local politics, the *Times*
was more reticent.

Coos County also opened a cannery in the summer of 1932 to put
up vegetables, fruit, and meat for distribution during the winter
months. The county urged truck gardeners to donate surplus stock to
make the program a success.[18] But as elsewhere, voluntary relief
projects did little to alleviate the poverty that had settled on the bay.
Although federal programs, especially the massive New Deal work-
relief projects, dwarfed voluntary efforts, most people still had little
money. They resorted to longstanding subsistence practices to survive.

The Civilian Conservation Corps (ccc) was the first federal relief
program to have an impact in southwestern Oregon. The Forest
Service and the Oregon Department of Forestry operated several
camps in Coos County that provided food and shelter, low wages,
and conservation-oriented work for young men. The "ccc boys" constructed roads, fire trails, and lookouts, fought forest fires, and promoted forestry on county, state, and federal timberland. Some of the
ccc enrollees came from far places, and Coos county youth were not
always exceptional hosts to the newcomers.[19] But the ccc remains to
this day the most popular of all the New Deal programs in southwestern Oregon.

The *Times* probably spoke for most of its readers when in 1938 it
applauded the ccc on its fifth anniversary:

> The ccc experiment has been so much of a success that it is being continued.
> Anything that prevents soil erosion, builds new forest highways, opens new park
> projects, sets out new trees, saves the old ones from fires—anything that does such
> things is of lasting value to the country. Coos County has been fortunate in having
> her share of the camps, varying from two, as at present, to five or six.[20]

New Deal programs were responsible for other projects on the
south coast. The Civil Works Administration (cwa) put 200 unemployed men to work on county and municipal undertakings in November 1933. The cwa, intended as a "reemployment" scheme,
eventually placed more than 500 area men in temporary jobs. cwa
projects included county road construction, filling small sloughs in
Marshfield and North Bend, improving local parks, and street drainage and maintenance work. The agency concentrated its county
efforts in Marshfield and North Bend, where unemployment was

most acute. Although it recognized that rural families were short of cash, the agency referred to them as "self supporting."[21] That was probably an accurate assessment, because conditions in urban settlements were much worse than in the countryside. The allocation of additional New Deal economic recovery funds through the Federal Emergency Relief Administration (FERA) and the Works Progress Administration (WPA) followed a similar formula.

The construction of the coast highway was the largest of the depression-era projects in the Coos country. Using both state and federal funds, the state highway department constructed bridges over the major rivers and bays on the Oregon coast during the late 1930s. One of those, the McCullough Bridge completed over Coos Bay in 1936, eliminated ferry travel between North Bend and the highway to the north. Because the bridge had to be high enough to allow ocean-going vessels to pass underneath, the construction project was a complicated engineering matter. Its cantilever span of 1,700 feet was the longest in the Pacific Northwest at that time.[22] Work on the bridge provided employment for a large number of people.

Although he did not participate in the emergency employment programs, Cliff Thorwald believes the New Deal projects "were a godsend." Those "gangs of men with shovels and wheelbarrows," he recalls, accomplished a lot of good work. Forrest Taylor was employed on several federally subsidized jobs in the North Bend area—city projects, the building of the North Bend dock, and construction on the airport.[23] At the very least, those public-works jobs enabled people like Taylor to earn a small income at a time when there were few employment prospects anywhere. In the larger picture, as many writers have pointed out, the relief schemes alleviated social discontent, helped preserve civil order, and assured that the basic structure of the American economy would survive the depression.

At one point, the district WPA office bragged that Coos County had achieved complete employment. In November 1935 the agency ordered every person who had applied for relief in the county to work on local projects. The office posted lists of names and directed relief applicants to specific jobs. When the WPA transferred 300 people from Coos County to distant projects, there were rumblings of dissent. Workers who did not want to be separated from their families opposed the move and declared they "would remain at home and starve rather than move." The *Times* speculated that the WPA strategy was to force men from public payrolls back into the private sector.[24]

Arbitrary decisions like those eventually brought into being a national organization, the Workers' Alliance, to speak for people who were on relief and at the mercy of agencies like the WPA. As a young adult, Valerie Wyatt joined a local chapter of the Workers' Alliance along with her father. The Wyatts, who were officers in the Coos Bay local, and other alliance members organized WPA workers to help them gain better conditions and higher wages. But the alliance did even more. It protested to the relief administrator when that office reduced payments and pensions; it pointed to instances where people who needed medical assistance were being neglected; and it asked local authorities to pressure county and state officials for more funds for direct relief and pensions. W. L. Harris, a local spokesman for the alliance, put it bluntly: "It's only through mass protest that we can get anywhere. There must be other ways to cut taxes than to deprive the needy."[25]

Even with a slightly improved lumber economy in the late 1930s, the WPA still employed a large number of Coos residents. At the close of 1938, the county provided work for 644 men and women, its entire quota of WPA jobs, and public works projects other than WPA employed more than 800 people well into 1939. The county's population at the time was about 30,000. At the same time, the number of people receiving some form of direct relief—surplus food, aid to dependent children, old-age assistance, and a category called general assistance—increased sharply.[26] Those conditions on the south coast point up the obvious—the depression remained a fact of life until war orders began to boost the American economy in 1940.

Despite the absence of public relief at the outset, the depression of the 1930s was not as severe in the bay area as might have been expected. In recent years it has been fashionable for defenders of the American social system to praise the "safety net" that federal welfare programs have provided for the unemployed. But during the 1930s, unemployed people were able to find refuges from hardship that, in many cases, are no longer available. Residents of cities and towns were only one generation removed from the family farm; therefore, returning home was always a possibility. Moreover, in a less interdependent world—at least in the ability of a people to feed themselves— there were other means to cushion the effects of unemployment and poverty.

That was especially true for rural areas like southwestern Oregon. Wood for heating and cooking was readily available, and the nearby rivers and ocean provided a variety of fish and seafood. Wild fruits, especially blackberries, were abundant in season and could be preserved easily and cheaply. And, as always, poaching deer was fashionable and widely practiced. Moreover, prices in the United States dropped an estimated 33 percent, and there is evidence that food costs may have dropped even more.[27] The abundance of subsistance resources available in the Coos country undoubtedly mitigated the severity of the depression.

Many of the people who lived through the 1930s in southwestern Oregon support that argument. The depression brought poverty and suffering to the Coos communities but no starvation and little social trauma. Mills operated sporadically at best and some failed altogether; but for people accustomed to seasonal layoffs and periodic closures, the hard times were simply longer in duration. As for the many young people who wandered away to the far points of the Pacific slope in search of jobs, they always had the option of returning to the security of the family home. At least there they could find shelter and food and the means of getting by until the mills and logging camps reopened.

Eleanor Anderson, who maintained close ties to the Scandinavian and Finnish communities, did not recall her friends going hungry during the depression: "People went without work, that's true, but I don't think anybody starved." But a large number of them, she said, left Coos Bay, "especially the young boys." Many young Finnish women went to San Francisco where "there were rich families and a good chance for maid work." As a group, her immigrant peers survived better than some, she believed, because "they were always good caretakers and savers."[28] The fact that her husband, Axel, worked steadily at Evans Products undoubtedly tempered Eleanor's recollections of the depression.

One of those who left southwestern Oregon to look for work was the youthful Dow Beckham. When he could not get a job in his native Coquille country, he went to Portland where he observed the desperation that drove men to do "anything to make a living." He worked for a short time in Portland pumping gas, and then went to the Olympic Games in Los Angeles in the summer of 1932. From there he passed through southwestern Oregon on his way to Spokane, Washington, "to sell real silk hosiery." After selling one box of hose and going hungry, he left with seventy-three cents in his pockets and rode a freight train back to Portland. That, he remembers, "was really in the depression." At a brief stop in Pasco, Washington, Dow bought a bowl of beans for one of his fellow passengers "who hadn't eaten for days." His most vivid memories about the Spokane trip—and the depression—were that "you could get awfully hungry and awfully cold, but you weren't alone."[29] He returned home and remained in familiar surroundings for the rest of the 1930s.

His aunt and uncle's home provided food, shelter, and a warm place to sleep. The uncle was a logger and worked "when he could," which mostly meant during the summer months. The couple canned vegetables and meat, and they raised their own cows and pigs, doing the butchering and putting the meat up in the fall. The family also had an ample supply of deer meat to supplement other foods for the rainy winter months: "People planned on having food in that manner. So you did not have a lot of money to buy clothes, and you didn't need it to buy groceries except staples like sugar and flour."[30] Sugar, flour, and salt, whether one lived in town or the countryside, were the most common purchases made at the grocery.

Dow Beckham followed his brother's example and attended college when he had saved enough money to enroll for a semester or two. For the rest of the depression he worked occasionally as a logger, taught school, and sold advertising; when the war heated up in Europe, he was selling automobiles. His brother, Curt, who also logged and taught school during the depression, agrees that survival was easier in the countryside: "It was tough to get a job in the big town, harder in the rural community. Here the depression hardly touched people as far as eating is concerned. They made their own fun. My uncle lived on Sandy Creek. They had a big garden; they had deer; they had fish; they raised beef, pork; they had a smoke house. But the money part, they didn't have." Curt remembers his uncle hauling home a 100-pound sack of sugar, quantities of flour, and coffee for the family's winter supply. His aunt and uncle were not unique, because most "of the local people did the same thing."[31]

When he finished high school in the late 1930s, Harold "Cardy" Walton went to work in the woods. But his job was a seasonal one: "There was very little winter work. When it started raining, every-body was out of work." Like most other families in his small logging community, the Waltons "ate pretty good, but as far as anything extra, you didn't have that." Not everyone fared as well as the Beckhams and the Waltons. Garnett Johnson lived in a small rural community in the early 1930s and remembers the want and hunger in her aunt's house. "They had beans that had been given to them that had weevils in it. They ate them. They had fried potatoes with no salt and no pepper, no seasoning, and they had two children to raise." Garnett's grandmother, who "was one to put up things," shared her food with the struggling family.[32] But the evidence suggests that most people, whether they lived in the countryside or in town, did not go hungry.

Barter, a common practice in money-short economies, was wide-spread in southwestern Oregon during the depression. Moonshiners exchanged goods with nearly everyone; workers labored for room and board; people exchanged legal and illegal fish and venison for necessities like salt, flour, and sugar; and farmers traded produce for needed items in the towns. Quentin Church and his family raised potatoes and then bartered them for groceries and cash at stores in Marshfield and Coquille. Many logging familes picked ferns for the "greenery business" to earn petty cash. The ferns, according to Curt Beckham, sold for two cents for a "bunch" of fifty-five. After deducting one half cent for hauling, "you'd get a dollar and a half for a hundred bunches." For men accustomed to falling huge Douglas fir trees, he believes it must have been "degrading for them to say, 'I've got to go undercut some fern today.' "[33] But that was not a dramatic change in lifestyle for a people long accustomed to seasonal and market-induced unemployment.

For some outsiders, like Pennsylvania-born Charles Reigard, the logging camps and lumber towns of the Pacific slope offered greater opportunity than the industrial centers of the East. Reigard left the family home outside Pittsburgh in 1936 and "headed for the West Coast"—age fourteen. He hired on with small logging outfits and began a "life of moving around a lot." Until he joined the army at the outset of the Second World War, Reigard worked in several camps and for small gyppo mills "picking up a few dollars here and there." Even when logging bosses were not hiring, "they would let you stay for the day, or for the night if it was getting towards evening." After a rest, a good meal, and sometimes a sack lunch, a person was fixed with the essentials to "look for a job some other place." Not an idyllic existence, but for young Charles Reigard it was better than staying at home.[34] In the logging country of the Pacific Northwest there were hundreds of young men without the security of family and friends who drifted from one logging camp to the next in search of employment. But those circumstances existed everywhere—in the industrial mill towns of the Northeast, the cotton country of the rural South, and in the Corn Belt states of the Midwest.

Because the southern Oregon coast was isolated and away from the main automobile and railroad arterials, there were fewer transients moving through the area. Bill McKenna got the surprise of his life when his American Legion baseball team traveled to Klamath Falls—a town on the mainline of the Southern Pacific—for a playoff game. He remembers how shocked his teammates were when a freight train rumbled by the ball field: "We were playing along, the second or third inning, and here comes this freight train, and of course, all the kids on the coast, we were just flabbergasted. There was not a clear space on that train. Any place. On the top. In between. All over. There was no effort—it would have been impossible to put those people off the train."[35]

Still, southwestern Oregon was no lotus land. Sporadic employment and the lack of money were daily points of reality, especially for people who lived in town. Victor West's father and mother raised a garden, kept a few chickens, and canned vegetables and salmon. The little cash the family had came from his mother's earnings in a box factory "when it was running." For Everett Richardson's father, the early depression meant selling the family car and hitchhiking to Portland where he got a job that ended abruptly with the great longshoremen's strike of 1934. His mother bailed out the hard-pressed family when she found employment on the bay; the elder Richardson supplemented that with WPA work. Finally, the father hired on with the rejuvenated pulp mill in Empire in the late 1930s.[36]

Bunker Hill residents Phil Therrien, daughter Marguerette and son-in-law Henry Brainard peeled chittum, picked ferns and huckleberry brush, and caught salmon. "My husband, my father, and I were very poor," Marguerette recalled later in life. With great pride she tells the story of the family tearing down old cabins on Isthmus Slough, rafting the lumber to a spot near their home, and building "a beautiful chicken house." In the later 1930s when he was approaching adolescence, Marguerette's son, Bill, picked blackberries and hustled beer bottles under the waterfront docks to earn money to see a movie.[37] The Therriens and Brainards, like many others, survived on garden vegetables, fish, and whatever was available and useful in the immediate environment.

One of Cliff Thorwald's unforgettable memories of the depression was of small children standing in front of the Bunker Hill store, "pressing their noses against the glass, looking in there at all the food and stuff." Among the boys from the neighborhood, very likely, was the inquisitive Bill Brainard. For his part, Thorwald worked sporadically during the early depression, but with the help of friends and his wife's family, they always had plenty of food. On one occasion, he recalls, they had a deer in the bathtub waiting to be dressed, a large salmon, a string of trout given to them by friends, and a "gunny sack of clams in the back yard." And no freezer! "You can imagine the work—cut up and can, cut up and can." There was no reason to go hungry "if you could get around, or if you had friends who could get around."[38] But that abundance might not have been available to people who lacked familial and social contacts or technical knowledge and skills.

Subsistence and barter were also important to Valerie Wyatt's family during the 1930s. Because her father poached deer like everyone else, the family usually had enough meat on the table. In exchange for labor, he brought home vegetables and meat from area ranches. Although the Wyatts had "no new clothes to speak of for several years," neither did their neighbors.[39] The experiences of the Wyatts and others were a far cry from the good life eulogized in the success journals of the 1920s, but with patience and struggle they survived the worst economic collapse in the nation's history.

For fishermen like Harold Morris and Jack Randleman, getting enough food was no problem. Although ocean troll fishing was excellent, the daily catch was at the mercy of a weak market. Still, selling a few fish was better than starving, according to Harold Morris: "You couldn't get a job; there was no unemployment compensation; there was relief, but you had to be at the bottom." Morris is proud of his self-sufficiency during those years. Although he lived on a "float house" much of the time, he "never crossed a picket line, never would, and never drew unemployment either." Jack Randleman remembers simply, "I ate a lot of fish."[40] The marine environment provided Morris and Randleman the basic foods that the Coos Indians had lived on for centuries. The progressive destruction of salmon spawning beds and industrial damage to the estuary would make that form of subsistence a precarious undertaking fifty years later.

Holding a steady job was no assurance against hardship. Beth Wood was a young teenager in the early 1930s and lived with her family in downtown Marshfield. Unlike many of their neighbors who were unemployed for long periods, Beth's father was a mailman and never missed a day of work. But her parents had other problems. They were "poor money managers," and Beth and her brother frequently went hungry, or, as happened for a two-week stretch, the family "had nothing to eat but potatoes." When her brother graduated from high school, he enlisted in the CCC and eventually spent three years with the corps. After that hitch, he left for California and found a job. Beth still pictures groups of men standing on street corners in the waterfront area when the Big Mill was closed. Now living in Albany, Oregon, she remembers Coos Bay as a place where people stayed "whether they found work or not. And if they left, they never did come back."[41] Her recollections are probably mistaken, because many people returned to the bay after testing the job prospects elsewhere.

Don Brown was one such person. He grew up in logging camps in the coastal area, attended the University of Oregon where he majored in journalism, and then went south to Oakland, California, and a job with the postal service. But when he was laid off in 1929, Brown returned to the familiar surroundings of the Oregon coast where he "did about everything you can imagine, some legal, some illegal." He was hired by a Reedsport mill, with the stipulation that he also put his talents to use on the local baseball team. He worked there until the longshoremen's strike of 1934 when he joined the picket line in support of the workers. The next year Brown was on Coos Bay, beginning a career that made him one of the most prominent union organizers on the coast.[42] In the process, he helped forge a legacy of union sentiment that endures in the bay communities to this day. Like many young men, Brown returned to the south coast during a period of great hardship. But his course was unusual in one respect; he committed himself to struggle for a better life for working people.

Coos Bay's lumber economy achieved a partial recovery in the last half of the 1930s. A growing export trade with the Orient, improved harbor facilities, better access to the great stands of Douglas fir, and declining timber reserves in the Puget Sound and Grays Harbor region contributed to the improved conditions. Shipping out of Coos Bay—the best indicator of the region's economic health—reached a volume of 652,958 tons in 1937, approaching the previous high of 712,197 tons set in 1923. Local mills established that level of production in the midst of a prolonged maritime strike that tied up all West Coast docks between October 1936 and February 1937.[43] Rail shipments, mainly of battery separators destined for the industrial markets of the eastern United States, added to the total output.

But tonnage statistics do not translate accurately into jobs, because much of that volume was in the form of logs or cants that were shipped to Asian markets, principally Japan. According to George Vaughan, whose family had been logging on the south coast for decades, "the only thing that kept the bay area in groceries was the log export business."[44] Although those shipments kept the logging camps and longshore crews busy, they did little to put mill workers back on the job. And, even that market was unreliable, depending on construction activity and the fortunes of war as Japan expanded its sphere of influence in the Far East.

The large number of unemployed people was a constant reminder that economic recovery was still in the future. Low prices for lumber and the drying up of the export market caused the Coos economy to slow again in 1938. Although there was no cessation of industrial activity like that of the early 1930s, brief shutdowns, curtailed hours, and single-shift operations left many people without work. To make matters worse, the pulp mill in Empire, employing more than 200 people, was closed for most of the year after Japan, the major purchaser of pulp, cancelled all orders. The brightest hues in the employment picture were the cedar specialty plants. Good prices and an upturn in automobile production made cedar manufacturing the most consistent of all bay industries.[45] They also placed heavy demands on the rapidly diminishing stands of Port Orford cedar, an ill omen for the future.

As the depression lingered on, the aggressions of national socialism in Europe and the growing competition between the United States and Japan in the Far East increasingly affected the lumber trade. By the beginning of 1940 the battery separator plants were on heavy production schedules, lumber prices were beginning to improve, and the pulp mill had reopened. But the southwestern Oregon economy continued to lag—home construction remained "disappointingly slow," and unemployment remained high. The *Times* was perplexed:

> This area suffers, as does much of the United States, from almost chronic unemployment of some needy citizens. Youth particularly is finding it hard to gain steady employment. Relief loads are heavy but by the combined efforts of the federal, state and county governments, are being met.[46]

Although war orders from England and elsewhere brightened the picture for 1940, the lumber trade was lethargic, seasonal unemployment the accepted norm, and the "greenery business" the common stopgap for out-of-work loggers.

Rumors that a family could make a living picking ferns, salal, and "brush" attracted Dorotha Richardson's parents to Coos Bay in 1941. Idaho newcomers with little cash, the Richardson's lived in their car during their first week on the bay. Dorotha remembers using service station restrooms to wash up in the morning. Then the family bought coffee and "lunch meat and bread" before commencing the day's round of job hunting.[47] Those conditions changed abruptly for the Richardsons and others with the bombing of Pearl Harbor; large war-related orders for lumber and the wholesale drafting of young men into the armed services created a shortage of labor. The Coos country was on the verge of a great economic boom that, for a time, would bring full employment, regular paychecks, and greater control over job conditions for working people. That achievement, accomplished through struggle on the picket line and at the bargaining table, was a consequence of the Second World War and the booming construction industry after 1945.

CHAPTER 7

The Second World War

There was so much work, it's almost unbelievable. We are working so much we hardly had time to spend our money.

Everett Richardson, 1981[1]

The Second World War had a profound and disrupting influence on most American communities. It brought an abrupt end to years of unemployment and economic stagnation, and it revolutionized the work force when thousands of women took jobs outside the home for the first time. It uprooted people and sent them into the armed forces or to centers of defense manufacturing. The drain of labor to the military and to defense jobs created an acute shortage of workers in traditional occupations like agriculture and lumbering. What had been a plentiful labor supply before the war became one of scarcity after 1941. People who had experienced long periods of unemployment during the Great Depression suddenly found their labor in demand. Despite long work days, the inconvenience of rationing, food shortages, and military conscription, the wartime years meant improved economic conditions for most. It was a heady experience for families who had suffered through decades without steady work.

When the war ended, the region's forest products industry entered a prolonged period of expansion. Log production, which had plummeted during the early years of the depression, more than doubled in Coos County during the 1940s and increased another 25 percent in the 1950s. The completion of the sprawling Weyerhaeuser plant in 1951 augmented the region's productive capacity even more, and further concentrated manufacturing facilities on the bay.[2] The immediate postwar years saw the emergence of hundreds of small outfits, some of whom made good money over the short haul. Although gyppo and small mill operations multiplied during this period, large corporations like Weyerhaeuser still dominated.

The effects of war in Europe and Asia came early to centers of natural resource processing like Coos Bay. When Japan diverted civilian ships to assist with its imperial conquest of China in 1937, the Coos Bay Logging Company had to curtail production, because it relied on Japanese ships to market its logs in Asia. In January 1938 the

Coos Bay Pulp Corporation, almost totally dependent on the export of
pulp to Japan, found itself without a market when the Japanese
suddenly cancelled all their orders. Japanese traders informed Wylie
Smith, the manager of the pulp mill, that they could not obtain import
permits. Smith believes the Japanese warlords probably were more
interested in purchasing "scrap iron and oil for their armament program."[3] But that was only the beginning of the disruption of normal
trading channels for the Coos Bay forest products industries.

The pulp mill was closed for eighteen months until the fortunes of
war in the Atlantic led to the reopening of the plant. When Germany
invaded Poland and sent its ships into Scandinavian waters in 1939,
that power play effectively cut off imported pulp supplies to the big
converting mills on the East Coast. Those buyers immediately placed
large orders for pulp with West Coast mills. According to Wylie
Smith, international events were directly responsible for the pulp mill
resuming production in the fall of 1939. When its Seattle investors
sold the plant to the Scott Paper Company in 1940, the new corporate
owners retained Smith as resident manager.[4] Although logs were in
short supply during the war, the Scott Paper mill operated steadily
with a complement of more than 100 employees.

Because of its isolated location, Coos Bay was not an important
recipient of defense contracts. Although the Navy awarded the Kruse
and Banks shipyard in North Bend an early contract to build four
mine sweepers, those shipbuilding orders did not create many jobs.
Even so, the Coos Bay *Times* exulted that the area was entering "the
defense picture with a sizable order" and stood "on the threshhold of
a boom." When the Navy announced plans to station antisubmarine
boats and other small craft on Coos Bay, the newspaper was even
more ecstatic.[5] But that editorial crowing for anything that promised
jobs ended when people began to leave in large numbers for the
armed forces or to defense jobs in Portland, Seattle, and California.

Nevertheless, the construction of new defense plants, especially in
southern California, helped to revitalize a moribund lumber market
by the early spring of 1941. Although the *Times* reported that unemployment "was virtually nil," that condition probably reflected people
leaving for the armed forces and to defense plants more than a sharp
increase in local employment. Despite the enthusiasm of some of his
writers, Sheldon Sackett, the publisher of the *Times*, was no un-
abashed worshipper of defense-related employment as the road to
economic recovery. More desirable, he argued, were conditions that
would keep people "at work after the rearmament rush has subsided." Still, he was optimistic. Defense spending "had thawed out

frozen money and idle labor." Now that "the old crate has been started again," Sackett believed, full recovery would follow.[6]

There were other signs that the local economy was improving. The Moore Mill and Lumber Company of nearby Bandon opened a plant at the site of the old Empire Lumber Company mill on outer Coos Bay in April 1941. The new Cape Arago Mill, set up as a cargo operation to supply lumber to the eastern market, employed more than seventy workers on one shift. The operation, the *Times* pointed out, took its place "in a community that is prosperous and busy, bothered but little by labor-employer troubles, and much above the average . . . in the matter of continuous employment." The increase in industrial activity, moreover, was not part of the defense boom, because the lumber business had passed "the peak of cutting for army and navy construction."[7] For its part, the Cape Arago work force strained an already dwindling labor supply, and bay area employers became increasingly anxious about the loss of skilled workers to Portland shipyards and the airplane plants in Seattle and California.

As the Japanese-American struggle for supremacy in the Pacific approached the boiling point, Coos County officials established voluntary committees to handle communication and transportation problems during "the present national emergency." Defense committees organized volunteers in each community to guard docks, shipyards, bridges, and utility plants. To cope with the manpower shortage, the Marshfield employment office advertised for white-collar workers to fill the early evening shift in local mills. Evans Products and the Irwin-Lyons plant, it reported, needed both semi-skilled and unskilled part-time help.[8] That feverish activity was a marked change from nearly fifteen years of underemployment.

For most of 1941 the West Coast lumber industry operated at full production. Although the manufacturers did little milling of logs for purposes other than defense, the West Coast Lumbermen's Association reported in October that mills were "working above capacity" to fill orders for the construction of Army and Navy installations and defense plants, especially in southern California. In the late summer, a minor crisis occurred when the federal government banned all non-defense construction. Because of the Roosevelt administration's directive and the lack of "bottom space" for shipping to the Atlantic, West Coast mills were forced to curtail production. But the *Times'* fears about a "recession in lumber" literally went up in smoke with the Japanese attack on Pearl Harbor. Shortly thereafter, federal officials flooded Coos area mills with orders for spruce and other specialty lumber products.[9] The critical production problem henceforth would be the short supply of labor.

Ultimately, the diminished size of the labor force and drastically altered marketing arrangements sharply reduced the volume of lumber shipped over the Coos Bay bar. Although rail shipments increased and demand was high, the drain of Coos residents to the armed forces and to defense jobs had reduced the work force to the point that it affected production. Beth Wood's entire family "left and went to California to work." Valerie Wyatt, the young union activist, spent the war years working for Columbia Aircraft Industries in Portland.[10]

By the spring of 1942 the labor shortage in the West Coast lumber industry had reached crisis proporations. According to Vernon Jensen, the best authority on the subject, "the lumber industry labor problem [was] one of the most critical in the nation by midsummer of 1942." In April, one Congress of Industrial Organizations' (CIO) official estimated that he could find immediate employment for at least 1,350 men in Columbia River mills and logging camps alone. He cited the "mass trek" of loggers to the shipyards and military conscription as the chief cause of the short supply of labor.[11] Under those changed circumstances loggers and millworkers suddenly found themselves in a sellers' market.

Finally, the state Selective Service office ordered Coos County officials "to make as few inroads as possible into the labor supply" for logging and lumbering. Because the labor shortage in the camps and mills was "acute," the office instructed local draft boards to classify with great care "fallers, buckers, riggers, log truck drivers, loaders, sawyers, ratchet setters, and green chainmen." But heavy war demands for lumber—new barracks, housing for war workers, government construction, railroad needs, and building material for Pacific islands like Hawaii and Midway—continued to place great strains on the industrial work force. On Coos Bay the supply of logs was only a few days ahead of the mill cut, a problem endemic throughout the West Coast lumber industry.[12] Loggers, who were accustomed to frequent job changes, left in droves for the shipyards or for better-paying jobs in other defense industries. And without logs, sawmills could not operate.

The federal government's War Manpower Commission attempted to rectify the production problem when it issued an order "freezing" workers in "certain essential occupations," including logging and lumbering. The restrictions prohibited loggers and millworkers from changing jobs unless they obtained the approval of the local employment office.[13] The essence of the plan was to halt the pirating of workers through the offer of better wages or working conditions. Although draft-age residents in the Coos Bay area admitted that the measure may have placed some curbs on the movement to better-paying jobs, labor mobility remained high for the duration of the war.

Fred Scherer, the manager of the Marshfield employment office, appealed to workers who were performing "essential war work" to remain on the job. Changing employment, he said, hurt production, and because wood products workers were "vital to the war effort," they should remain on the job and meet their patriotic obligation. Elsewhere, William Greeley of the West Coast Lumbermen's Association told a United States Senate committee that the coastal lumber industry was operating with a manpower shortage of 20 percent.[14] Federal coercion and appeals to patriotism, however, did not resolve the labor shortage in the lumber industry. At war's end one of the major criticisms of government policy was its inability to stimulate greater lumber production during the conflict.

The Second World War brought great change to the Coos country. Because of the manpower shortage, employers devised new schemes to speed production, placed a premium on labor-saving devices like the chain saw, accelerated the introduction of other technological innovations, attracted workers from other parts of the country, and brought women into the work force in large numbers. For logging operations, the shortage of help meant longer hours, and in some instances, even faster and harder work. At the same time, loggers and millworkers were in a position of greater strength and were better able to exact a "pound of flesh" in exchange for their labor.

For Garnett Johnson the war meant a new occupation—"punking whistle." Although she had never worked as a logger before, she "had heard those whistles" all her life and "had some idea how fast they had to go in and how correct you had to be." She remembers the amusement at the employment office when she filled out her work card: "SEX—female; OCCUPATION—logger." But her bosses considered her "a good whistle punk and a careful one," and they "never complained." Dow Beckham, responsible for a young family and with an aversion to the violence associated with warfare, left his teaching job to return to logging—"an essential industry." In a short time he became one of the key men splashing logs on the Coos River for the Irwin-Lyons Company. Until the firm built a second splash dam in 1944, he was constantly fighting log jams with a "very small" crew.[15]

An acknowledged "camp inspector" during his younger years, Pete

Kromminga quit his waterfront job during the war and returned to the woods. His deferment was assured because he was a high climber. Kromminga recalled the government's freeze on jobs and knew several loggers who had "quit and wound up in the Army." And once they were drafted, "there was no getting back." The war meant longer hours of hard labor for Kromminga. Logging outfits always were "shorthanded," because the "cost plus" work in the shipyards attracted "lots of men." But he and his logging friends used the "labor problem" to gain better wages and improved working conditions.[16]

According to Dow Beckham, the purpose of the job freeze "was to keep the lumber people from raiding each other's crews" and to prevent men from "running off to work in the shipyards in Portland and San Francisco." Although Beckham "kept mostly the same crew" during the war, he noted that there was a serious problem in the woods.[17] The exodus of laborers to the shipyards and other high-paying defense jobs placed a premium on experienced loggers. Operating with a smaller work force and faced with profitable defense orders, logging bosses used every means to speed production. Before the job freeze and the threat of the draft curbed job itinerancy, loggers simply told the boss to "shove it" when wages or working conditions were unsatisfactory or the operator was running a highball camp. Government restrictions and the threat of being drafted undoubtedly deterred some movement between jobs.

But organized logging crews were able to gain a better shake at the bargaining table when operators made unreasonable demands to increase production. Pete Kromminga remembers one outfit that wanted its cutting crew to "go busheling" (being paid by the thousand board feet rather than an hourly wage). In that instance, the CIO local and the bosses "traded a few things" and the fallers went busheling; after the deal was made, "the cutters made big money."[18] Although busheling was not a new practice, the use of the chain saw—which enabled fallers to cut far more timber than they could with a crosscut saw—encouraged falling by the thousand. It also meant tying pay to productivity, a dangerous practice in hazardous physical settings like the steep slopes of the Coos country.

During the war loggers also began to assert greater control over working conditions. When the demand for lumber increased in 1941, Pete Kromminga's crew was in the woods "just as soon as it got daylight." But when the company started charging the loggers "two bits a day" for bus transportation to the logging site, the crew objected. At a meeting of his union local, Kromminga told the members that on the waterfront the bosses furnish the transportation. Although some of the members thought he "was kind of a rabble rouser," it was not long before the companies furnished the transportation. His fellow workers, he remembers, "found out it was a damned good thing."[19] In any event, the logging operators undoubtedly were more interested in the handsome profits they received when the fir, cedar, and spruce logs were delivered to the mills.

The federal government used a variety of incentives to urge experienced loggers to return to the woods. On one occasion, more than 300 loggers left their jobs in the Kaiser shipyards in Portland to go back to camps in the Columbia River country. The men reportedly left the shipyards at the request of War Manpower Commission chairman Paul McNutt, who declared that logging was the "Number 1 manpower problem in the West." Although the dire need for labor attracted a few newcomers to the south coast, there is no evidence that shipyard workers returned in large numbers until the war ended. Victor Graham, an Allegany logger serving aboard the USS Black Hawk in the Pacific, told readers of the Coos Bay Times that "old time loggers" were the answer to the labor shortage. He pointed to the perils of hiring inexperienced men to work in the mountainous coastal forests. Give such a man "a pair of caulks and stick him out on the end of a springboard where you can spit 40 feet down the hillside, and see what happens."[20] But neither "old time loggers," newcomers, nor women ever resolved the inadequate labor supply during the war.

The labor problem and the shortage of materials affected the entire West Coast lumber industry. The lack of logs in Puget Sound and Grays Harbor caused mills to close periodically, and the plants on Coos Bay also experienced shortened work weeks. The War Production Board's procurement division, which purchased lumber for the government, occasionally allocated logs among local mills according to defense needs for a particular dimension. Wylie Smith of the Scott Paper mill recalls one instance when the federal agency directed his firm to turn over two million board feet of logs to a local sawmill "that was filling some government order."[21] But despite a persisting shortage of logs and labor, the pulp operation ran continuously.

Logging bosses and mill foremen also used variations of the "speed up" during the war. The Coos Bay Lumber Company, according to Cliff Thorwald, "speeded up all they could, and paid more money." Both the Coos Bay Lumber Company and Evans Products used "time studies" and established quotas to increase production. And to keep workers on the job, logging operators frequently violated the Wage Stabilization Act of 1942 and granted raises. The evidence also shows that widespread violation of the act and the lack of uniform wages contributed to a high labor turnover.[22] Those conditions persisted well into the postwar era; loggers simply showed their dissatisfaction with wages and working conditions by walking off the job.

Women from all walks of life took wage labor jobs during the war that traditionally had been the province of males. After a morning of "punking whistle" somewhere deep in the coastal mountains, Garnett Johnson ate lunch with the rest of the logging crew. Dorotha Richardson worked for Evans Products, and as the labor situation worsened, she and other women did "men's work" in the plywood end of the company's operation. Other women, like Valerie Wyatt, left for the Portland shipyards.[23] Participation in wartime work for wages influenced the attitudes of women like Johnson, Richardson, and Taylor for the rest of their lives.

Jobs on Coos Bay were plentiful for women during the war. At Evans Products, where females numbered 800 of the 1,200 employees, turnover was high. Women quit to seek other lines of work, according to Dorotha Richardson, because making battery separators "wasn't that glamorous." But, she points out, the union local forced the company to pay the same wages for men and women doing the same job. When the war ended, Evans laid off a large part of its work force, in part because plastic was replacing wood in the manufacture of battery separators. Richardson also believes that Evans "did not want women in plywood." Although her union negotiated for a token percentage of women in the plywood plant, when Evans began to phase out its Coos Bay operations in 1959, there were only twenty women working in plywood.[24]

Several women worked at the Empire pulp mill, which had to operate continuously because of the difficulty of shutting down and restarting the pulp-cooking process. That meant four shifts of forty hours each, with one shift working eight hours of overtime to cover the 168-hour week. Wylie Smith, now in his seventies and the manager of the old pulp mill, hired inexperienced women to work in the "wood room" even though there were "no jobs there that women could do that well." He overcame his reluctance because "we were clear down to where we couldn't obtain enough men to keep the mill running."[25] However inexperienced, women workers helped managers like Smith meet government contracts and make good profits.

The war in the Pacific ended shipments of logs to Japan; thereafter, only sawed lumber was shipped out of Coos Bay. But cargo mills like the Coos Bay Lumber Company and the Irwin-Lyons Company turned out a large volume of cants for military purposes. The *Times* marvelled at the "remarkable" production of the mills, "because it was entirely made up of lumber while in past years the number of board feet of logs has been included." Of more than 300 ships leaving the port in 1941, all but five were bound for domestic ports.[26] Although the destination of lumber shipments changed once the United States began its "island hopping" campaign toward the Japanese mainland, the federal government was still the largest purchaser.

Because of the large overseas shipments of goods and the heavy use of wood in boxing and crating, the demand for lumber continued to exceed output. At the close of 1943, the War Production Board blamed a short-handed work force for a 10 percent decline in the production of lumber for the year. For Oregon and Coos Bay, the *Times* pointed out, "the situation means as steady production at the mills and in the woods as there are men available to do the work."[27] Operating within a myriad of wartime restrictions on jobs, wages, and prices, and the rationing of food and material goods, workers in the Coos country took advantage of the healthy job market to better their situation.

Despite modestly improved economic conditions for most Coos Bay residents, lumber capitalists, as elsewhere, benefited the most from the Second World War. The Coos Bay Lumber Company and Evans Products, the oldest and for many years the largest manufacturers on the bay, produced huge orders for government contractors. War-related markets also brought fortune to two self-made lumber entrepreneurs on the bay—James A. "Jimmy" Lyons and Al Peirce—two men whose business activities played a significant role in shaping the postwar era in southwestern Oregon. But the Lyons and Peirce operations differed from the corporate empires of the Coos Bay Lumber Company and Evans Products—both represented "home grown" capital.

Jimmy Lyons was a buccaneer of sorts, willing to take financial chances where others feared to tread. For Dow Beckham, who directed the Irwin-Lyons boom system on the Coos River, Lyons was an innovative and daring lumberman, "a strong individual mentally, quick to make decisions," a man who attracted strong friendships and loyalties and who made equally powerful enemies. Although his financial woes during the depression years were legendary, many of Lyons' employees, like Victor West, remember him as "good to work for" even though "he pulled a lot of fast ones."[28] Combining business shrewdness and a willingness to "get his hands dirty" along with the rest of his crew, Jimmy Lyons emerged from the war financially solvent.

War contracts enabled Lyons to pay his employees on a regular basis for the first time. Teaming with Howard Irwin, a Portland investor who was treasurer of the company, Lyons contracted to sell timber to the government on a cost-plus arrangement. According to Dow Beckham, the company "was able to produce the kind of lumber that the Army and Navy needed for building docks in the South Seas." The government required long, squared timbers, and Lyons put his entire operation into producing lumber to meet those contracts. "The more timber we cut and put through that sawmill," Beckham recalls, "the more money he'd make. It was just that simple." And Lyons "was willing for us to get all that we could" in overtime wages. During the war the Irwin-Lyons sawmills turned out a prodigious volume of lumber, many times outdistancing the production of "the big mills."[29] The operation also was in a good position to take advantage of the building boom expected when the war ended.

Although it was not one of the major lumber producers on the bay, the small Al Peirce mill cut piling for government contracts. Shortly after the war, Peirce built a new sawmill designed to process small and middle-sized logs and to employ more than 100 workers. According to Gene Wechter, head sawyer at the mill for nearly thirty years, Peirce "was on a shoestring" at first, but eventually "made it" through shrewd marketing. In Bill McKenna's view, Al Peirce "hit the market" at the best possible moment.[30] Although the mill was medium sized and geared to specialty markets, it began producing lumber at a propitious moment—the onset of the great California construction boom.

Like other newspaper editors, Sheldon Sackett of the *Times* began to turn his attention to the postwar era as allied victories in Europe and Asia began to turn the tide against the Axis powers in early 1943. The bay area, he noted, was "a gateway to the Orient," uniquely suitable for expanded trade. Asian countries "will be needing our goods and we'll be needing their orders." The effusive editor even predicted great prospects for that most elusive of local businesses, the coal industry. Then, in phrasemaking reminiscent of the great robber barons of the previous century, Sackett pointed the way to the good society: "If we're going to have full employment and full production . . . after the war, we're not going to make 'reserves' out of great resources of raw materials and foods, we're going to look for even more."[31] The editor's stirring invitation for open season on natural resources—especially in timber and fisheries—would turn a sour note thirty years later.

Lumber orders for rebuilding ravaged European cities began flooding Pacific Northwest mills before hostilities in Asia had ended. For his part, Sackett predicted that the demand for lumber meant there would "be no immediate worry of unemployment." Bay area employers, he reminded readers, would "welcome the influx of workers from shipyards, aircraft plants and the armed forces." Sackett estimated that local industries needed at least 1,250 more workers. The rehabilitation of foreign nations, national housing needs, and the expansion of industry in the United States indicated "a rosy future for the region." Coos Bay, Sackett said, was more fortunate than other areas, because it lacked "large, temporary wartime payrolls."[32] That unbounded optimism characterized public and private conversation on the south coast for nearly two decades after the war ended.

Sackett's words became prophetic when foreign and domestic orders for lumber products increased dramatically after 1945. The immediate postwar era—referred to as the "boom years" by Coos residents—was a time of high employment, the easy availability of good-paying jobs, and an influx of people from all parts of the country. A major regional newspaper dubbed Coos Bay the "lumber capital of the world," a distinction that was borne out in huge lumber shipments. Although producers sold a large volume of lumber all over the world, the burgeoning home-building industry in California was the bread and butter market for the Coos economy.

When Bill McKenna left Coos Bay to join the Army in 1940, unemployment lay heavily on the local communities. Vacant houses were everywhere, "lots of them, and they were cheap." Although Evans Products had orders to cut battery separators for "what they called submarine stock for Italy and Germany," he remembers that it was not unusual for the plant to shut down for five or six days at a time. McKenna married his hometown sweetheart during the war, and then settled in Portland for a year after his discharge. When the young couple returned to Coos Bay in 1946, striking changes were apparent on every hand—"times were pretty good, and everybody was working." For the McKennas, however, it was "a time of tremendous adjustment for people who had come immediately out of the service and out of the depression." Bill McKenna remembers that his sense "of what a house was worth was all out of kilter, because all of a sudden, here's this tremendous shortage."[33] The lack of housing reflected the large influx of working people seeking jobs. For their part, producers were eager to supply lumber to the frenzied home-building industry in California where old time loggers are fond of saying, "houses were being built by the section."

The high demand for labor continued for nearly two decades, and the easy access to jobs during and after the war gave workers strength at the bargaining table. The expansive economy, coupled with an increasingly sophisticated technology, vastly stepped up the pace of exploitation in the forests of the Coos country. Although some foresters were aware of the declining timber inventories, the men and women who worked in the mills and woods generally were not privy to that information. It was still an age of optimism, and it seemed to many that the timber would last forever.

Lumber Capital of the World

"TIM-BER-R-R!"
That lusty cry, first sounded on the banks of Maine's Kennebec, then boomed from the lips of the Saginaw loggers, is today echoing in full volume among the hills and crags of Oregon's southwestern coast.

Portland *Oregonian*, June 8, 1947

At the end of the Second World War, southwestern Oregon had one of the largest remaining stands of old-growth timber in the United States. Covering a vast four-county area, much of that forested wealth was tributary to Coos Bay, the best shipping port between San Francisco and the Columbia River. The timber also was close to California, soon to be the center of a booming home-building industry. Because lumbermen already had cut over most of the privately owned and easily accessible timber along the Columbia River and in the Grays Harbor and Puget Sound region, timber holders in the Coos country confronted great marketing opportunities. Within two years of the Japanese surrender, newspapers were heralding the Coos Bay region as the "lumber capital of the world."

The healthy California and foreign lumber markets placed heavy demands on both labor and the timber resource in southwestern Oregon. The communities in the Coos country literally hummed with activity in the postwar era as new mills opened, gyppo operators multiplied, and immigrants flocked to the area. Coos County's population grew more than 30 percent in the 1940s and 1950s, an increase that is comparable to that of many areas in California during those two decades.[1] There were periodic housing shortages on the south coast, especially during the summer months when migrant laborers flocked to the area to work in the woods or in the mills on the bay.

The lack of housing and the abundance of jobs contrasted sharply with the late depression years when, according to one resident, there were "lots of houses for sale" and "times had not gotten all that good."[2] But the shortage of houses and apartments and the movement of people through the bay communities were symptoms of the time. In the years after 1945 Americans were a people in motion, frequently changing employment and moving to new locations for better-paying jobs or improved working conditions. For people who were raised in the tradition of packing their bedroll and leaving for the next mill town or logging show, those experiences were not new.

107

As was true elsewhere after the war, there was a heady optimism in the bay country, an atmosphere that suggested the good times would go on forever. Because of the excellent growing conditions and the fact that the largest timber holders in the Coos Bay district were "treating timber like a crop," the *Oregonian* predicted bright prospects for the long-range economy of southwestern Oregon. Forecasters, it said, "look for no end here to the song of the ax and saw." For working people like Bill Brainard, a young, proud, and self-conscious Indian, that meant confidence and a willingness to move on if "somebody didn't say good morning to you right." And those options were available to everyone, he insists: "You didn't have to stay any place you didn't like."[3] Until he took a permanent position with a utility company in 1962, Brainard worked at a variety of jobs—gyppo logging, rafting on the river, operating a towboat, and short stints in the Menasha and Weyerhaeuser mills.

According to Bill McKenna, the good times of the postwar era convinced people that an economic collapse like the Great Depression "could never happen again. Bad times were a thing of the past." McKenna remembers that he "had no qualms about quitting" a job because it wouldn't be hard to find another one. He sold plywood, "gyppoed for a while," worked for a local dairy, and when that company wanted to transfer him, he quit and entered the teaching profession. McKenna's work experiences during the 1950s were living testimony to Bill Brainard's claim that "if you wanted to do something, it was here to do."[4]

Ross Youngblood, a young graduate forester from Oregon State College, began a thirty-year tour of duty as head of the new Coos Bay district for the General Land Office in 1944 (Bureau of Land Management after 1946). Because the war had delayed the introduction of caterpillars and gas and diesel donkeys, a few operators were still using steam-powered engines, he recalls. Marshfield "was just a sort of little coastal town with a fishing fleet, and loggers that logged into the water." But shortly after the war the city began to grow, and during Youngblood's period of residence the area "was really booming." Foreign ships made regular visits to load lumber, there was a "lot of tourist trade," and a thriving fishing industry developed.[5] If the region was less than a worker's paradise, it seemed to offer enough opportunity for a person to make a decent living.

The late 1940s were years of transition for the Coos Bay lumber industry. Although large companies were still the most important factor in the volume of production, the great demand for dimension lumber, especially for the California construction industry, brought new sawmills into being and encouraged other entrepreneurs to form fledgling logging enterprises. The California building boom launched Bill McKenna on a short career as a gyppo logger. For Chappie McCarthy, it meant purchasing a "cat" through surplus military sales and doing salvage logging on his father's timberlands where he earned "spending money" and saved enough to pay his way through the University of Oregon.[6] That great surge in the demand for lumber placed a premium on labor, especially during the summer months, and meant that the good job market of the early 1940s would continue.

But even during the best of times employment remained largely seasonal, and occasional slumps in the building industry still affected the timber-dependent communities on Coos Bay. Ross Youngblood remembers "a little dip in '46" and another in 1952 when "things slowed down." For Bill McKenna, struggling to make it as a gyppo logger during the 1950s, "the market was not always that good." There were "lots of pitfalls and traps" and many people went out of business. Wylie Smith, co-owner of the Coos Head Timber Company, remembers "a pretty serious cycle in '49, when everything kind of hit the skids." Although Coos Head's three mills ran steadily through most of the postwar years, the company put on a second shift only "if the market justified."[7] But those market-induced downturns during the 1950s and the 1960s were temporary, and workers could always look forward to another round of building activity, the rekindling of extra shifts and overtime in the mills, and daybreak-to-dusk operations in the woods.

During the rainy season, the southern Oregon coast and the rest of the Douglas fir region had some of the highest unemployment rates in the country. Even in the dark winter months, however, everyone expected that the slackening of the rains would brighten job prospects. Rehirings and the opening of small logging operations normally began to pick up in February and March, and by late spring, when building and highway construction was in full swing, jobs usually were abundant. On occasion, the local employment office would issue a call for more loggers and sawmill workers. Those pleas brought newcomers to the area from nearby states—and a few from as far away as Oklahoma and Arkansas—and further strained an already tight housing situation.[8] Those seasonal and market-related conditions persisted throughout "the great boom."

When the lumber market was soft or labor disputes, particularly waterfront strikes, tied up lumber shipments from the bay, workers sometimes left the area. During the maritime strike of 1948, the *Times* reported a sharp rise in unemployment and workers leaving for "points in the state not as yet affected by the shipping labor troubles." But job prospects always improved following strikes or market slumps. When the local economy was booming, as the director of the local employment office noted in 1954, southwestern Oregon was "greatly dependent upon a summer influx of outside labor."[9] Newspaper reports and census tabulations in the postwar era support the stories still current in the bay area about the influx of "Okies and Arkies."

Although the large companies set the tone for the post-1945 employment and production conditions on the bay, the hundreds of small operators who moved on the periphery provided employment for thousands of workers. The *Oregonian* reported in 1946 that "one-family sawmills were springing up like mushrooms" in the Coos Bay region and were "contributing to the all-out drive of the lumber industry to supply the needs of the nation's home builders." At the same time, a local banker estimated that there were 100 small portable mills in operation in the area.[10] But that was only the beginning of the emergence of small, independent units as a major force in forest products manufacturing on Coos Bay.

The immediate postwar years in southwestern Oregon were the heyday of the storied gyppo logger and sawmill operator, the hardy individual who worked on marginal capital, usually through subcontracts with a major company or a broker, and whose equipment was invariably pieced together with baling wire. In his great novel *Sometimes a Great Notion*, Ken Kesey features the gyppo logger in classic form through his account of the fictional Stamper family. "Never Give A Inch"—the family motto—is the symbol for the Stampers' struggle to survive in a world progressively dominated by outside capital and large labor organizations.

Reckless and daring gamblers, always ready to move on to the next stand of timber, the multitudes of gyppos were unique to the postwar era in the Douglas fir country. Opposed to labor unions and government regulations, they were a throwback to an earlier day of independent entrepreneurship. The voracious California construction industry, the availability of easy-to-reach small tracts of second-and third-growth timber, and access to modest credit marked the emergence of gyppo logging and sawmill operations. Varying in size from three to fifteen or twenty employees, those small units were important contributors to the Coos economy between 1946 and 1960.

George Youst, who came to the bay area from southwestern Washington, where he milled railroad ties and bridge planks, was one of the earliest of the modern-day gyppos in the Coos country. He set up a sawmill in Coos County in the late depression years with a $900 loan on a half section of timber he owned in the state of Washington. His son, Lionel, explains that gyppos commonly set up their mills on a hillside and from there they would "shoot the slabs down into the canyon." Once the canyon had filled with waste wood, the operator would "set fire to the slab pile and burn it and then start over again."[11] Sometimes the mill burned too, as happened to the Yousts on one occasion. With a donkey engine salvaged from the fire, George Youst simply moved his family and equipment to another stand of timber.

Operations of that kind made a profound impression on Jerry Phillips when the state forestry department hired him as a logging inspector in Coos County in 1952. At that time, he recalls, there were about 500 small mills in Coos and Curry counties, most of them cutting cross ties for the nation's deteriorating railroad system: "From a high point you could see dozens and dozens of columns of smoke coming up all the time, because everywhere you looked there was a small mill employing between five and fifteen men that was cutting timber from some ranch. They had built these small mills, and they had a slab and sawdust pile that was constantly on fire." Although "few of those fires got away and caused damage," when they did, Phillips said, they usually spread from the slab and sawdust pile into the mill. Those grease-soaked planks and wooden structures usually burned easily.[12]

When the state began requiring sawmills to install burners, the conical metal structures that eventually were used to contain the burning slabs and sawdust, the added expense put many gyppos out of business. Regulations of that kind, usually favored by the larger companies, were ruinous to small operators.

Large mills, or in some cases, brokers, would subcontract work to gyppo loggers and sawmills. According to Quentin Church, who worked for small outfits between 1946 and 1948, the big mills bought the rough-cut planking or boards, and then processed, planed, graded, and packaged the lumber for export. Bill McKenna points out that many of the small outfits were financially tied to one of the big mills "to such an extent that if you really looked deep enough," the operation probably belonged to a large mill.[13] Gyppo logging and sawmilling enterprises, whatever their financial ties, were risky ventures. To survive in that intensely competitive world required great skill and mechanical ingenuity.

After traveling about the Pacific slope for nearly fifteen years,

Chuck Reigard decided to make Coos Bay his home in 1954. But not to settle in one job. Reigard remembers "there was a little mill stuck back in every little nook and cranny at that time." He ran a logging outfit for his brother-in-law, worked at both Weyerhaeuser and Coos Head, and then for several small mills where he "was getting into the millwrighting end" of the business.[14] Because gyppo mills moved frequently, employees like Reigard acquired great skills in the process of dismantling and setting up the machinery.

"They were very ingenious, some of those fellows," recalls Ross Youngblood. George Vaughan, whose logging family was well known in Coos County, agrees; gyppos had "much to do with improvements in sawmilling because of the necessity of keeping manpower costs down." They were adaptive and used innovative and efficient devices to save labor. But when the big trade organizations like the West Coast Lumbermen's Association pushed for grade-marked lumber, Vaughan remembers, it hurt gyppos, because they manufactured "poorly graded stuff."[15]

The major trade groups and the U.S. Forest Service had been urging lumbermen to adopt standard grades and cuts of lumber for several decades. The National Lumber Manufacturers Association and its regional affiliates aggressively promoted "standardization" during the 1920s. The large companies, which wanted to eliminate smaller competitors, determined trade-organization policy. That was especially apparent in the South during the 1920s and 1930s where the Southern Pine Association proposed lumber-grading standards as a means to eliminate the smaller, "peckerwood" mills.[16] When the West Coast Lumbermen's Association took up the charge in the 1950s, their object was to impose specific requirements on the smaller mills, most of them unable to cut systematically to accurate dimensions.

But for a time the overheated California lumber market served gyppo mills well. The Al Peirce Company, Coos Head, and the Cape Arago mill purchased both logs and rough-cut timbers from gyppo outfits and then milled and shipped the finished lumber to their distribution yards in California. Although Coos Head marketed lumber all over the world, Wylie Smith says that anything that did not "make the export grades" went into the category of "common lumber" and was sold in California, primarily for framing houses. Al Peirce operated on a similar basis, purchasing gyppo logs and cutting those into framing lumber on a gang saw, a device that increased output but produced lower-quality boards. At Cape Arago, head sawyer Dave Mickelson remembers his mill's "peanut machine" that turned gyppo planks into two-by-fours by the dozen. Combined with the large volume from its own "head rig," that meant a constantly loaded "green chain."[17] And lots of overtime.

Chappie McCarthy, one of the few independent loggers still operating in southwestern Oregon, supplied logs to the Al Peirce mill. Because he "was impressed with the people who were making money at it," he decided to go into logging full time when he graduated from the University of Oregon. Although he became disheartened after his brother died in a logging accident, his family had money tied up in the contract, so they "decided to go back in and complete it." With a cat, an old loading machine, and a yarder, the McCarthys supplied logs to the Al Peirce mill and later to the Coquille Plywood Company. Because his father was well known, Chappie found it easier to get credit, "and that's the thing you operated on."[18] In a world dominated by the likes of Weyerhaeuser and Georgia-Pacific, the McCarthy operation still survives.

Many gyppo outfits were family-run shows. In his travels through the Coos country for BLM, Ross Youngblood encountered dozens of struggling enterprises where every member of the family contributed to the operation. He remembers steam donkeys and long-outdated Model A trucks used to yard and transport logs, and steam and Model A engines to power sawmills. In one family-operated steam-powered mill, "the mother did the firing for the steam engine, the father was head sawyer, and the son ran the dogs on the carriage. Two other sons did all the other off-bearings from the saw. They did all right."[19]

And some of them, like George Youst, even bounced back from adversity. After his mill burned, Youst moved his charred but operable donkey engine to another stand where he entered into a cooperative arrangement with the owner. "That was really a gyppo operation," recalls his son, Lionel, who was about five years old at the time: "My dad was running donkey. Ernest Peterson, who owned the timber, was falling timber. My cousin was setting the chokers. My mom was punkin' whistle. And my brother and I were just kids and she would babysit us while she was punkin' whistle." One day as his father was hauling in a log across a county road, a passerby was crushed to death when a guy line broke and the spar tree fell on him. "A bad day," Lionel's childhood recollections tell him. He felt even more distressed when his cousin remarked, "God, they can really hook a guy for this." Out of his boyhood fears, Lionel imagined "them a hooking my dad with a big hook." Although it was "a pretty scary deal," nothing came of it.[20]

The life of a gyppo was an endless round of work and time-consuming "business trips" looking for a fresh stand of timber. While George Youst was operating in one setting, he would spend weekends traveling about the countryside seeking the ideal location for his next mill site. Because he had no heavy equipment, the setting had to be such that "you could log to the mill." On one occasion, Youst bought a large stand of timber high in the Coast Range, and the family spent six years logging the area. Lionel recalls that his father put in a "skyline" and used his donkey to yard the mill equipment up the mountainside to the site. George Youst hand hewed the timbers for the mill and built a lumber chute to send the sawn boards 1,000 feet across a county road to a field. He used a large log with a rubber tire on the end of it to cushion the boards as they reached the end of the chute. Because the larger timbers would split when they hit the log, Youst "found out that the only thing he could shoot down there was two-by-fours."[21]

George Youst was a skilled sawmill man who had spent most of his adult life assembling and disassembling mills. "That was what he was specialized in, and he was pretty good at it," according to his son. He could set up a sawmill with a "minimum of expense and by hand," and although he made a lot of mistakes, "he remembered most of them." When Youst was not busy fixing something at the mill on weekends, he was on the road looking at other mills. "There wasn't anything else," Lionel remembers. The family lived on the bay while Lionel was growing up, yet they never had a boat and "didn't do anything unless it was connected with sawmills." No fishing, no hunting, just sawmills—"that was about it."[22] There are no complaints from the son who admired the father whose lifelong obsession was sawmilling. But for George Youst and many other small operators the sands began to run out in the mid-1950s.

Sawmilling was becoming complicated. Electrically powered units were replacing the old mills powered by one engine and driven by a maze of belts. When George Youst put up his last mill in the mid-1950s—"just like he had built all the other mills"—Jerry Phillips, fresh from college to the Oregon Department of Forestry, told him he would have to build a wigwam burner to dispose of his slabs and sawdust. That, according to son Lionel, was "totally out of his experience, so beyond his comprehension." But, he complied, and from there moved to California where he put in an electrical mill and went bankrupt. "It was too much of an expense, and too many regulations."[23] The new world of sawmilling made little sense to George Youst. Simply put, he did not belong.

Gyppos always were marginal capital undertakings to begin with. Therefore, when government agencies imposed requirements that operators had not figured in their original calculations, it often made the difference between success and failure. As for his father, Lionel Youst says, "he got into something he didn't have any business getting into." Those were inauspicious years for gyppos and other "self-made" men on the bay. Jimmy Lyons was killed in a hunting accident in 1953, Al Peirce died in an automobile wreck in 1958, and George Youst went broke the same year. For young Lionel Youst, just discharged from the Air Force, "it was just like the world had kind of crumbled."[24] The late 1950s were, in truth, a period of transition in which large mills were once again setting the tone for business activity in the Coos country. George Youst's failure was merely a sign of the times.

Another problem for small operators was access to timber. The farm and ranch holdings that had sustained many of the gyppos since the war had been cut over, and it was difficult to purchase small tracts from the larger owners. Bill McKenna and his logging partner got out of the business at that time. "We were lucky," he says, because they were able to sell their equipment just as available farm timberland began to run out. Although he did not think that large mills conspired to put gyppos out of business, Dow Beckham concedes that the likes of Weyerhaeuser "could bid on government timber easier than the gyppos." The prime reason for the diminishing number of small operators, he believes, was a tapering off in the California construction industry. "When that market began to decline," he argues, the big operators captured the remaining sales.[25] Although they still did not have the field to themselves, by 1960 it was apparent that only firms with large timber holdings and extensive marketing arrangements would survive the newly emerging order.

During the 1940s the Weyerhaeuser Company announced plans to build a large sawmill facility in North Bend. The prospect of a lively lumber market and the maturing of its Coos timberlands undoubtedly prompted the decision. "Why Coos Bay," the *Times* asked? "Because the timber was there, the know-how was available, and an ocean highway was a rifle-shot away."[26] The newspaper might have added that Weyerhaeuser was the first multinational corporation to conduct the lumber business in a truly integrated way. It would not be the last.

Before its mill began sawing logs, Weyerhaeuser began building maintenance shops and a network of roads into its timberlands; it commenced dredging operations for a log dump on one of the waterways, and it conducted extensive surveys of its vast holdings to determine which areas to harvest first. Loggers equipped with powerful chain saws were at work by mid-1950, falling timber that would be trucked and then rafted to the mill.[27] Meanwhile, the company's public-relations apparatus extolled the permanent nature of its Coos Bay venture and the benefits the additional payroll would bring to the area.

And there was impressive statistical evidence to support that claim. Up to that time, Weyerhaeuser had sold only a few select parcels of its Coos holdings. A few months after the mill opened in 1951, the company employed more than 500 people in its milling and logging operations, and in the next few years it continued to expand its manufacturing facility on the bay. The Weyerhaeuser plant brought new people to the area, once again strained the available housing supply, and added a powerful political voice to local decision making. At the time the mill started up, the Army Corps of Engineers began dredging the Coos Bay bar and channel to a depth of forty feet to make possible the full loading of large offshore ships.[28] For the next thirty years Weyerhaeuser would be the most influential interest, though not the only one, calling for the commercial development of Coos Bay waterways.

A major symbol of the growing concentration in timberland ownership and wood processing after the Second World War was the emergence of the Georgia-Pacific Corporation as a multinational forest products firm. From a small financial base in Georgia, the corporation extended its network to the Pacific Northwest in the 1950s when it made large purchases, including the huge Coos Bay Lumber Company manufacturing plants and 120,000 acres of timberland in 1956.[29] The Georgia-Pacific "buy out," as it is called on the southern Oregon coast, was a momentous development. Suddenly the most aggressive of the expanding forest products empires occupied a central place in the area's economy.

The Dant and Russell Company of Portland was the major shareholder in the Coos Bay Lumber Company at the time of the Georgia-Pacific purchase. Shifting family fortunes after the death of the company's founder, Charles E. Dant, persuaded the survivors to sell the firm's timber holdings and manufacturing plants on the Oregon coast. The primary attraction of the purchase, according to the *Oregonian*, was the large acreage of old forest, the "timber-rich jewel" in the Coos Bay Lumber Company holdings. Those timber reserves, estimated at six billion board feet, represented "one of the largest private holdings in Oregon." Handled by Blyth and Company, a Chicago firm, the deal was closed in July 1956.[30] Unlike other Georgia-Pacific purchases during those years, the Coos Bay Lumber Company buy out was no simple matter.

Because the company had expanded so rapidly during the early 1950s, Georgia-Pacific found it necessary to create a cash flow and sell part of its standing timber in southwestern Oregon to swing the purchase. Wylie Smith, who was present at the sale in San Francisco, recalls that the transaction involved "cash on the barrelhead:"

> I was there at the closing in July of 1956 in the board room of the Bank of America, with probably 100 people in the board room, numerous lawyers and notary publics, a few stenographers. And the principals were there from G-P, and the principals were there from Baker-Fentress, who controlled a lot of the Coos Bay Lumber holdings, also Dant and Russell people were there, and all the Coos Bay Lumber head people were there. And some thought the transaction would never come together right up to the last hour, but it did come together. The money was paid, and papers changed hands, and G-P acquired a fine stand of timber. And what they had left, they sold large volumes to help produce the cash to pay it off.[31]

To create that cash flow, Georgia-Pacific sold large blocks of old-growth Douglas fir to the Coos Head Timber Company, the Moore Mill and Lumber Company (owners of the Cape Arago mill in Empire), the U.S. Plywood Corporation, and other small mills in the Coquille Valley. Thus, with a booming lumber market in California, there began what Jerry Phillips calls the "rapid liquidation phase" of the old Coos Bay Lumber Company timberlands. Ross Youngblood, who left Coos Bay in 1957 to direct the BLM office in Medford, believes that Georgia-Pacific had no alternative, because they had "to liquidate to get their money out of it." His final word on the quick sale of timber: "That's private enterprise, and that's the way the cards turn."[32] Georgia-Pacific, which had moved its corporate headquarters to Portland, Oregon, in 1954, made additional timber sales to mills in southwestern Oregon; it also increased the harvests of logs supplying its own manufacturing plants.

For the short run, the sudden availability of a huge volume of old-growth fir helped to sustain sawmills that otherwise would have closed because they lacked timber. Harold "Cardy" Walton, who worked for the Coos Bay Lumber Company, does not believe the medium-sized mills could have survived on government timber contracts alone. The sales to Coos Head and Moore Mill "boomed the work in Coos County." The rate of harvest was augmented further, Walton points out, when Georgia-Pacific "immediately jumped" its own cutting quota and hired additional loggers.[33] Georgia-Pacific's rapid liquidation of its timber holdings eventually would wreak disaster on the communities along the Coquille and on Coos Bay.

At the time of the buy out, the Coos Bay Lumber Company was the sixth largest lumber producer on the Pacific Coast; it had purchased the Coquille Plywood mill from Smith Wood Products in 1945, and in 1951 the firm built a hardboard manufacturing plant in Bunker Hill at the head of the bay. At that point the company employed about 1,700 workers in its mill and logging operations.[34] Except for the opening of its new plants and minor administrative changes, the basic structure of the Coos Bay Lumber Company had remained substantially unchanged for more than thirty years. Even after Dant and Russell became major shareholders in 1944, the firm's resident manager made most of the decisions. All that ended with the Georgia-Pacific purchase in 1956.

According to Cliff Thorwald, purchasing agent for the Coos Bay Lumber Company at the time of the buy out, Georgia-Pacific restructured the entire operation. Hitherto, Thorwald had answered only to J. W. Forester, the manager, who "was king of everything—camps, mills, hardboard plants." Forester, in turn, answered to Dant and Russell. With Georgia-Pacific, however, Thorwald worked through the company's director of purchasing in Portland; Forester and most of his key assistants were gone; camps deteriorated, and the new management began to phase out the cook houses and bunkhouses and to purchase crummies to transport workers to the woods. Those were difficult times for Thorwald, who had to work for people who "couldn't understand local conditions" and who asked "some very foolish questions."[35] But that was only the beginning of the disruptions that Georgia-Pacific would bring to the south coast.

The bay-area communities generally had looked favorably upon the Coos Bay Lumber Company, according to Jerry Phillips. That "was an image problem that G-P had to overcome when they came here, because one of their first actions was to reorganize the company and to retire early a lot of the Coos Bay Lumber senior personnel." That created ill will, and many area residents felt that "good people were being put out to pasture as a corporate cost-cutting measure." Although Cliff Thorwald decided to "grin and bear it," he recalls that Georgia-Pacific's new personnel created all sorts of problems: "They were insecure, and that made them arrogant." Camp and mill bosses quit; the logging superintendent quit; and the master mechanic in charge of the company's trucks also quit.[36] Those changes affected mill workers, the yard crews, and loggers as well.

The coming of Georgia-Pacific ended the relaxed control Dant and

Russell had exercised over its holdings. Although the buy out of 1956 might seem little more than a changing of corporate bosses, in reality, effective management and decision making of the old Coos Bay Lumber Company holdings had passed even further from the community. Of Dant and Russell, Cliff Thorwald remembers, "we knew the name, that's all." J. W. Forester, who was "the ultimate man to see" regarding company policy, lived in the community and was always visible around the mills and frequently visited the logging camps.[37] Under Georgia-Pacific, the revamped lines of authority had managers and bosses answering to the corporate heirarchy in Portland rather than to a single individual on the bay.

For the Coos Bay *Times*, the large new corporate venture presented bright prospects for the future. When Georgia-Pacific announced plans to build a plywood plant on the site of the old C. A. Smith paper and pulp mill in Bunker Hill, the decision seemed to confirm the paper's earlier prediction. The 260 workers in the new plant would provide "another large quantity of jobs" and would "permit the company to make better utilization of its large timber holdings in Coos County." The move would further stabilize Georgia-Pacific's operation and would "go far to guarantee a longer span of job creating in the area." The *Times'* executive editor, Forest W. Amsden, who later headed KING broadcasting and television stations in Portland and Seattle, pointed out that the Georgia-Pacific announcement "served notice that it is here to stay—an active, wealth-producing, valued member of the Southwestern Oregon community."[38]

Shortly after the Georgia-Pacific plywood mill opened, the company purchased a series of advertisements in the local newspaper— perhaps to refurbish its tarnished image in the bay area:

> Production at G-P's Coos County plants is geared to a long term timber harvesting schedule. Better recovery from each log used, new products manufactured from previously discarded waste, and utilization of portions of the tree formerly left in the woods, all have the effect of increasing the quantity of raw material available. The basis of Georgia-Pacific's entire forestry program is to insure, over successive years, that we will grow a volume of timber at least equal to the volume harvested.[39]

During the boom years of the 1950s, the business community and its newspaper allies were more concerned with market conditions than with the extent of the timber resource. Lumber spokesmen extolled the production of molded plywood, complained about "Canadian competition in our own American markets," and bragged about the annual volume being shipped over the Coos Bay bar. Although the *Times* occasionally warned about the region's dependence on lumbering, its major emphasis was on "more development of natural resources" and new industry.[40] Bay-area promoters, in short, wanted more of everything—cheaper electric power, deeper water in the harbor, better east-west highways, stronger tariff protection for lumber, and more federal money to improve the harbor.

Not everyone agreed that more development and growth would benefit the Coos country. North Bend resident Fred Hand criticized community leaders who were "hollering for more roads, more industries, more chain stores, more this and more that." Although the bay settlements would never return to prewar conditions, he thought the area was "still a fairly decent place to live." And it would remain so "IF people will understand that more money, more roads, or more of anything—except learning to be content with what we have—will not solve our problem." He even chided promoters of tourism: "Yes, we have a good product to sell, all right. So did Esau. He sold his birthright for a mess of pottage, too."[41] But those words of caution were lost in the roar of chain saws and log trucks and big profits for the forest products firms.

Despite occasional slumps in the lumber market, Oregon's timber-dependent communities from Eugene south to the California border prospered during those years. The seven counties that made up Oregon's fourth congressional district grew faster than any other part of the state immediately after the Second World War. The Coos Bay communities had their own mini housing boom, local merchants enjoyed a thriving retail trade, and the local newspaper headlined Oregon's prowess as the leading lumber producing state in the nation.[42] The region's economy remained strong even after the decline of the small sawmill operators in the late 1950s. The expansion of the Georgia-Pacific and Weyerhaeuser facilities and a thriving fishing industry easily took up the slack in the lost gyppo-created jobs.

But there were warning signs as well. Beginning in 1960, forest products employment began to decline; although mill failures and mergers into fewer competing units accounted for some of the reduction, the increased mechanization of mill and logging operations was of far greater consequence. As the larger production units extended their control over the Pacific slope, capital investments increased and the number of mills and workers steadily declined.[43] Although Oregon's south coast was one of the last areas to feel the effects of that trend, the substitution of machines for labor was ominous for the future of the region.

The shifting fortunes of the large forest products firms affected the Coos economy, even during its most expansive phase. When battery manufacturers began substituting plastic for wooden battery separators, Evans Products phased out its local separator plant and sharply reduced its work force. The firm continued to run the plywood plant until 1961, when company executives decided to close its entire Coos Bay operation. Slumping plywood prices, antiquated mill machinery, and more lucrative investment possibilities elsewhere prompted the decision. Dorotha Richardson, who had worked at Evans since 1944, was put out of work in the first wave of layoffs. For her fifteen years with the company, she received nothing—no pension benefits, no severance pay.[44]

In the years before it closed, Evans Products sold timber to other firms, but for reasons of its own the company did not modernize the equipment in its Coos Bay mill. When its sawmill closed in 1959, the firm cited inadequate timber supplies and a soft market as an explanation for its decision.[45] Evans was the first of the major firms to operate with outdated machinery until its profit margins no longer justified keeping the plant open; it would not be the last. But at the time Evans shut its doors, displaced workers still were able to hire on with other area mills.

Economic conditions on the south coast were still relatively good through the 1960s and early 1970s. But there were increasing concerns about the rapid depletion of timber, worries that were unheard of in the booming optimism of the immediate postwar years. With the accelerated harvests of the postwar years, it was obvious that the mature timber was receding further back in the mountains—a fact that was apparent to loggers who had to spend up to four hours a day traveling to and from work. That was a far cry from the time when loggers felled trees into the waterways adjacent to the bay.

CHAPTER 9

Timber Forever

We don't want one big mill in one section cutting all the timber, then, when it is gone,
to shut down—throwing many out of work.
Ferdinand A. Silcox, Chief, U.S. Forest Service,
Portland, Oregon, August 18, 1934[1]

Frank Younker knew timber. He remembers the huge logs rafted down the South Slough on the ebb tide. As a boy, he delivered supplies to Camp Four, the old C. A. Smith logging camp, and for most of his life he hunted and fished, and on occasion, used the South Slough country as a base for his moonshine operations. Looking wistfully at an old photograph of the magnificent spruce, cedar, and fir that once grew along the slough, he told an interviewer in 1975: "You see, that's what trees looked like in the old days. We don't have trees like that no more, no more."[2] To see an old-growth forest today, Younker would have to travel miles into the Coast Range where he might find isolated patches on Forest Service or Bureau of Land Management (BLM) property.

Less kind and charitable old timers are more outspoken about the logs being hauled to the mills today. "Sticks," one of them grumbles. Others refer to the young trees presently being harvested as "pecker poles." Dow Beckham, who remembers the big timber stands on the Coquille and Coos drainages, says the companies are "logging brush these days." When he began working in the woods in the 1920s, loggers "would not take a tree that didn't have at least twenty inches in diameter on the small end." Today, he says in amazement, "that's a big log." Jack Johnson, a boisterous and friendly timber faller for Weyerhaeuser for nearly twenty-five years, says the company is cutting "dog hair these days."[3] But despite their friendly disdain for the size of the trees being harvested, neither Beckham nor Johnson is overly critical of the rapid harvest of the old-growth timber stands.

Frank J. Fish, a native of Myrtle Point, also remembers the days when there was "real timber" in the Coast Range. Fish, who worked as a timber locator in the early twentieth century, recalls falling a tree that was eight feet, nine inches in diameter on the stump. The tree took one hour and fifty-eight minutes to fall and scaled out at 32,000 board feet. When Stephen Spoerl moved to the Gold Beach area on the southern Oregon coast in 1908 because of its "wildness and remoteness," both the size and the extent of the old-growth forest impressed him. He told an interviewer that he thought loggers would never cut trees in the isolated Gold Beach area. There was "so much timber closer to the mills and easier to get out, you'd wonder why they would ever monkey with this stuff." But, viewing the cutover slopes of the south coast in 1975, he remarked: "it's a different ball game in this day."[4] The depleted timber inventory in southwestern Oregon at this writing testifies to the truth of Spoerl's observation.

Like other retired loggers, Frank Fish and Stephen Spoerl look at the past with a tinge of nostalgia and regret. They miss the big trees, but understand the social, economic, and technological forces that brought an end to the old-growth forest. Loggers who worked in the days of crosscut saws and steam donkeys had reason to think the resource was endless. "We didn't think we would ever run out of trees," Dow Beckham recalls. "We knew that it would last forever. They were in the way, and it was growing back so fast." Curt Beckham, who quit logging in 1946 at a time when the woods operations were becoming increasingly mechanized, agrees with his brother: "In my time trees were growing as fast as we were cutting. I believe that. I don't believe we would have ever seen denuded hills. Even the big camps, they couldn't cut the timber as fast as it was growing, because we could only get out so much timber per day, per year."[5]

For most of the years the Beckhams worked in the woods, hand labor and steam power dominated the production system. It took a large work force to satisfy the volume of timber required in the mills. For several decades, therefore, the constraints of technology, manpower, and markets limited the output of the woods operation. Gasoline, diesel, and electrically powered mills meant little to loggers who had to fall trees slowly and laboriously. Those restrictions slowed the liquidation of the old-growth forests in the Coos back country at least until the Second World War.

There were other factors, including a limited sawmilling capacity, that restrained the rate of harvests in the Coos country. Unlike Washington's Grays Harbor district where a great many mills were sawing lumber by the 1920s, only two large plants operated on Coos Bay—the Coos Bay Lumber Company and the old Simpson mill (and its successors). Those were cargo mills, manufacturing for the export market either in California or the Far East. Although a railroad linked the bay area to the outside by 1916, it was not an important factor in lumber shipments until the Second World War. By contrast, Grays Harbor had access to a major transcontinental railroad by the 1880s.[6] More than most lumber manufacturing centers on the Pacific Coast, therefore, Coos Bay has always been oriented to the sea.

In addition, timberland ownership was more concentrated in the Coos Bay region than in most of the Douglas fir country. Those circumstances—a limited technology, a less-abundant labor force, and fewer competitors for south-coast forests, slowed the liquidation of the resource. Moreover, the first stands of second-growth timber were not ready for harvest until the Second World War. Equally important, until the 1940s a perennially glutted market meant that only the clearest of old-growth lumber could be effectively marketed. After 1945 a revolutionary technology and a booming lumber market combined to bring on the "rapid liquidation phase" of Coos forestlands.

Along most of the Pacific Slope agrarianism was not a factor in timber harvesting. In earlier lumbering centers in North America, it was necessary to remove the trees to make way for agriculture. Wielders of the axe traditionally prepared the way for the plowman, the sure sign of progress in what many believed to be a natural transition from forest to farmland. Removing the forest to open the way for pastoralism in New Brunswick, New England, Pennsylvania, and Minnesota was an obvious objective, but there is no indication that similar motives prevailed in the Coos country. Although land speculators, especially in Washington, hoped to profit by selling cut-over timberlands to prospective farmers, no one in southwestern Oregon argued that clearing the forest was the first step to an agrarian society.[7] Agriculturalists very early recognized that tillable soil was limited, confined to the narrow bottomlands in the Coos drainage and the broader valley of the Coquille.

Although a thriving dairy industry developed in the open pastures of the lowland, Coos County's timber resource was the central attraction for most newcomers. From the time Dennis McCarthy first cruised timber for the county government in 1911, lumber industry investors and manufacturers, town developers, newspaper editors, and foresters have been interested in the extent and volume of the area's forests. Although there were no reliable estimates until the Forest Service began making extensive surveys in the 1930s, most people assumed that the timber would last forever.

And there was abundant testimony to support that claim—from the loggers who struggled daily through tangles of vine maple beneath the forest canopy and the promoters who told one and all that the

Coos country held the largest remaining old-growth forest in the United States. What the area needed, the boosters argued, was more sawmilling facilities. When the *American Lumberman* published an extended supplement on the C. A. Smith operations in 1911, the journal informed its readers that the company's forests were under "the supervision of a trained forester" and that timber fallers were leaving "seed trees" for the purpose of producing second growth. Those conditions, it predicted, would lead to "perpetual lumbering" on the company's "enormous timber holdings" because annual growth would equal the rate of harvest.[8] Skeptics were few during those years. When someone raised an occasional voice of caution, the impressive timber stands adjacent to the coastal area seemed to mock such nonsense.

Professional foresters were the first to urge caution in the exploitation of the forest resource. Oregon's timberlands, although still relatively untouched in the first decade of the twentieth century, were part of that concern. In his report for 1912, Francis A. Elliott, Oregon's state forester, pointed to the experiences of states like Michigan and Wisconsin which, he said, "proves the fallacy" that forests were inexhaustible. The "almost total depletion" of those great pine forests, he said, should teach Oregon to harvest its stands "in such a way as to insure future crops." Elliott warned again in 1919 that large acreages of private timber were "being rapidly mined . . . and then left unproductive."[9] Although a 1911 law required the state forester to encourage reforestation, during Elliott's tenure in the office, the state of Oregon devoted nearly its entire budget to forest fire protection— activities that major lumbermen strongly supported.

Long after he left the U.S. Forest Service, William Greeley remarked that the people in the state of Washington were "in the lumber business in the same way that the citizens of Iowa are dependent upon corn, and the folks of the South are subjects of King Cotton." Greeley's analogy also fit the neighboring state of Oregon and, to a lesser extent, the province of British Columbia. Because of the increasing timber harvests in the two states after the turn of the century, Washington and Oregon soon led the nation in the production of lumber. At the same time, the rapid liquidation of the forests in the more accessible locations became a growing concern. Henry Graves, dean of the forestry school at Yale University and Greeley's predecessor as chief, warned in 1925 of "a feverish haste to cut the choicest of the last remaining bodies of timber" in the Pacific Northwest with little effort to "restock the lands."[10] Although foresters like Graves warned about the rapid depletion of timber in certain areas of the Northwest, federal and state governments took no action to restrain private timber harvesting, nor did they establish policies to stabilize timber-dependent communities.

And yet, reports of depleted timber supplies and impoverished communities, especially in western Washington, continued to reach the nation's capital. A Pacific Northwest Forest and Range Experiment Station report in 1927 indicated that nearly half of the privately owned forestland in the Douglas fir region was not being adequately reforested. Two years later Forest Service chief Robert Y. Stuart remarked that the effort to stabilize the lumber industry "was more than an internal problem" and required federal attention.[11] Although federal interest in the "excessive" timber harvests in Washington and Oregon mounted during the Depression years, Congress took no action.

Western Washington was the first area to suffer the consequences of overcutting in the Pacific Northwest. For many years the major log-producing districts in the region were the magnificent old-growth forests in the Puget Sound, Grays Harbor, and Willapa Bay areas. The high quality of the timber, less difficult terrain, and easy access to water transportation attracted lumbermen in the late nineteenth century, and explain, in part, the early emergence of western Washington as a major timber producer. Although the state reached its peak in lumber manufacturing in 1929 and continued to lead the nation in timber production until the 1940s, the center of lumbering activity was gradually shifting south to the Columbia River.[12]

By the time of the Great Depression, several communities in western Washington were beginning to suffer. The experiences of Tacoma, smaller manufacturing towns on Puget Sound, and the Grays Harbor settlements suggest that little had changed in the long history of boom and bust cycles for forest-dependent communities. There was no economic incentive for lumbermen to conserve, to harvest on a sustained-yield basis, and to reforest cutover lands. The big profits were in cutting, stripping, and then moving on to the next stand. The dynamics and logic of a social system in which profit and loss were the major criteria for human decisions both created and impoverished the lumber towns in western Washington.

Under different social and economic arrangements, the Grays Harbor area might have served as a cautionary example for timber harvesting practices elsewhere after the Second World War. When western Washington timber production peaked in 1929, Grays Harbor County was the leading log producer in the Pacific Northwest. Yet only ten years later, Forest Service Region 6 forester H. J. Andrews described Grays Harbor as "vast expanses of cutover land largely barren of conifer growth."[13] In effect, two market-related disasters struck the area simultaneously—the Great Depression and a drastically depleted timber supply.

I. J. Mason of the Forest Service conducted a study of Grays Harbor in 1935 to determine the causes of the sudden collapse in the area's economy. The sawmills in the district were obsolete, he learned—they had been built before 1920 and many were more than forty years old. Lumbermen had constructed plants "with no consideration of permanent timber supplies, but only as to a timber supply adequate to depreciate them." The "excessive sawmill installations" had brought the end of the present industry in sight. Those dynamics, according to Mason, were market oriented. Although the Grays Harbor sawmill industry lasted for sixty years, that was "not due to any planning on the part of the timber industry but rather to the . . . huge original timber supply and the restrictions on production imposed by general market conditions."[14]

The Washington State Planning Council published a study in 1941 of the small town of Elma, located on the eastern edge of Grays Harbor County. The planning council chose the Elma area for an extensive survey because it "had been denuded of its principle [sic] economic asset, timber." The "sobering and grave problem" for those communities, according to the Elma report, was "how to maintain and perpetuate a community which had depended largely on the logging of timber and the manufacturing of lumber products."[15] For timber-dependent settlements elsewhere, the Elma survey provided a harrowing preview of mill closures, population decline, and the inability of a community to meet its social obligations.

Because of the interests of its editor and publisher, Sheldon Sackett, the Coos Bay *Times* kept its readers informed of broader currents in the world of forestry. When the Forest Service sent its experts into the Coos Bay district in 1931 to survey the area's forestlands, the newspaper pointed out that southwestern Oregon had "the greatest stand of merchantable timber left in America," greater than that on Puget Sound, Grays Harbor, the Columbia River, and Humboldt Bay. Two years later the *Times* quoted a Bank of America report predicting that the Far West would soon produce 80 percent of the nation's lumber.[16] Heady prospects for owners of timberland in southwestern Oregon, but also reason to pause and look to the experiences of other timber-dependent areas.

Sackett was no mere worshipper of production records. In his personal "Crow's Nest" column, he warned readers that a single industry, "however numerous its plants, will not maintain local prosperity." When Forest Service Chief Ferdinand A. Silcox warned a Portland audience in 1934 that "quick liquidation instead of sustained yield" was bringing distress to timber-growing states, the *Times* gave the talk front-page coverage.[17]

Forest Service Region 6 Chief C. J. Buck told the Northwest Regional Planning Council in 1934 that sustained-yield management was the only way Oregon and Washington could avoid "a day of social and economic reckoning." Buck pointed to conditions in Clatsop County, Oregon, and Grays Harbor County, Washington, to show "the effect of our present 'cut-out-and-get-out' policy upon families and communities." The remedy, he told the planning council, was a sustained yield of timber that would protect both the region's economic structure and its cultural and civic life.[18] In the absence of effective controls over the rate of timber harvests on private land, however, stable forest communities would remain largely the dream of state planning boards and progressives in the forestry profession.

The federal forestry agency brought its agenda to Coos County in November 1935 when H. L. Plumb, an assistant regional forester, warned that "an appalling tragedy" would take place in the area unless the citizens took immediate action. Under present conditions, he told residents, the supply of Port Orford cedar would be exhausted in twenty-five years. When the *Times* learned that the private stands of cedar would be gone in twelve years at "the present rate of cutting," it expressed even greater alarm. The newspaper pointed out that private owners, "harrassed by taxes, fire risks, and compound interest," were cutting their Port Orford cedar "and letting tomorrow take care of itself." It criticized the sale of logs to Japan and San Francisco, because "Coos county gets not a whit of payroll for manufacturing the raw material." The *Times* also urged the federal government to purchase the "distressed tracts of Port Orford which are now glutting the market," and recommended that private holders be required to "log their stands carefully."[19]

Career forester Edward I. Kotok joined the growing number of Forest Service officials who were concerned about Pacific slope lumbering communities. Kotok feared that Pacific Coast states would repeat the old cycle of cut and run. Although the region had not "reached the final stages of exploitation," he indicated that "some of the adverse symptoms" were already evident. Still, Kotok thought the region's forest problems were "yet in the making." In its annual report for 1940 the Forest Service expressed its concern again for the lumbering districts in western Washington where payrolls had dropped by 75 percent in a decade. The report mentioned abandoned communities and a declining population—the social consequences of the rapid liquidation of the forest resource.[20]

The establishment of planning councils in Oregon and Washington in the 1930s gave some legitimacy to sustained-yield proposals. The Oregon State Planning Board outlined a sustained-yield program for the state in 1936 that would provide existing sawmills with a continuous supply of timber. "The present 'cut-out and get-out' policy of forest cutting," the report stated, "will result in a brief period of industrial activity, followed by inevitable economic and social disaster." The study also indicated that Oregon, because of its large virgin timber stands, was one of the few states where a sustained-yield program could be put in operation without curtailing production.[21] Although those proposals may have been appealing in the abstract, they did not move anyone to action.

When Oregon's short-lived planning board issued its timber study in 1936, sustained-yield proposals were popular. The *Times* thought the report was "startling in its bold facts on the rate of depletion in Oregon's timber," but it feared that the recommendations would be "tucked away in some official vault" and forgotten. Because timber owners could not view the matter "from the standpoint of the long distance interest of the state," the *Times* urged the governor and legislature to "take concerted, prudent" action.[22] But the Oregon legislature, where the lumber industry's presence loomed large, did not act on the planning board report.

The Northwest Regional Planning Council published a brief informational pamphlet in 1940 that outlined "the basic facts concerning Forest Depletion in the Pacific Northwest." The council pointed out that forests, despite their significance to the region's economy, were "being depleted at a dangerous rate." Annual harvests in the Northwest were more than twice the annual growth rate, and the "numerous ghost towns" in the region were "grim indicators of what happens when the timber supply gives out." Unless the rapid depletion of the forests was checked, the council warned, "serious economic and social dislocation is inevitable." The answer to the problem, it indicated, was placing forests "under sustained yield management."[23] But sustained-yield proposals soon gave way to the push to increase lumber production during the Second World War.

Although the war opened up new opportunities for people who lived in impoverished towns, it did not lesson the rate of timber harvesting in the Pacific Northwest or elsewhere. In fact, the resurgence of patriotism gave industry leaders the opportunity to pursue wartime production goals unhampered by moral appeals to community stability. George Harris Collingwood, a forester with the National Lumber Manufacturer's Association, told Forest Service Acting-Chief Earle Clapp that trees were less important than human lives, and the country might "have to sacrifice future needs for immediate demands."[24] Production and profit making, therefore, not appeals to forestry and community welfare, would dominate politics during the war.

Despite the wartime effort to increase production, the warnings continued. In 1942 the Forest Service again singled out the Pacific Northwest, where "concentrated and unnecessarily destructive cutting" was jeopardizing "opportunities for sustained-yield operations." Under those conditions, the service warned, "many communities are bound to suffer." Words of caution, however, meant little to lumbermen who were operating on cost-plus contracts.[25] For those districts with large stands of old-growth timber, the supply problem lay somewhere in the future.

With the ending of the war, both the technology and the markets were suddenly available to dramatically increase the rate of timber harvesting on the Pacific Coast. When he stopped logging in 1946, Curt Beckham recognized the great changes taking place in the woods—the power saw, the bulldozer blade, the development of durable trucks, and movable power equipment like the steel spar. "The old things were done away with," he says. Where once a good pair of timber fallers could fall eight to ten trees a day, "now they can go in with power saws and mow it down."[26] For Beckham, currently the director of a logging museum, today's mechanized operations are a different world from the steam-powered equipment of his youth.

One man with a chain saw could cut far more timber than several sets of fallers with crosscuts, Dow Beckham points out. Another innovation, the diesel-powered donkey, enabled loggers to haul timber to landings easily. It "was the best-developed piece of machinery" for the woods operations, the younger Beckham said; it had more power, loggers "didn't have to bother with water lines, and you didn't have the fire hazard you had with steam donkeys." Wire cable companies using higher-grade metals began to manufacture better steel rope for use with the more powerful engines. And the development of the bulldozer also "made it easier to build better roads, faster." As a symbol of that increased productivity, Beckham cites the example of a lone gyppo logger: "Just one guy goes out, he cuts the trees down, he cuts it up in logs, loads it on his truck, and takes it to town all by himself."[27]

Before he went longshoring in the mid-1950s, Pete Kromminga lived through the revolution in logging technology. He worked out of Reedsport in 1948 for a "thirty-one-man outfit that had all hand fallers and buckers." At that point the company sublet its timber falling to a contractor who employed seven men to fall the same amount of timber with chain saws. "Twenty-four people displaced," he observed, with a grim nod to the new technology. The same thing happened when gasoline engines came to the woods. A "steam pot," according to Kromminga, required a fireman, two "wood splits," a person to run the drag saw, and a loading pot that also needed a fireman. "When those things were converted to gasoline or diesel, you didn't need those five men."[28] Although operators used gasoline-powered machinery on the south coast in the late 1930s, the shortage of material during the war delayed the full transition to internal combustion engines until the postwar period.

Bill Brainard, who worked "in the brush" in the early 1950s, is blunt about the new technology and its affect on both humans and the forest environment. "They're wood butchers out here," he says. Whereas it "took two guys to run the hand briar, now you've got a power saw that weighs fifteen pounds and just goes like hell." The increased horsepower of the diesel-powered yarding machines and the manufacture of bigger log trucks were additional technical advances that speeded the movement of timber to the mills.[29] While the new technology may have been impressive, some—like Bill Brainard—are critical of its overall impact.

As construction activity picked up after the war, there were signals that pointed to trouble for the south coast. Even before the Weyerhaeuser Company opened its large plant in 1951, the lumber manufacturing capacity of the Coos area already exceeded the annual growth of timber. Local mills, according to the *Times*, could not "operate at capacity without depleting the supply of green timber." To correct that situation, "some adjustment will need to be made to assure permanence." To "rationalize" the timber supply, the newspaper suggested larger single ownerships and "firm pledges to the government" to establish diminished but steady harvesting schedules. The *Times* indicated that it was well aware of developments in other lumbering centers of the Northwest: "The alternative of timber exhaustion is a bitter one to contemplate. . . . It is now later than we like to think even for Oregon with its top-rank timber resources, to continue timber cutting without regard for the new, balanced growth, coming on."[30]

But with a heavy demand for lumber in California, permanence of operation and sustained-yield production were not the center of attention in the postwar period. Rather, the building of new Weyerhaeuser mills, the opening of virgin timber stands, the construction of all-weather roads, and the monthly production figures of the sawmills made headlines in Oregon newspapers. Boosters of southwestern Oregon enjoyed the flattery and attention showered on Coos Bay as the "world's largest lumber port." And the major companies buttressed that optimism with assurances that they were operating on a permanent basis.[31] The future seemed bright and full with promise.

And who would doubt that hope? Certainly few who read the assessment of Harrison Hornish, managing editor of the *Times*, who flew over the southwestern Oregon backcountry in the summer of 1949. He reported "looking down on mile after mile of treetops, a vast green blanket that seemed from the Coos-Douglas county line to stretch in an almost unbroken series of waves of green clear to the ocean." Hornish concluded that the area "would seem [to] . . . have an inexhaustible supply of trees." But the combined production of the gyppo operations and the increased output of the large mills began to take their toll on Coos area timberlands. And reports indicated that timber in the upper Williamette Valley, an area bordering on the Coos country, was becoming scarce.[32] Those mills began to look outside the valley, some of them to drainages north of Coos Bay, for their log supplies.

Some Coos County mills were beginning to scramble for access to timber by the mid-1950s. The BLM precipitated some of that concern when it lifted marketing restrictions on its timber sales. Beginning in 1947, the agency had tried to ensure and stabilize employment by requiring that timber harvested within designated "marketing circles" be processed in the same area. When Secretary of the Interior Douglas McKay, an Oregonian, lifted the restriction, the *Times* accused him of bowing to upper Willamette Valley lumbermen.[33] The real issue, however, was the dwindling supply of timber available to mills in the Eugene-Springfield area.

"Local Timber Belongs Here," a *Times* editorial headline declared. Because of the "overcrowding of mills," lumbermen in the upper Willamette Valley "have almost depleted their private timber." Now that BLM has abolished its marketing circles, the article continued, Eugene lumbermen "are casting covetous eyes" at the rich forestland north of Coos Bay. Operators in the Coos Bay district protested that the exhaustion of timber in the upper Willamette Valley was "no justification" to change the marketing circle system. The result, the newspaper reported, would be "high bids that will freeze out local bidders." To which a valley operator offered a bare-knuckles rejoinder at a Portland hearing: "If the Coos Bay and Reedsport area mills can't compete with us, that's their tough luck."[34] Despite the protests and hearings, McKay's order stood and log trucks soon began to rumble towards Eugene-area sawmills.

Reduced to its naked essentials, the controversy marked the beginning of a protracted struggle for access to public timber. By the mid-1950s private inventories were diminishing rapidly in some areas, and lumbermen were increasingly looking to the public lands for their log supplies. For operators on the south coast, the BLM order meant more competition for government timber. Market forces were alive and well.

There were other developments that had a great impact on the volume of timber harvesting in the Douglas fir region after the war. One of those was the emergence of the Georgia-Pacific Corporation and its large purchases in the Northwest, including the Coos Bay Lumber Company. What happened to the "last great stand" in the Coos country is a story common to corporate practices in market-oriented resource economies. The Georgia-Pacific buy out set in motion what Jerry Phillips calls the "heavy liquidation phase" of the old Coos Bay Lumber Company timberlands. The firm's large sales of old-growth forest marked a dramatic shift in the harvesting policy on those lands. Corporate profit needs and the booming lumber market in California, not a social commitment to sustained-yield forestry and community stability, guided the Georgia-Pacific liquidation program.

Residents of the south coast assumed that the Coos Bay Lumber Company was operating on a 100-year cutting cycle. According to Ross Youngblood, the local BLM forester, the Coos Bay Lumber Company was not "liquidating in a sense of what occurred as a result of being sold to G-P." When he left the area in 1957, "there was still volumes of timber left"; however, his colleagues "recognized real quick when G-P took over, they were liquidating the timber." Youngblood estimates that the company may have tripled the harvest—"you could see it was being rapidly depleted beyond its growth."[35] He speculates on what would have happened if the holdings had been kept under the original ownership.

Cardy Walton, who went to work for the Coos Bay Lumber Company in 1949, remembers officials of the firm discussing their 100-year cutting cycle. As a matter of policy, the company also puchased all government timber sales that bordered on its properties. On one occasion, the logging superintendent told Walton that he "would probably never live to see the day" when the company's holdings were logged off. "Now," Walton says, "it's all gone." While the Coos Bay Lumber Company cut between thirty million and thirty-five million board feet a year from one of its main units, Georgia-Pacific "immediately jumped that to about 100 million, plus selling a tremendous amount" to other mills.[36]

For Cliff Thorwald, Georgia-Pacific's purchasing agent, the rumors and innuendo about diminishing timber supplies were worrisome. "Beautiful timber was sold to Roseburg outfits just so they [Georgia-Pacific] could raise money," he recalls. According to union leader Jerry Lantto, the Coos Head Timber Company cut a large volume of old-growth trees, "beautiful wood," that came from Georgia-Pacific timberlands. Lantto argues that selling timber "to generate cash flow" was "the worst thing G-P did" to south coast communities.[37]

Georgia-Pacific's revolutionary timber management decisions created a great deal of concern in southwestern Oregon. The company's dramatically increased harvests were common gossip among loggers and union people who were well aware of the lumber industry's propensity to cut and run. The sizable timber sales "raised eyebrows" in the industry, according to the Portland *Oregonian*, because most companies were seeking to acquire, not dispose of, old-growth timber. Georgia-Pacific executives responded in 1958 with a news release announcing plans for a thirty-five to forty-year cutting cycle for its second-growth stands. Company president Robert Pamplin told the *Oregonian* that the firm planned the sales when it made the purchase; moreover, the timber sold was "outside the sustained-yield working circle."[38] A strong lumber market and rising timber prices undoubtedly made that a profitable business decision. But the long-range consequences for southwestern Oregon communities were fraught with danger.

Georgia-Pacific was not the only large timberholder to increase its cut during those years. Through the 1950s the Weyerhaeuser Company harvested timber from its own lands only to satisfy the needs of its new plant on Coos Bay. According to Jerry Phillips, the company "could have sustained that cut, if they had chosen to, forever." But the firm's executives decided otherwise. In the early 1960s Weyerhaeuser elected to increase the volume of its annual harvests—it sold timber to firms in Eugene, and it began a major log export program, primarily to Japan. Phillips notes that many people became aware that Weyerhaeuser was "cutting a great deal faster than they could sustain."[39] It was obvious, too, that the sale of logs to Japan was costing the area jobs, an issue that became more controversial when the work force in the forest products industry began to decline.

Statistics support the increasing concern about depleted timber inventories and declining employment opportunities in the Douglas fir region. In an important study of log production in Oregon and Washington published in 1972, Forest Service economist Brian Wall underscored the significance of private timber harvests in the 1950s and 1960s. By 1952 the "Oregon timber industry was in high gear in southwestern Oregon" and harvesting rates remained high in Lane, Douglas, Coos, Curry, and Jackson counties through the 1960s. But, he warned, the rapid inventory depletion and inadequate reforestation indicated "that the extremely high rates of log production in parts of western Oregon have a limited future." Although the total output in Oregon remained fairly constant during the 1950s and 1960s, public harvests were making up an increasingly larger share of production.[40] Those words of caution pointed especially to southwestern Oregon, where the liquidation of private timber was still in full swing.

There were other warnings. In the year of the Georgia-Pacific purchase, a study estimated that private ownerships in the area tributary to Coos Bay "will be reduced to minor commercial value in about 30 years." The report warned: "The experience of other areas in this regard should not be ignored." Charles Stanton of the Roseburg *News-Review* in neighboring Douglas County, told his readers that southwestern Oregon counties should not be "flattered" by production statistics showing their leadership in national lumber production. Other counties had held that distinction in the past, he noted, and "some of the former champions" were not doing so well.[41]

The heavy drain on the timber inventory in southwestern Oregon began to take its toll in the 1960s. At the peak of production for gyppo mills in 1952, Coos County supplied 1.7 percent of all logs harvested in the United States. That percentage dropped to 1.2 in 1962 and in 1970 to 1 percent. Coos County's total employment in the forest products industry also peaked in 1960 and then began a slow but steady decline. The closure of the Evans Products plant in 1961 was the standardbearer for the future.[42]

At the onset of the 1970s, growing evidence pointed to a shortage of timber in southwestern Oregon. The BLM and the Forest Service were adopting rules that reduced the annual harvests on federal timberlands. Georgia-Pacific's liquidation program, Weyerhaeuser's expanded cutting rate, and indications that smaller mills in the district were coming to the end of their merchantable timber brought matters to a head. The convergence of those factors, according to Jerry Phillips, showed "that there was a greater installed capacity in the mills than there was a permanent timber supply.[43] The concern about depleted timber stands in southwestern Oregon led to legislative hearings and a study of timber inventories in the state. But market conditions, not the future stability of timber-dependent communities, continued to guide harvest decisions.

Next to Gifford Pinchot, William Greeley is the most prominent forestry figure in the first half of the twentieth century. In a revealing letter in 1946, the aging forester warned that western states were "rapidly approaching the end of their virgin forests." He urged northwesterners to organize their forest industries on a "crop that is maintained steadily, without violent fluctuations from one decade to another":

> . . . if we are going to maintain stable forest industries and support their communities with dependable, continuing payrolls, the business must be organized on a volume of lumber or pulp that can be kept up steadily in the future. Otherwise Western States would simply have the same sort of migratory forest industries and often ghost towns that have been characteristic of the great forest regions of the East. The mills now sustained by virgin timber would cut out and dismantle. There would be a break of many years time in the industrial life of the community. Then when a new supply of timber had been grown, some new mills would doubtless come in. Meantime, what happens to the people, the workers, the stores and other community facilities, the schools and churches—everything that gives American living its stability?[44]

To Jerry Phillips, sustained yield was "a rather naive, elementary, oversimplified concept," and the forestry profession has "disavowed it." Each timberland owner, he believes, "should choose responsible goals for himself and the community." It is important to understand, Phillips says, "that every area of the world has had its turn in the bucket in going through from the old-growth to the young-growth cover-type stage." Although the process can "destabilize employment in a community," it is necessary to liquidate the old growth and convert to a tree-farming regime. As for southwestern Oregon, Phillips notes that the conversion stage "has taken a hundred years, 1880 through 1980." The Coos country, the forester says, is "one of the last places in the world to complete that conversion."[45]

Lumbermen largely ignored William Greeley's prescription. For its part, the industry was playing to the same set of cultural values and social virtues that characterized its historical movement across North America. Corporate profit-taking rather than human social needs defined forestry practice. In practical terms, the market ruled supreme and sustained-yield forestry, at least as it applied to private timberlands, became obsolete by the end of the Second World War. The harvesting practices of the forest products firms on the south coast—and elsewhere—proved indifferent to the social needs of dependent communities. Jerry Phillips's "conversion" model is an explanation (and excuse) for allowing the market rather than human requirements to determine the harvesting rate.

The extraordinary harvests of the postwar years in southwestern Oregon repeated a pattern played out on other forest frontiers. In the mid-1970s the state forestry board commissioned a study to forecast the state's timber supply prospects. "The bellwether of Oregon's economy," the research team found, was in trouble. The study forecasted a sharp decline in timber harvests for the rest of this century. That decrease, it predicted, would be especially stressful for the timber-dependent south coast, where harvests were expected to fall by 35 percent.[46]

But the once-booming lumber district was merely a microcosm of forest-dependent communities everywhere in the Northwest. The excessive harvests of the postwar years, the resurgence of the southeastern forest products industry, and upward-spiraling interest rates combined to bring economic disaster to many of those communities in the early 1980s. When the depression struck the forest products industry, seven out of ten jobs on Coos Bay were timber related, a higher percentage than in any comparable area in the state. A Portland *Oregonian* columnist remarked that Coos Bay might "serve as a cautionary example for all of Oregon."[47] For people in southwestern Oregon, the depression and mill closures were shattering experiences. The future seemingly had disintegrated in the midst of high unemployment and a declining population.

Bosses and Workers

I used to think my Dad was cuckoo for being an IWW. Since then I found out he was right on the ball.

Don Brown, November 11, 1980[1]

Until the period of intensive mechanization following the Second World War, most of the natural-resource industries in the United States were labor intensive. Rank-and-file workers dominated the labor force in the coal-mining counties of West Virginia and the copper towns of Montana, as well as the logging communities of Washington and Oregon. Although their efforts produced great profits for the owners of capital, people were not passive in the face of arbitrary decisions made in faraway places. Rather, laborers everywhere struggled, often against great odds and under harsh and demanding circumstances, to gain their share of the wealth.

The major urban centers of the North Pacific slope and the small logging towns tributary to them share in that tradition. From the establishment of the first lumbering settlements along the coastal waters until well into the twentieth century, laboring classes have dominated life and culture in the region. Although mill owners and managers and their allies in the business community usually controlled the political system, a large and sometimes vocal working-class constituency tempered decisions and helped forge a political culture that embraced, in part, the hopes and aspirations of common people.

Unskilled and skilled workers in the Coos Bay area have always outnumbered middle-level management and professional people. That remains true to the present day with the dramatic expansion of minimum-wage jobs, especially in the service sector. Southwestern Oregon residents have always been proud of their working-class traditions, a heritage that has been rich with struggle in one of the most volatile sectors of the American economy. Mercurial production cycles, seasonal employment, and the lumberman's persistent effort to force labor to bear the burden of the industry's problems were constant points of reckoning.

The seasonal character of work on the south coast and the shortage of labor during the summer months directly influenced wage scales and the bargaining strength of workers. As early as February 1888,

138

the Coos Bay *News* reported that shipowners had reduced the wage
for longshoremen, because "men are plenty and they can get all they
need." But, the newspaper predicted, "when the logging camps open
up, it will be the longshoremen's turn."[2] Because of the highly mobile
work force and the uneven character of the coal and lumber economy,
the demand for labor continued to fluctuate. During the rainy season
logging bosses and mine managers were able to exact concessions
from workers, but when the economy was healthy and labor in
demand, the tables were turned.

George Chard, whose working career began in the late nineteenth
century, typifies many of those who shifted between a variety of jobs.
Chard got his first job in the coal mines with his father when he was
twelve years old. Although he worked in the mines more than in any
other enterprise, Chard also delivered coal, hired on with road-build-
ing crews, operated a riverboat, and like many young men in the Coos
country, served a stint with the Smith-Powers Logging Company.
After he retired, Chard reflected that his jobs were "all hard work."[3]
Like others of his kind, George Chard was a "working stiff" who sold
his labor for daily wages or piecework production in the mines.

Although sporadic union organizing took place in the bay area in
the early twentieth century, most of it centered on crafts and was of
short duration. Moreover, there was little solidarity and many of those
fledgling unions worked at cross purposes with one another. The
most prominent of those early organizations, according to newspapers, were welfare and annuity associations that provided accident
insurance and a variety of benefits to their members. Carpenters and
joiners, shipwrights, and other skilled trades formed such "benefit"
societies, but there were no permanent membership groups for the
largest pool of laborers—coal miners, loggers, and sawmill workers.

Longshoremen were the only local industrially based trade to attempt to organize during those years. Forty dock workers formed a
local of the International Longshoremen's Union in 1901 and gained
the support of the Coos Bay *News,* because, the newspaper reported,
the great trade associations being established in the United States
were themselves "an invitation, if not a demand, for labor to organize." When West Coast longshoremen struck in 1906 for higher
wages, the *Times* reported that several local companies "could not pay
the increased wages." And when San Francisco dock workers settled
for a higher wage, the Oregon Coal and Navigation Company of Coos
Bay informed the *Times* that it could not afford the rate agreed upon in
California.[4] Because Coos Bay was a small port with limited traffic, its

longshoremen were vulnerable to San Francisco merchants who threatened to boycott shipments to the Oregon port when laborers protested. Those threats often prevailed, because labor cooperation among the several West Coast ports was still in its infancy.

The volatile coal and lumber market continued to wreak havoc among local longshore workers. The onset of a prolonged depression in the lumber industry and the virtual ending of coal shipments to San Francisco by 1910 meant an extended period of sporadic employment. The Coos Bay *Harbor* reported that longshoremen were "continuing to hang on to their property and to their place in the union with the hope that the old times will return." But, the newspaper indicated, it "has been hard sledding for the men who have determined to wait."[5] That period of waiting did not bear fruit until the great victory in the longshore strike of 1934.

Real power for longshore workers meant strong organization and solidarity on Coos Bay and efficient coordination among the locals in every important West Coast port. For the first thirty years of the century, employer organizations kept the upper hand although major strikes occurred in 1906 and 1916. During the 1920s, when the American business community aggressively asserted itself in every walk of life, the International Longshoremen's Association (ILA) lost most of its influence on the Pacific Coast. Companies controlled hiring halls in Seattle, Portland, Los Angeles, and in Coos Bay; only in San Francisco, where the ILA maintained a shadow influence, did longshore workers maintain a semblance of organization.[6] To make matters worse for dock workers, federal and state authorities did not recognize legitimate longshore unions as collective-bargaining agents until 1934. Even then it was the militant rank-and-file longshore locals in every major Pacific port who forced the issue.

The more progressive working-class elements on Coos Bay expressed themselves through ethnic socialist organizations and in their support for socialist candidates for public office. In the presidential election of 1904, Eugene Debs polled nearly as many votes as the Democratic candidate, Alton B. Parker. Two years later a local newspaper remarked that "socialists number some of our best and foremost citizens." Debs again received about 12 percent of the Coos County vote for president in 1908. There is other evidence of working-class sentiment during those years: socialist picnics, a "Russian-Finn Socialist Society" in the community of Eastside, an organization of socialists in Marshfield, the regular appearance of socialist speakers, and socialist candidates for local offices.[7]

When the Industrial Workers of the World (IWW) became active in the bay area in 1911, local newspapers took a sharply critical stance. The *Times*, although it supported a "square deal for every man," did not believe "that a band of idle braggarts . . . should be permitted to duplicate on Coos Bay the disaster that has followed in their wake wherever they have been permitted to obtain a foothold." Because the IWW threatened "legitimate enterprise," the *Times* charged, it should not be tolerated. These "industrial perverts" threatened the entire community; therefore, the "businessmen and officials of Marshfield" should "meet and master the situation promptly."[8]

The *Times* carried on its editorial vendetta against the IWW for more than fourteen months. "Theirs is a doctrine of destruction, dynamite and deviltry," it accused in a May 1913, editorial. Because Coos Bay would never enjoy industrial peace with the IWW present, citizens should move positively and promptly: "The time to act is NOW." Such advice was unnecessary in the logging camps where foremen already were acting on that premise and dismissing any worker suspected of belonging to the IWW. To put a fair face on its editorial vigilantism, the *Times* reported that most local members of the organization were "recent arrivals."[9] It did not occur to the editor that working conditions in the camps and mills may have created an ideal environment for Wobbly organizers.

For the commercial classes on the bay, an IWW strike call for higher wages and an eight-hour day, scheduled for mid-May 1913, was the last straw. Logging bosses told employees who were dissatisfied to "roll their blankets and roll out," an order supposedly aimed at IWW sympathizers. Although there were no reports of trouble, a large number of local businessmen were enrolled as special law enforcement officers. Newspaper editorials and commercial organizations on the bay had created an atmosphere of hatred against the IWW by May 13. Despite those odds, the IWW closed one logging camp and in other camps men quit in protest against low wages and long hours. Nevertheless, the strike danger had passed within a week. According to the *Times*, the mayor of Marshfield had put down a potential threat of street preaching when he warned that the jails would be filled with those who broke the law.[10]

The local newspapers' rantings against the "anti-American and anti-social" IWW finally came to a head on June 24, 1913, when a "citizens" group marched to IWW headquarters and escorted its two organizers out of town. (One of them, Wesley Everest, was later martyred in the "Centralia Massacre" in Washington State.) The *Times* praised the "decisive" action:

Coos Bay has cause today to be proud of the character of its citizenship, in one of the most remarkable demonstrations ever witnessed in any American city, this community has given notice to the world that there is no retreat or refuge on its hospitable shores for the anarchist agitators of the iww. . . . There was no violence and no excitement. The coolness and courage of conscientious citizens who were loyal to their homes, their city and their country, marked every move.[11]

Two weeks after Marshfield's iww leaders were sent packing, businessmen in the small town of Bandon "peacefully removed" from the town a local chiropractor and socialist, Bailey Kay Leach. That action brought an investigation from the governor's office and a charge that logging boss Al Powers and Bandon lumberman George W. Moore, were behind the deportations. Although Governor Oswald West's special investigator, the state's attorney general, absolved Marshfield and Bandon officials of any wrongdoing, the governor persisted in his accusations that southwestern Oregon leaders had violated the civil liberties of the two iww organizers and Leach. The attorney general's whitewashing of the issue probably had more to do with election-year politics than the merits of the case. When a grand jury appointed to investigate the deportations returned a deadlocked verdict, the county issued no indictments.[12]

Once again, the iww chose not to openly test the deportation of its organizers. The area was isolated and hard to reach—there was no rail connection to Coos Bay from the Willamette Valley until 1916. In those cases where iww members made their famous "free speech" stands, packing the jails with waves of volunteer orators, rail transportation was readily available and there were usually major population centers close at hand.

Between the two world wars Coos Bay continued to be a region of many workers and few bosses. And for most of that period, experienced loggers and mill employees normally outnumbered the jobs available. The high rate of turnover in the woods also suggests that workers were often "on the move" to the next camp or "slave market" (hiring hall). Although mill employees were less itinerant, frequent layoffs, arbitrary firings, and unemployed people standing at the gate were commonplace.

During the 1920s and early 1930s there was little redress for most working people. For Eleanor Anderson's Finnish and Swedish female friends, those conditions meant employment as a domestic in a Coos-area home, working in one of the cedar-veneer plants, or leaving for San Francisco to work for wealthy households.[13]

Although employment opportunities for women improved during the First World War, theirs was still a world of meager wages and assembly piecework in a local box or veneer plant. When the economy went sour, bay women kept their jobs only by dint of hard work and a willingness to accept low wages. Only with the formation of strong unions in the 1940s did the arbitrary power of the bosses and managers begin to erode.

The capricious behavior of foremen and supervisory personnel made the work environment a formidable place for many people well into the twentieth century. A few of the more notorious logging bosses, like the Coos Bay Lumber Company's Jack Dashney, are still remembered for their harsh treatment of workers. They were men who played fast and loose with their work force, and—especially when labor was plentiful—firings and hirings were as regular as the seasonal rains.

As always the loggers' main weapon against highball operators and poor working conditions was simply to walk away from the job. Even after unions had organized most logging outfits in the late 1940s, the easy availability of jobs still meant a high turnover. But it was on the waterfront, not in the woods or mills, that workers first successfully asserted their power over wages, conditions of employment, and safety in the work place.

Don Brown grew up in the timbered back country of the Oregon coast where his mother and father worked as camp cooks. Because of the isolated location of the logging outfits, his parents "didn't come out very often," and their frequent job changes meant that the son attended thirteen schools before he finished the third grade. After wandering to California as a young man, Brown returned to Oregon's south coast in the early 1930s, became involved in the great longshore strike of 1934, and converted to industrial unionism. He spent the rest of his wage-earning life working the docks and serving his union in a variety of capacities.[14] Like the great labor leader and American socialist of the early twentieth century, Eugene Debs, Brown learned the importance of unions from his own experiences, not abstract theories or outside organizers.

Lewis Barnekoff and his two brothers—like their father, who was a charter member of the Bandon local of the ILA—became longshoremen. To support his family in the tiny port town south of Coos Bay, Lewis's father worked in the woods and fished to supplement his longshoremen's wages. His experiences were typical of many who worked on the docks before effective union protection—unsteady employment, back-breaking work when ships were in, insecurity, arbitrary treatment from bosses, and the always dangerous conditions brought on by "speedups." For Alvin Monk, another Bandon long-shoreman, the "old days" meant being available when the ships came in, hiring on through the "random method," and then suffering the abuses of mates and loading bosses. "If you was a good worker," he recalls, "you'd get hired again."[15]

On Coos Bay, Cliff Thorwald remembers the conditions under which longshoremen worked before the 1934 strike. Bribery, rampant in virtually every West Coast port, was a fact of life on the Coos waterfronts. Thorwald recalls that longshore workers had to "pay a mate ten bucks or so" to get on a crew. Even then, shipboard bosses were abusive and used a variety of techniques to speed the loading process. Because most of the evils centered on the fear of losing one's job, dock workers normally toiled until the ship was loaded with lumber, even if the task took up to eighteen hours.[16] Those conditions made a ready field for union organizers.

In most West Coast ports, including Coos Bay, waterfront employers hired men through the "shape-up" process—gang bosses chose workers from a daily line-up at specified dock locations. The system encouraged bribery, favoritism, and pitted worker against worker and one waterfront gang against another. But with the passage of the National Industrial Recovery Act in 1933, which guaranteed labor the right to bargain collectively, the ILA, long dormant on the West Coast, successfully organized most Pacific ports. Longshore workers struck on May 9, 1934, against an accumulation of grievances that had been building for at least fifteen years.[17] The 1934 strike was the opening shot in a protracted series of longshore work stoppages that lasted into the 1970s.

From the vantage point of the Coos Bay Lumber Company's machine shop, Cliff Thorwald remembers the longshore walkout of 1934 as "a vicious strike." Lumber piled high on the company docks and the firm ordered its employees to load ships. Striking longshoremen verbally harassed scabs and others who were packing lumber, including Thorwald, who was pressed into service to load logs. That incident made a lasting impression, and to this day he is reluctant to talk about the strike.[18] Because of its inability to move lumber, the Coos Bay Lumber Company had to close the Big Mill for the duration of the strike.

The *Times* praised the Marshfield longshoremen's union, because unlike the ILA in San Francisco and Los Angeles, local strikers were "reasonable in their demands, fair in their representations, and willing and anxious to resume work." When the strike lasted into the summer and violence mounted in the West Coast ports, the *Times* pleaded for Coos Bay employers and workers to declare their "independence from localities which for more than two months have robbed us of hundreds of thousands of dollars." Despite strong local support for Harry Bridges and the rest of the emerging leadership of the West Coast ILA, the *Times* attempted to sow discord among dock workers by reporting that union men were "disgusted" with the actions of Harry Bridges who reportedly was attempting "to continue the tie-up."[19]

Local longshoremen ignored the *Times*. They showed their solidarity by refusing to move a stick of lumber until the ILA and the employers association signed an agreement to submit their differences to binding arbitration. Don Brown, one of the local longshore leaders, says that Coos Bay dock workers were solidly behind the strike. When employers tried to bring in strikebreakers from outside, there was sporadic violence—strikers threw rocks at scabs and they overturned a bus in the town of Empire.[20]

Coos Bay was not a major focal point of the longshore strike. Seattle, Portland, Los Angeles, and San Francisco played center court. In the latter port the labor dispute led to violence, death, and a citywide walkout. The four-day general strike was called off on July 19 and longshoremen finally returned to work on July 31 when waterfront employers and the West Coast ILA agreed to submit their differences to federal mediation. A board of arbitration subsequently awarded the longshoremen a substantial victory—increases in pay, a thirty-hour week, a jointly operated hiring hall (with the dispatcher appointed by the ILA), and lastly, a coastwide settlement.[21]

The strike had a profound influence in the Coos country. It marked the opening wedge for working people who would increasingly seek collective solutions to their problems. From a relatively weak organized labor movement at the onset of the 1930s, the area soon moved to the forefront in the percentage of its labor force committed to union principles. To this day, rank-and-file union members recognize the importance of the 1934 strike in establishing a precedent for worker successes in southwestern Oregon.

Longshoremen like Alvin Monk are proud of their achievements since 1934, especially the abolition of the "random method" of hiring and the establishment of union halls. Monk also witnessed the emergence of Harry Bridges and the formation of the International Longshoremen and Warehousemen's Union (ILWU) in the mid-1930s. The ILWU, he points out, was different from the ILU because of its rank-and-file nature "where membership decides matters." Lewis Barnekoff, a member of the Bandon local like Alvin Monk, recalls the close cooperation among longshore workers during the 1934 strike. To support themselves, they cut firewood, fished, and raised garden vegetables.[22] Workers would use similar practices in future, sometimes longer, strikes.

The successes of the longshore union did not have an immediate impact in the sawmills and logging camps. But Marshfield longshoremen continued to lead the way in labor militancy, because the experiences of 1934 showed they had the power to bring the bay-area economy to a standstill. Waterfront tieups usually meant the immediate closure of Coos Bay Lumber Company mills and logging camps. Moreover, picketing dock workers were even able to stop Southern Pacific trains from moving oil and gasoline on certain occasions.[23] Those lessons in worker assertiveness eventually spread to other industrial sectors.

American Federation of Labor (AFL) organizing on the south coast was still in its infancy when the federation's Lumber and Sawmill Workers locals went on strike in most of the major lumber centers of the Pacific Northwest in 1935. Central to the strikers' demands were higher wages and a forty-hour work week. The strike, which was more widespread in Portland, Tacoma, and the huge Long-Bell and Weyerhaeuser plants in Longview, Washington, lasted for about forty-five days and was only a modest success. The agreements ending the walkout did not include union recognition and the right to arbitration.[24] Those victories would wait another day and more militant activity.

Although the Lumber and Sawmill Workers established a local on Coos Bay, its members did not take part in the 1935 walkout. When the AFL union attempted to establish a chapter in Powers, the meeting had to be postponed because of the absence of several prospective members. For their part, longshoremen refused to handle "unfair" lumber, but the Coos Bay local indicated that it would continue to work until further developments in the lumber industry. When the labor dispute had passed, the *Times* praised the Coos Bay Lumber Company for already paying the minimum wage sought by mill workers elsewhere, and it applauded the "good judgement and restraint of workers" for realizing they were "getting a fair deal."[25] Although the newspaper criticized "radical elements" in the lumber strike, it was no blind worshipper of the lumbermen's associations. Rather, the *Times* advised management and labor to seek arbitrated solutions to their differences.

Despite setbacks, the Lumber and Sawmill Workers Union con-

Steve Prefontaine *(University of Oregon Archives)*

Florence Berg *(photo by George Case)*

Richard J. "Chappie" McCarthy *(photo by George Case)*

Valerie and Forrest Taylor *(photo by George Case)*

The Lindblad family, Paula seated center (*courtesy Paula Lindblad Laurilla*)

Dow Beckham (*photo by George Case*)

Paula Lindblad Laurilla (*photo by George Case*)

Pete Kromminga *(photo by George Case)*

Dorotha Richardson *(photo by George Case)*

Lionel Youst *(photo by George Case)*

Jack Johnson
(photo by George Case)

Bill Brainard
(photo by George Case)

tinued its efforts to organize local mills. In July 1936 Evans Products workers won recognition for their union—a one-year agreement to arbitrate differences and the union's assurances that it would not strike during that period. The Lumber and Sawmill Workers Union won another victory later that summer when it successfully organized the big Smith Wood Products Company, the largest payroll in the town of Coquille.[26] That strike marked the beginning of protracted labor conflict on the south coast.

Once again the longshoremen's union led the way. Between October 1936 and February 1937 the Coos Bay locals joined their Pacific Coast affiliates in a protracted strike against maritime employers. That conflict had dramatic consequences for southwestern Oregon, because the Pacific Coast longshore locals left the AFL and formed the International Longshoremen and Warehousemen's Union (ILWU) under the Congress of Industrial Organizations (CIO). West Coast workers recognized the strength of the militant ILWU and that influence translated into greater effectiveness for CIO organizing efforts. By the summer of 1936, H. J. Leaf of the Coos Bay Lumber Company admitted that the local longshoremen "seem to dominate the labor situation to a very large extent."[27]

One consequence of the dramatic growth of CIO locals was the formation of the Coos Bay Area Industrial Union Council, an organization to promote industrial unionism. With the support of the ILWU, the council established several CIO affiliates on the bay. According to Don Brown, longshoremen "went up and talked to loggers" about the benefits of industrial over craft unionism. As an organizer, Brown told prospective recruits that cooperation at the craft level simply would not work. "It bubbles up your thinking" to believe that "you can get things done" as a craft.[28]

Valerie Wyatt (now married to Forrest Taylor), a young woman with progressive political views, helped with petitions, handed out leaflets to workers leaving the mills, and served as secretary to the industrial union council. As an industrial unionist, she was involved with the CIO's International Woodworkers of America (IWA) in a jurisdictional dispute with the AFL's Lumber and Sawmill Workers Union in an effort to organize employees of the Coos Bay Lumber Company. The "spirited battle for membership" between the two unions lasted into 1940 when workers voted to decertify the Lumber and Sawmill Workers local.[29] That move was prelude to the IWA emerging as the bargaining agent for the Big Mill.

Plant managers and logging superintendents used a variety of tactics to fight the growing militancy of the work force. Employers played one union against the other, closed mills over the slightest of disagreements, and attempted to discredit union organizers as "outside agitators." Through paid advertisements in newspapers, a district employers' organization, the Associated Industries of Southwestern Oregon, described the union movement as destructive of the community's welfare. "Are You an American Citizen?" one full-page advertisement asked. It charged that union organizers preached "violence as opposed to reason," strived "to pit class against class," ignored the "welfare of the many," and undermined "the spirit of cooperation and teamwork" in the community. "Such forces," the ad concluded, "are un-American."[30] Despite the employers' efforts, union membership grew dramatically on the south coast.

Unions benefited from the shortage of labor during the Second World War. When the federal government began rationing gasoline and rubber tires, AFL and CIO loggers in the Pacific Northwest threatened to strike for free transportation to and from work. According to Pete Kromminga, he had little difficulty convincing his IWA associates to demand free transportation to the logging shows.[31]

Despite the patriotic appeals of employers, during the war mill workers and loggers staged temporary work stoppages to gain higher overtime pay, union shops, and increased benefits. On one occasion, the *Times* called an IWA "job action" to force a logging operator to dismiss two non-union employees "deplorable." The newpaper's editorial claimed that "times are too crucial for cessation of work." Although the *Times* said it did "not know enough about the facts . . . to form a fair opinion," it chastised workers for stopping production in a national emergency.[32]

But job actions during the war were few. As a shop steward and eventually president of an IWA local during the war, Kromminga argues that there were no major problems until 1945: "We didn't have any serious trouble, because the employers were making so much money they didn't fight us."[33] With the ending of the war, however, labor-management relations became more volatile. A booming housing market in California kept the demand for lumber high, placed a premium on labor, and gave unions added strength at the bargaining table. But the proliferation of gyppo operators, most of whom paid well, made employment with union outfits less attractive over the short haul.

The jurisdictional struggles between the CIO and the AFL also continued into the postwar years. In one case involving the IWA and the Lumber and Sawmill Workers, CIO loggers threatened to cut off the supply of timber to a plywood mill if its employees voted to join the

AFL. Because it was the more militant of the two unions, the IWA often pushed the Lumber and Sawmill locals to more progressive positions—demands that the AFL leadership disapproved of. Many loggers were critical of the Lumber and Sawmill Workers for being timid in supporting worker grievances. In those situations, Pete Kromminga recalled, "you just gathered your stuff and left. There was lots of work anyway."[34]

In a move that originated during the war, business executives laid plans to curb union strength and to reassert corporate dominance in American life. Lumbermen were part of that effort to regain the initiative in determining standards of wages and conditions of employment; only a self-confident and assertive work force stood in their way. The struggle between the two eventually was joined when lumber bosses in the Pacific Northwest attempted to break the power of the unions, especially the IWA, early in 1946.

The lumber industry employers demanded: (1) the employer's right to determine eligibility for union membership; (2) the denial of vacation benefits to strikers; (3) the reintroduction of piece work; (4) the elimination of night-shift pay differentials; (5) minimum pay rates and no overtime benefits for fire fighters; and (6) denying union representatives access to company property without a pass. The IWA immediately asked for a strike vote and demanded that employers renew existing contracts.[35]

When IWA workers acted in advance of the strike vote and walked off their jobs in early May, industrial activity in the Coos country came to an immediate halt. Because most of the logging crews were IWA members, the strike closed down AFL mills as well. But the attractions of the burgeoning California lumber market proved to be the trump card for the IWA. Northwest lumber capitalists agreed to extend most of the provisions of the 1945 contract for the following year and thereby avoided a region-wide shutdown.[36] Coos Bay companies, which normally followed the settlements made in the large "flag" mills on the Columbia River, withdrew their demands for contract concessions and the area was soon humming with activity.

But the labor situation remained volatile in southwestern Oregon, and jurisdictional disputes between AFL and CIO locals periodically disrupted the area's economy. Dorotha Richardson, an Evans Products employee during those years, recalls that rival unions devoted as much time to raiding each other's membership as they did to fighting management.[37] Employers tried to capitalize on these divisions. In an effort to undermine the militant longshoremen's union, the Waterfront Employers' Association signed agreements with AFL locals and then insisted that CIO strike actions were illegal because of binding contracts with the AFL unions.

Two employer initiatives of that kind, one in 1946 and another in 1948, brought lumber production on Coos Bay to a standstill. In the notorious *"Rolando* incident" in the summer of 1948, the Irwin-Lyons Lumber Company hired an AFL crew for below-deck work on the firm's vessel. That move threatened jobs that were traditionally the province of the CIO union members.[38] The real issue, however, was the employers' efforts to curb the growing influence of the CIO locals. As the most militant of the CIO unions, the ILWU suffered the brunt of employer attacks.

When CIO engineers and cooks claimed that their contracts gave them the right to crew the *Rolando*, the ILWU joined the CIO maritime unions in picketing the AFL crew aboard the ship. Despite the boasts of the local AFL building trades, "to crash any CIO picket line," long-shoremen prevented the loading of the ship. In fact, the Irwin-Lyons Company had to close its sawmill when the AFL Lumber and Sawmill Workers' Union refused to cross the picket line. That occurred in the face of a telegram from William Green, national AFL president, direct-ing the local to return to work. Tensions heightened when Harry Lundberg, head of the AFL sailors' union in San Francisco, accused "CIO communist stooges on the waterfront" of causing the strike.[39] Although that was not the first incident of red-baiting, thereafter the tactic became a standard maneuver in labor disputes. It also indicated that Coos Bay was closely integrated with the politics and economics of a much wider stage.

When the Coos Bay Lumber Company closed its doors over the *Rolando* incident, the local ILWU charged that it was "just another attempt on the part of the company and the Waterfront Employers Association to bring pressure on the longshoremen, as well as force public opinion against them." There were incidences of violence and eventually nearly 100 state police in riot gear were called in to patrol the waterfront. But the strike continued to hold and the mills re-mained closed.[40] Because the 1948 dispute was coast-wide, its settle-ment awaited the outcome of negotiations between the CIO maritime unions and the employers associations.

Tensions in Coos Bay and in other ports remained high as the Waterfront Employers Association tried to break the CIO unions. One employers association official told the *Oregonian* that the strike would be a long one, because the time was right "to get rid of bad conditions forced upon us during the last 15 years." Longshoremen accused shipowners and waterfront employers of wanting to drive workers back to the "dark ages." By mid-September 1,500 people were out of work on Coos Bay, and there were reports of loggers migrating to the Eugene area to look for jobs. And the red-baiting continued, especially in the form of thinly veiled rumors in the Coos Bay *Times*. The newspaper reported that many longshoremen were ready to return to work but that "if they speak out they're apt to be beaten up." That judgment runs counter to the recollections of Alvin Monk and virtually every other longshore worker who remembers those years.[41]

For three months the Pacific Coast Waterfront Employers Association insisted on an anti-communist clause and employer-controlled hiring halls as a precondition for discussions with the ILWU. But in early November the group dropped those demands and resumed negotiations with the CIO and the longshoremen. Finally, after three months of what some referred to as an employers' "sitdown," the association gave up its effort to break Harry Bridges and the ILWU. But the ramifications of the *Rolando* dispute lingered on until April 1949, when the National Labor Relations Board granted the AFL jurisdiction over below-deck shipboard workers.[42] Although the ILWU lost the local battle, on a wider scale the union won the war.

During the 1950s logging and sawmill workers were more aggressive in seeking better wages and benefits and improved safety conditions. Those struggles, and occasional region-wide strikes, brought higher pay and health and vacation benefits. The successes also contributed to a complacency among workers that left them without contractual protection when mills in southwestern Oregon began to close. Dorotha Richardson points with pride to the three-month strike of 1954, when workers displayed a solid front and won an arbitrated settlement that granted a sizable wage increase. Yet when her employer, Evans Products, began to phase out its operations in 1959, many of the workers lost more than their jobs—there was no severance pay and Evans employees lost their pensions.[43]

Postwar workers increasingly defined their objectives in terms of wages, fringe benefits, and vacation time. Overtime work was plentiful, and the docks were crowded with lumber waiting shipment out of the bay. "We were working so much," Everett Richardson remembers, "we hardly had time to spend our money." With relatively strong unions dedicated to gaining decent wages, life for working people seemed secure, even after Evans Products departed in 1961. The tough battles appeared to have been won; unions were a force to be reckoned with in the bay country. According to Forrest Taylor, a union progressive and an elected official in the local ILWU at the time, "this was a fairly good union town."[44]

The greater Coos Bay area remained solidly union through most of the 1970s. It was one of the few districts in Oregon to give George McGovern a plurality in the Nixon landslide of 1972. Local unions have sponsored popular Labor Day picnics that draw huge crowds, and labor officials have actively supported the local community college, the only one on the isolated southern Oregon coast.[45] In addition, the area's fishing industry prospered through the 1960s and into the 1970s. But disaster was approaching.

CHAPTER 11

Hard Times and Survivors

"I'm very, very glad that I'm old and not young and have to try to figure out how to feed a family."

Dorotha Richardson, 1984

Before he came to the Coos Bay area in 1973, Jeff Manley had worked for a Kansas police department, as a probation officer on a juvenile court, as a labor organizer, and had helped develop a land recovery program for the Pottawattamie Indians. After a year at Boise State University, he was hired to direct the North Bend Community Action Agency, which served ten communities on the southern Oregon coast. His first impression of those settlements was their unusually high rate of unemployment. In the old logging town of Powers, where Georgia-Pacific had just closed its mill, Manley estimates that unemployment was around 80 percent. The fear of impending mill closures, he recalls, was widespread in other small south coast communities—Port Orford, Gold Beach, Bandon, and Myrtle Point.[1]

Other features of the region's economy caught Manley's attention. Although the mills "paid good money," they "were always opening and closing," and even in the best of times employees had to "save and prepare for that time you wouldn't work." At the same time, the options for young people were beginning to narrow. There was, in fact, a growing division in the work force. For adolescents there were no boom times in the 1970s. Although youth unemployment was high and many young men and women were leaving the area, "the old line people who had gotten on at Weyerhaeuser, who had gotten on with other large outfits, their good times were still going on."[2]

Simply put, the mechanization of the forest products industry was diminishing the size of the work force. The changes in the south coast economy reflected a general transformation that has affected the North Pacific slope lumber industry, especially during the last twenty-five years. Dramatic technological and capital shifts—increased mechanization in the woods, the introduction of automated mill equipment, and centralized production in fewer plants—have altered both the productive base of the industry and the size of the work force. While larger population centers with diversified economies like Portland, Seattle, and Vancouver, British Columbia, have been better able

153

to withstand those dislocations, that has not been the case with smaller, timber-oriented communities.

That phenomenon, moreover, has been worldwide, affecting forest industry workers from the pine plantations of Tasmania to the boreal woodlands of eastern Canada. The growing tendency of the giant natural resource corporations to shift capital to arenas of highest profitability has compounded the difficulties for single-industry communities. Business leaders owe their allegiance to stockholders and corporate dividends and pay little attention to the social health of the communitites that produce their wealth. According to a Forest Service economist, in the wake of the postwar housing boom the timber industry lost interest in federal programs to stabilize dependent communities. That lack of concern, he argues, has placed southwestern Oregon counties in a "vulnerable stage of development."[3]

To make matters worse, there has been no social or resource planning for the future, and in few areas has the absence of a broadly based social strategy been more harmful than on Oregon's southern coast. Even when depleted timber supplies were becoming obvious to everyone, the market was the only restraint on the rate of harvesting on private lands. The Coos country in the postwar era, like other forested areas around the globe, was little more than a resource outpost, an extensive tree farm for the large forest products corporations.

Although the Coos County population remained relatively static in the 1960s, a growing service sector and an expanding number of public jobs brought a sharp increase during the 1970s. There also was a growing retirement community in the Coos Bay vicinity and especially in the area around the small coastal town of Bandon. For Jay Dow, who came to the bay country after a career in the Navy, economic considerations were most important; it was a good place to retire, he notes, because the "cost of living compared to many areas is cheap." Table 4 indicates changes in the county's population during the last fifty years.[4]

More significant—and ominous for the stability of the area—was the shift in employment from manufacturing to non-manufacturing jobs. The former had declined steadily from nearly 50 percent of the work force in 1960 to less than 30 percent by 1980. At the same time, non-manufacturing employment has increased from slightly more than 50 percent in 1960 to more than 75 percent in 1980.[5] Although the forest products industry appeared strong during the 1970s, structural changes in the local economy were beginning to take their toll.

TABLE 4.   Coos County Population, 1930–1980

Year	Population	Percent Change
1930	28,373	—
1940	32,446	14.4
1950	42,265	30.3
1960	54,955	30.0
1970	56,515	2.8
1980	64,047	13.3

The erosion of the industrial work force was a gradual one. Because of the decreasing number of gyppo operators in the 1960s, people became increasingly dependent on employment in one of the large mills or in government or service-sector jobs. Cal Thompson, who retired after a long career with the Coos Bay Lumber Company and Georgia-Pacific, recognized the changes that had taken place by 1975: "Now it's like everything else, it's big outfits. You have to be big or you can't operate. The little guy can't compete with the big ones."[6] Thompson might have added that the south-coast economy was in a precarious situation, overly dependent on employment with the large companies and without a significant safety net of jobs in any industrial category other than forest products.

Although there were no massive layoffs in the North Bend and Coos Bay mills for most of the decade, there was a steady attrition in the size of the industrial labor force. According to Shannon Chamness, who worked in Georgia-Pacific's plywood plant during that period, "as people left for one reason or other, whether it was retirement or just quitting, they just didn't replace them." Chamness remembers being out of work for three weeks on one occasion, but that was a market-related and temporary shutdown.[7] Chamness, of course, was one of the "old line people" whose jobs were relatively secure through the 1970s.

That was not the case with Dorotha Richardson, who was put out of work when Evans Products closed its doors at the onset of the 1960s. She lost pension benefits earned over a fifteen-year period and received no severance pay. To supplement her family's income, she worked as a janitor at the Eagles Lodge and at the Coos Bay Labor Center. Although she is retired now, she has been working part-time as a secretary for the Central Labor Council. Because of the drastic decline in union membership since 1980, the Labor Center was forced to eliminate her wages. But she continues to volunteer her time to union causes because she "likes the work."[8]

Paul Rudy, who grew up in the logging country of northern California, was appointed in 1968 to direct the University of Oregon's Institute of Marine Biology, located on the outer Coos Estuary. Although he was accustomed to the appearance of lumbering towns, he was struck by the poverty, run-down buildings and "one bit of ugliness after another" on Coos Bay. The forest products industry was still providing a solid base of jobs, but it was obvious that antiquated mills were being operated to the detriment of the environment, and there were no long-range schemes to protect the resources on which the region's economy depended. As an appointee to Oregon's first state-wide planning body, the Land Conservation and Development Commission, Rudy tried to convince others that "it was the sensible thing to do to protect your resources."[9]

For a time Rudy and his supporters made some progress in getting the worst of the pollution cleared from the bay. Helped along by a friendly state legislature and relatively good times in the early 1970s, most people seemed to agree with his argument that the bay communities had to take a long-term view of the use of their resources. But that climate changed dramatically in the early 1980s with the rash of mill closures and rampant unemployment. For people who lost their jobs or whose employment was threatened, Rudy points out, it "changed the whole philosophy and the way they looked at things."[10] But unlike many mill workers and loggers, Rudy did not become a victim of the industrial wreckage that has blighted the 1980s. That story will form the remainder of this chapter.

When Don Baldwin joined the state employment division in Coos Bay in 1971, the lumber industry was in "a bit of a recession" and unemployment averaged between 10 and 12 percent for the year. But that figure, he claims, was misleading, because unemployment was seasonal and normally "quite a bit lower in the summer." Many people looked forward to a month or two of leisure when the mill was down to hunt and fish or to look for another job. For most of the decade, Baldwin remembers, "other than temporary adjustments when production needed to be cut to keep inventory down," there were no mill closures of any consequence. Evans Products and Menasha Corporation's plywood mill had closed in the 1960s, a decade when the economy was "kind of stagnant."[11] But jobs for experienced mill workers and loggers still were available, that is, if one were patient and enthusiastic.

Up to the mid-1970s local firms still hired people at the gate, although usually when an employee failed to show up for work. One mill supervisor told Don Baldwin that he liked to see eager people outside his office with gloves "slapping in the palm of their hand to show they've got them. If they've got a lumber-pulling apron, they might as well wear it when they come in here. These are the things I'm looking for." But Chris Short, a heavy-equipment operator for Weyerhaeuser until he was elected field representative for the International Woodworkers of America (IWA) in 1982, remembers that jobs were slowly "tightening down" by 1974 and 1975. Conditions had changed dramatically from 1964 when Weyerhaeuser hired him three days after he applied for a job.[12] Even for experienced workers, therefore, options were narrowing by the late 1970s.

At the same time, Short points out, his employer had strengthened its position in the labor market:

Weyerhaeuser had the reputation when I went there of being a school for the young and a home for the old. It's where you could go, if you didn't know anything, to get trained, and once you got some training, you could go to work for a gyppo in the woods end of it and make some big money. And when you got older and wanted more security and slowed down a little, then you came back to Weyerhaeuser.

Those conditions came "to a screeching halt" in 1979.[13] Since the mill closures and massive layoffs, Weyerhaeuser has enjoyed a monopoly on the local labor market.

The Georgia-Pacific Corporation, which had harvested the remaining timber on the old Coos Bay Lumber Company lands in twenty-five years, led the list of mill closures in the summer of 1979. The company cited the high cost of bidding for public timber and the expense of converting the mill facilities to handle small logs as its reasons for shutting down. During the peak of its operations in the 1960s and early 1970s, Georgia-Pacific employed as many as 1,000 workers in its Coos Bay mills (in 1977 it still employed 700). The company already had announced the decision to move its headquarters to Atlanta, Georgia, effective in 1982.[14] Unlike the closure of the locally owned and managed Al Peirce mill, the Georgia-Pacific announcement was a shock that came without warning.

Harold "Cardy" Walton was at his union desk in the IWA hall on the afternoon of July 30, 1979, when a Georgia-Pacific public-relations man handed him a news release announcing the closure of the firm's Bunker Hill mill. According to Jerry Lantto, field representative for the union local, men and women on the swing shift heard about the plant's closure from the news media before they went to work, and many of those at the mill "heard it from people coming in." An advance warning "shouldn't have been that big an issue," Lantto points out, because large corporations like Georgia-Pacific know "years in advance when a plant was going to close."[15] The bitterness of the union's leadership and its rank-and-file members still lingers in the bay communities.

The corporate decision put 230 people immediately out of work. For Shannon Chamness, who learned about the closure "when the boss came around ten or fifteen minutes before it was time to go home," it meant a period of readjustment and eventually two part-time jobs to support herself. "Everybody was in a state of shock," she recalls, "then some people started getting angry and other people started worrying." Chamness was one of the worriers, because she had just driven her first new car "off the showroom floor and didn't have the license plates for it yet." To cover the purchase price of the car, she had extended her monthly financial commitments "up to my wage"; unemployment compensation would be less than half her weekly paycheck. Chamness told a newspaper reporter: "I bought a Cougar XR-7. I sure wish it was a Datsun now."[16]

Determined to keep her modest home and meet the car payments, Chamness accepted a transfer to a Georgia-Pacific plant in Springfield, Oregon. Removed from family and friends, she quickly became disillusioned: "I hated Springfield. I hated the people. I hated the town. I hated the mill. The whole bit. But I think in retrospect, it was homesickness. I'm happy here. I came home and got a job as a dishwasher." The dishwashing job in the basement of a Chinese restaurant for the minimum wage of $3.35 an hour proved to be "harder work than at the mill."[17]

Unlike many of her friends, Chamness survived the financial shake out. She borrowed money from her parents to pay for the car, found a more pleasant job in a "donut" shop (still at the minimum wage), and finally "managed to get on at the hospital for three days a week" where she earned $5.64 an hour and received medical benefits. Dining out, shopping trips to Eugene and Portland, and "going to the beauty shop every week" are no longer part of her itinerary. But she considers herself fortunate. Her ex-husband lost his home and nearly everything he owned, and a woman friend who worked for Georgia-Pacific is divorced and still in a "depressed state." For many of her co-workers, the economic disaster has meant a resort to alcohol, "broken homes and broken marriages." And Chamness wonders if the lack of medical insurance contributed to the early death of another friend.[18]

Although the closure of Georgia-Pacific's plywood mill was only the first of several on the south coast, it was the largest single plant to shut down in Coos County. According to Chamness, the community lost some of its top wage earners, and that had a reverberating effect on the "retail trade and everything else." When the Al Peirce Lumber Company stopped milling lumber because of the increased cost and short supply of logs in December 1979, the bay area lost another 125 industrial paychecks. There was more disaster in 1980—the "temporary" suspension of production at the Cape Arago mill (150 jobs), the shutting down of Georgia-Pacific's hardboard operation (130 jobs), and the permanent closure of the Coos Head Timber Company sawmill (250 jobs).[19]

The Coos Bay area had gained a reputation as the most depressed part of the state by the early 1980s. With their heavy dependence on timber-related employment, the bay communities were pacesetters for the epidemic of mill closures that spread across the North Pacific slope in the 1980s. The Coos Bay local of the IWA, reduced to fewer than 100 members, merged with the North Bend union, most of whose members worked for Weyerhaeuser. The latter company, with a firm hold on the area's labor market, openly threatened further layoffs in order to gain contract concessions as the decade advanced.[20]

In truth, southwestern Oregon was experiencing a dramatic shift in the way people made their living. While economists use the term "structural unemployment" to explain those changes, that approach tends to excuse the social consequences of the manipulations of capital in recent years and the trauma and suffering left in the wake of those decisions. "Structural unemployment" provides a conscience-easing explanation for increases in poverty, the uprooting of people's lives, and other socially disruptive influences associated with economic hardship. Residents of Coos County, whose world has been disrupted by the mill closures of recent years, offer a personal and human side to the cold statistics of the economist.

The Community Action Center in the old-town section of North Bend is housed in a multistoried turn-of-the-century building in need of paint and repair. One of the few remaining community action programs in the country, it provides assistance to poor people in the several population centers on the southern Oregon coast. The director of the agency, Jeff Manley, is a bright, husky, bundle of energy who speaks easily about the people and the constituencies he serves. He also has a practical working acquaintance with the exercise of power in the communities of North Bend and Coos Bay. Despite his sometimes outspoken challenges to bay-area leaders, Manley and the action agency have survived.

The mill closures, according to Manley, affected the Community Action Center in both a negative and a positive way. The unemployment was "dramatic in the negative," because it increased the workload of staff members handling cases of sexual and physical abuse of children, with spousal beatings, and with alcoholism. But growing deprivation and economic hardship was a boon to advocacy and organizing, because the action agency began to serve "people who understood that a willingness to work hard all their lives didn't guarantee or protect them from the system." Blue-collar workers who normally ignored Manley's office suddenly began to question community leaders.[21]

When the action office decided to bring a lawsuit against the City of Coos Bay for misusing a $3.8 million community development grant, Manley points out that "the working-class neighborhoods of Empire rallied to our support." The city applied for the grant to provide assistance to low-income areas; instead local officials diverted the money to fund "a new city hall and a new swimming pool in the richest part of town." Through the legal initiatives of the Community Action Center and with the support of the hundreds of people who turned out at public hearings, the courts ordered the city to return part of the money and to build a youth center in the Empire district and a senior center in downtown Coos Bay, and to improve water and sewer service to poor neighborhoods. With a chuckle, Manley remarks: "It was a good time for us."[22]

Because the mill closures put a heavy burden on social service agencies, the action center became more involved in the delivery of services than in political activism for the poor. The agency also had to dig and scrape for dwindling financial support. At the very time when unemployment was increasing, the state legislature made married men ineligible for public welfare. The function of the law was obvious, Manley remarks: "What they were really trying to do was cut the number of people on public assistance." Or, more pointedly, to force people to hunt for jobs where there were none.[23] An obvious effect of the budget pruning was an increase in the financial strains on the already overcommitted community agency.

But the people who walked through the doors of the Community Action Center were only a small part of a much larger population caught up in the mill closures. For the older generation of skilled workers, men like David Mickelson and Eugene Wechter, who were once the productive backbone of the timber-rich Oregon econom_ the events of the past few years have brought perilous times. They played by the rules, faithfully put in their time at the plant, purchased modest homes, and paid regular dues to local clubs. In the wake of the industrial layoffs, their jobs are gone as is the regularity and security of that world.

Mickelson, 57, and Eugene Wechter, 60, are justifiably proud of their abilities as head sawyers. Mickelson, who went to work for the Cape Arago Lumber Company in 1946, "pulled on the planer and green chain, worked on the resaw," and then became a head sawyer in 1957, a job he held until the mill closed in 1980. He enjoyed reading the grain of the timbers, "trying to outsmart the log," a skill that took years to develop. But all that is behind him now. Unlike some of the younger men at Cape Arago, Mickelson was not offered a transfer to the company's plant in nearby Bandon. When International Paper-opened a new mill in Gardner, twenty-five miles north of Coos Bay, Mickelson applied for a sawyer's job. "They were interested," he reports, "but when they found out my age, well, they were not interested anymore."[24]

After Cape Arago went down, Mickelson collected unemployment compensation through two extensions, drew upon a modest savings account, and finally went to work in January 1983 under the "Green Thumb" project, a federal jobs program for people over the age of fifty-five where "you only work twenty hours a week, minimum wage, for nonprofit organizations." Mickelson works for the nearby Charleston Fire Department for $3.35 an hour. At Cape Arago he was earning nearly $12 an hour. But, he notes with resignation, "you have to do something or a guy goes crazy." He also manages to "pick up a few odd jobs on weekends," mostly lawn and maintenance work.[25]

Although Mickelson's car and small home in the Empire district are paid for, he and his wife have struggled. He had to drop his medical insurance because the monthly costs were too high. His most recent worries are paying the property taxes on his home and his car insurance. Mickelson also has taken welding classes at the local community college, acquiring skills that may be salable if the Port of Coos Bay lands a contract to construct offshore oil-drilling equipment.[26] With a lifetime of friendships in the bay area, he is determined to hang on until he is eligible for Social Security and his retirement pension comes due.

Eugene Wechter, tall and husky, served as a flyer in the South Pacific at the end of the Second World War. After his discharge, he tried commercial fishing, the Evans Products mill, worked in the woods for a gyppo operator, and finally landed a job with the Al Peirce Lumber Company in 1949. Wechter learned the sawyer's skills and operated the mill's Swedish gang saw system until the plant closed in 1979. Wechter's two sons also lost their jobs at the mill. One was injured in 1983, and according to the father, will not be able to work again. The other son went to Texas to look for a job, but "got homesick and came home."[27] Wechter's difficulties, however, had only begun.

Because his home and family were in the area, Wechter did not consider looking elsewhere for a job. Like David Mickelson, he "had a few dollars saved up" and drew unemployment until it ran out. He logged for a local farmer, operated a fishing boat for awhile, and then "didn't do anything. I just stayed home." He faults the mill closure, in part, for his divorce: "It more or less broke up my family. I mean she wouldn't stick around; couldn't keep things going like we always wanted to." Through the winter of 1983–84, Wechter and his son have been working "off and on, not too steady" for a non-union mill in the Coquille Valley. Compared to the Peirce mill, his present situation "is not very good. It's just a job."[28] For Eugene Wechter the camaraderie and security of the Peirce mill are of another world.

Although "Cardy" Walton has returned to his old job with Georgia-Pacific's small woods crew, he will never forget the searing experience of the early 1980s. A quiet, relaxed man who has spent most of his life in the timbered back country, Walton is appalled at the effect of the mill closures on the older workers: "Losing their cars, losing their homes. People with their homes almost paid for. No way to finish it. Trying to sell out cheap to get to move somewhere to go to work. Losing their automobiles and everything else that they bought. Forcing the older people into early retirement, taking a reduced pension. Trying to survive."[29] The new economic conditions of the 1980s forced many well-paid and skilled mill workers into a marginal existence, struggling to get by on part-time employment and minimum wages.

For many former union members those circumstances have meant pumping gas, service employment at entry level wages, or picking ferns and cedar boughs. Walton knows several former Georgia-Pacific plywood workers who have not held a steady job since the mill closed in 1979. Expressing frustration at his inability to find work, one man in his mid-fifties told Walton: "I'm either too damn old or too dumb or something." Another husband and wife who were employed in the plywood plant now toil at minimum wages and are struggling to keep their home; they have already lost their car.[30] But the economic dislocations on the south coast had ramifications that went beyond the weekly paycheck.

Although local mills have employed women as hourly wage earners since the early 1920s, the rate of their participation in the work force outside the home has been lower on the south coast than in the rest of the state. Since 1970, however, women have entered the labor market in large numbers, both as primary and secondary wage earners. At the same time, the percentage of men employed has correspondingly declined. Those changes, according to Jim Mills, a family counselor, directly conflict with the area's "traditional values of men being in charge and being the bread winner, the woman playing a relatively subservient role in the home." Although the issue is more pervasive than its relation to jobs, "the unemployment situation has speeded up the process of catching up with the rest of the world."[31] One of the consequences has been an increase in spousal abuse and divorce.

"Cardy" Walton's daily associations with people are far different from the urban counseling world of Jim Mills. Yet Walton understands why so many of the "old members" of the union are getting divorces. "I would imagine," he says, "probably being around the house all the time, they irritate one another after a while, and sooner or later it's going to cause trouble." According to Mills, the extended presence of the principal wage earner in the home heightens existing tensions and leads to increased alcoholism, physical abuse, and in many cases, divorce.[32] Although those problems always existed, the economic disasters of the 1980s have made those difficulties more obvious.

There is yet another side to the story, and that involves the loss of dignity to people who have labored hard most of their lives and are proud of their ability to support their families. "They've worked steady, paid their taxes, supported their community," Jerry Lantto points out, "and all of a sudden it's all gone, just down the tube." That loss of dignity, according to Jim Mills, can be as disruptive as the loss of income and can impair a person's ability to function. Lantto is more emphatic:

> That's got to be quite a blow to a person's ego, or dignity, or whatever. Applying for food stamps, welfare, everything else. He's never participated in that system before in his life. Most of them wouldn't, didn't even know how to go about doing something like that. They've never done it. All they've done is work all their lives, contributed. They've become a receiver. It's got to be hard on them.[33]

From his position in the state employment office, Don Baldwin provides workers with information about unemployment compensation and job placement. Since the mill closures, his staff has noticed that women have been able to find work much more easily than men. They come to the agency "saying they've just got to get work because either their husband is unemployed or there is concern about the stability of his job." According to Baldwin, "two-income households or households where the woman has gone to work and become the primary wage earner" have increased sharply. Lower pay and prestige has also meant a higher turnover in the minimum-wage jobs.[34]

The transition to low-paying, part-time work was especially difficult for men who worked in the woods, according to Baldwin. For loggers who liked their jobs and believed "they were part of an important operation," there was little satisfaction in the menial work associated with the service industries. When it became apparent that the mills were not going to reopen, Baldwin and his staff also observed a latent anger among the people who visited the office. That "negativity," characteristic of areas with long-term, chronic unemployment, has affected state-agency employees as well. Yet, the employment office staff is "impressed and surprised about how people keep going" and are willing to consider new types of work.[35] But only so many doors can be closed before hope begins to dwindle.

That was certainly true for older workers whose skills became obsolete with the massive layoffs. "Looking for work is one of the hardest things a person can do," Baldwin remarks, "especially in an area that has high unemployment." And for people over the age of forty, leaving the area is not an option, according to Jerry Lantto. With only "plywood experience" to sell, "it's really a gamble for a man to sell his home and move somewhere else in hopes of finding a job." From the vantage point of his union office, Lantto has learned that "the odds are really against" older people competing successfully in a glutted job market. Sixty-year-old David Willis, still employed as a longshoreman, points to the obvious—it is difficult to be unemployed in a strange place: "In your own environment you have contacts, family friends, your own credentials, and your ear is tuned for the area."[36]

For skilled mill workers and loggers like David Mickelson, the future appears to offer little more than marginal employment in jobs that were once considered demeaning. Don Baldwin, who is reminded each day of those wrenching experiences, agrees that their prospects for finding employment are grim. "Anybody who believes that there's not discrimination against older workers," he says vehemently, "just is moving in a fairy land."[37] Although many displaced lumber workers have left the area, most of the older ones have remained.

But the economic problems on the south coast also have affected young people. Growing up in families where men (and some women) received good wages, the younger generation looked forward to similar conditions when they entered the work force. Although the events of recent years have shattered those expectations, Don Baldwin remembers a time when the employment office "got involved in reality training"—telling youthful job seekers to anticipate $4.50 as opposed to $10 an hour. At the moment, the fast-food chains in North Bend and Coos Bay are the most likely employment alternative for most.[38]

One high school counselor points out that student wages from places like McDonald's, Burger King, Dunkin Donut, and Pizza Hut provided the only family income during the early days of the mill closures: "The student was the one who was employed in the family because of the type of job they could get." Another counselor sees the growth of fast-food eateries as "a real boon to us, because that is where most young people find employment now."[39] Exodus from the south coast, generally soft-pedaled by the school counselors, is another choice that many young people have made.

The employment prospects for high school graduates have changed dramatically during the last fifteen years. Whereas their parents could look forward to a future as a logger, mill worker, or in one of the supporting industries, today most of those options are severely limited. A stagnant forest products economy, a sharply diminished inventory of harvestable timber, and mechanization have eroded the region's industrial base. There is more to the story—an expanding southeastern wood products trade through this writing, and imported Canadian lumber have captured markets that traditionally belonged to producers in the Pacific Northwest. Those developments suggest continued hardship for the region's timber-dependent communities.

Post Mortem: Reflections on the Present Condition

These are not happy times for resource-dependent communities like those in southwestern Oregon. But the timbered regions of western America are only part of a larger theater of action in what properly must be understood as the internationalization of trade and investment policy. Centers of finance and corporate power have the ability to shift capital from one geopolitical location to another and from one industrial sector to the next. Expressing itself through the aegis of the multinational corporation, late twentieth-century capitalism operates on an international scale and largely beyond the influence of any single nation.[1]

That state of affairs has contributed to the increased exploitation of hinterland areas dependent on timber, mineral extraction, or agriculture for their sustenance. Isolated, with relatively small populations, and lacking significant influence in the trade and exchange relation, natural resource communities are byproducts of industrial strategies and decisions made elsewhere. One consequence of that imbalance is the continued vulnerability of resource-dependent regions to market fluctuations. That, of course, is not new to the twentieth century.

Although those conditions exist in their most apparent form in the so-called dependent nations of the world, there are sizable regions and districts within the developed countries that function in a peripheral relationship to centers of capital. That is particularly true of Appalachia and many places in the American West where resource industries have dominated local economies, their infrastructures and financing, and their labor skills—for the benefit of stockholder dividends and to the detriment of the areas they influence. For their part, state and federal governments have fostered the needs of the natural-resource capitalists and have ignored the social requirements of the dependent communities.

In the American West and in British Columbia the development of the mining and lumbering industries share common historical features. Investment capital from the eastern United States, England, and Europe made possible the "opening up" of those areas to resource extraction. In essence, that form of industrialism was imposed from outside because of the limitations of indigenous capital. As a consequence, most of the benefits accrued to the investors—the real movers and shakers of western enterprise. The famous populist cartoon depicting a cow with its feeding end sprawled across the trans-Mississippi West and its milking apparatus on Wall Street is an appropriate analogy for the exchange relationship between western resource communities and the investors of capital.

In many of those areas the extraction of resources and the mining of soils has run its course. Once-thriving mining towns like Butte, Montana, are being turned over to historic preservationists and oral historians who are sifting through the physical and social wreckage in search of the essence of those communities. In truth, theirs is more than a symbolic gesture, because Butte, its mining counterpart in Bisbee, Arizona, the decaying agricultural communities throughout the American West, and the lumbering towns of the Douglas fir country are becoming anachronisms—that is, in the sense that they play a significant and influential role in the modern western economy.

Those traditional mining, agricultural, and lumber communities share common experiences and special difficulties—many of them related to the pervasive influence of modern capitalism and its vast network of exchange, investment policy, and ability to move on the national and international stage. For timbered regions that phenomenon has been worldwide, affecting forest-dependent communities from the pine plantations of Tasmania to the forests of eastern Canada. The wooded slopes of British Columbia, Japan, and those on Oregon's south coast have been turned into extended tree farms for the large forest products corporations. Weyerhaeuser, for one, exports logs from its Coos Bay holdings, and then mills the timber into merchantable lumber at its subsidiary operations in Japan.

For the Douglas fir region in particular, the shifting investment policies of the multinational forest products firms have been particularly stressful. But the flow of capital in recent years away from the region's once booming timber industry repeats a historic tradition—that resource capital in the United States has been extremely mobile; it has contributed to the development of towns and then devastated them. The mounting social and economic problems of those troubled communities are witness to that truth.

Immediately after the Second World War, the timber resource in southwestern Oregon was extensive and there was still time to develop a long-range resource-management strategy. However, as this study has made clear, the market prevailed and the social and economic stability of the region was never a major consideration in private and public decision making. Now that the resource base has been severely depleted and nineteenth-century social theories are fashionable in state and federal capitals, there is even less likelihood that those communities will escape from the strategies and investment decisions of the private corporations who control much of the land.

In the 1980s a rash of mill closures, a severe recession in the forest products industry, and large sales of Canadian lumber on the Pacific Coast have increased the hardships for the communities on Coos Bay. Empty office buildings and storefronts and vacant automobile dealerships are becoming regular features of the landscape. The area once billed as the "Lumber Capital of the World" with its tremendous production records in the postwar years is now taking its "turn in the bucket." The heavy harvests in the region since the Second World War and the expanding southeastern wood products trade suggest that those hardships will continue into the foreseeable future.

Many of the forest products firms see the eastern United States as the center of the industry's growth for the rest of this century. That shift, according to the Seattle *Post-Intelligencer,* "is an ironic retreat to the nation's early days when the lumber industry was concentrated in the Northeast and Midwest."[2] The "retreat" of those corporate enterprises to more lucrative investment arenas is part of the larger piece of the increased mobility of capital in recent times. In its wake it has left an impoverished social and economic environment.

Oregon's south coast was not alone in suffering the pangs of economic depression in the 1980s. In a prepared statement released on January 29, 1985, from its corporate headquarters in Stamford, Connecticut, Champion International Corporation announced plans to close eight hardwood, plywood, and lumber mills, laying off about 2,000 workers in Washington, Oregon, and northern California. The closures included a Champion mill at Gold Beach on Oregon's south coast and one in Lebanon, Oregon, with more than 830 workers. Sixteen-year-old Jim McElhinny, employed in the Lebanon operation, told a news reporter the next day: "I'm single and I'm going to be the first one out of town. . . . The closure is God's will, and I don't question God."[3]

Although it would be comforting to ascribe such social and economic disasters to divine judgment, even the most pious of forest products workers would find it difficult to believe that the recent epidemic of mill closures was a sign of God's benevolence. Red Russell, who presides over a dwindling International Woodworkers of America (IWA) membership, views the Champion International decision as "a devastating blow to the timber workers in this area." The termination of the Gold Beach operation, about seventy-five miles south of Coos Bay, put 322 people out of work and boosted sparsely populated Curry County's unemployment rate to more than 20 percent. The Champion closure in Lebanon and another one in a nearby community raised Linn County's unemployed population to a similar percentage.[4]

The departure or failure of so many forest products firms has made the timber communities in the Pacific Northwest even more dependent on and, therefore, vulnerable to the few that remain. On Coos Bay the Weyerhaeuser Company has stepped up its export of logs to Japan. Although the IWA sharply disapproves of log exports—they mean fewer jobs in the manufacturing plants—longshoremen favor the practice, because it provides work for union members and keeps the port busy in an otherwise depressed economy. Both the local IWA and the longshoremen's union, however, have muted their differences in the interests of labor solidarity.

As elsewhere in the United States during the slumping economy of the 1980s, forest products firms have taken advantage of high unemployment to pressure workers into contract concessions, or what organized labor calls "give-backs." Although the Louisiana-Pacific Corporation has led the trend in union busting, every major company has tried to erode union power and influence. As one of the "flagship" companies in the Pacific Northwest, the Weyerhaeuser corporation initiated a move early in 1985 to force unions to accept sweeping cuts in wages and benefits in their existing contracts. John Ball, secretary-treasurer for the regional IWA, accused the company of wanting to "push people back to the poverty level."[5] For its part, the company cited market factors and the need to lower production costs to remain competitive with the Southeast.

In a related development, the International Paper Company in Gardner, twenty-five miles north of Coos Bay, forced the IWA local to renegotiate its contract as part of an agreement to reopen its 800-employee sawmill. Red Russell, the IWA regional president, although disapproving of the break in the ranks of his union, has no quarrel with the Gardner local. "What would you do if you had bamboo shoots under your fingernails?" he asked in reference to International Paper's threat to keep the mill closed unless the union agreed to concessions.[6]

The glut on the labor market has played into the hands of the

companies in other ways. Charles Reigard, who is on medical leave
from the Weyerhaeuser plant on Coos Bay, points out that the number
of jobless people outside the gate has had an intimidating effect on
those who are working. Union strength, even in traditional strong-
holds like Coos Bay, has eroded since the late 1970s, and Reigard fears
that the movement will soon revert to the 1930s. "We have a one-
company market for labor, and it's going to be hard to combat that."
The situation has frightened rank-and-file members to the point that
they no longer support the union.[7]

Even independent loggers, once the bastion of the industry in the
postwar era, are a diminishing breed on Oregon's south coast. The
large companies play one independent against another, and in many
cases, contractors get work only by undercutting the bid of a com-
petitor. Chappie McCarthy, a survivor who has seen many of his
gyppo friends file for bankruptcy, sketches a Darwinian world for the
independents. Many operators, he notes, "corral a lot of work" and
then are unable to meet their financial commitments: "Their business
ability was not up to their greed. To be a logger, after all, you've got to
be a selfish, greedy son of a bitch to survive. Actually, you've got to be
a little bit crazy too. Where else would you find somebody try to make
a profit out of an expense?" To stay in business as an independent
logger, he muses, "you've got to be able to pay your bills and take
something home to pay for the groceries."[8] Although the family
logging outfit has experienced "down times" during the rainy season,
McCarthy and his brother have managed to survive the recent shake-
out on the south coast.

While Oregon's Economic Development Commission chases the
high-tech mirage in an effort to boost the state's ailing economy, the
Port of Coos Bay has been aggressively promoting the estuary as a
staging area for offshore oil-drilling platforms and as a potential
stopping place for "Love Boat" cruises. Frank Martin, the agency's
new director, fresh from the Port of Chicago, regularly captures
newspaper headlines in his effort to attract business. A local high
school teacher also created a flurry of excitement when he suggested
that coal production still remained a viable way to create jobs. Others
further removed—and perhaps better informed—are skeptical about
those options.

One of them is Dow Beckham, now in his mid-seventies and relatively healthy after undergoing quadruple bypass surgery. Although
he finds it "kind of sad" that the economic boom in the Coos country
has come to an end, he points to a fundamental truth: "This is not

new. It's happened in the West in the mining business, and now in the timber business." And for better or worse, he predicts, "the main thing in our economy will be the timber industry," although it will operate at 50 or 60 percent of its postwar capacity.[9]

Like Dow Beckham, Bill McKenna comes from a logging family and has spent most of his life in the Coos country. His parents came to the bay area from Michigan when "that country had been practically skinned." But the Douglas fir country and the southern Oregon coast, in particular, are different from his parents' homeland: "This area is made to grow trees. Face it, that's why we're backward. We're a tree farm."[10] McKenna believes the area will remain so.

Let Paula Laurilla—who still toils in the kitchen of Lindblad's, the tavern-rooming house that her father opened for business in 1913— have the last word. Located on U.S. Highway 101 a few hundred yards from the site of the Big Mill, Lindblad's is the oldest working-class tavern on Coos Bay. Once a thriving social establishment for mill workers and loggers and a place where gyppos discussed business propositions, Lindblad's has come upon hard times of late. Business is down, Paula reports, "and you don't know if it's going to go up again." Asked if she is optimistic or pessimistic about the future, she replied, "I'm tired! I'm tired of guessing what comes next!"[11]

Notes

Preface

1. John Dargavel to the author, May 1, 1984.

Introduction

1. Portland *Oregonian*, Nov. 29, 1981; Eugene *Register-Guard*, Nov. 29, 1981.
2. *Register-Guard*, Nov. 29, 1981.
3. *Life*, 73, no. 7 (Aug. 18, 1972), 52; and Los Angeles *Herald-Examiner*, June 1, 1975.
4. Interview with Shannon Chamness, April 18, 1984.

Chapter 1. Poor Man's Paradise

1. Marjory K. Cowan, "Historical Sketch of the Coos Bay Country" (B.A. thesis, University of Oregon, 1913), 1.
2. For accounts of the Pope and Talbot venture and the early Pacific lumber trade see: Edwin T. Coman, Jr., and Helen M. Gibbs, *Time, Tide and Timber: A Century of Pope and Talbot* (Stanford: Stanford University Press, 1949); Stewart Holbrook, *Holy Old Mackinaw* (New York: Macmillan, 1938); Thomas R. Cox, *Mills and Markets: A History of the Pacific Coast Lumber Industry to 1900* (Seattle: University of Washington Press, 1974).
3. Stephen Dow Beckham, *Coos Bay: The Pioneer Period, 1850–1900* (Coos Bay, Ore.: Arago Books, 1973), 31.
4. Oregon *Statesman*, Oct. 18, 1853; Oregon *Spectator*, Sept. 16, 1853.
5. Emil R. Peterson and Alfred Powers, *A Century of Coos and Curry* (Portland, Ore.: Binfords and Mort, 1952), 425–426, 580.
6. Beckham, *Coos Bay*, 22–27.
7. Stephen Dow Beckham, *The Simpsons of Shore Acres* (Coos Bay: Arago Books, 1971), 1–15; Cox, *Mills and Markets*, 166–167, 171–172.
8. John A. Allen and Ewart M. Baldwin, *Geology and Coal Resources of the Coos Bay* (Portland: Oregon State Department of Geology and Mineral Industries, 1944), 60–63; George Case, "The History of the Port of Coos Bay, 1851–1952" (M.A. thesis, Pan American University, 1983), 104–105.
9. Quoted in Peterson and Powers, *A Century of Coos and Curry*, 394, 533.
10. Beckham, *Coos Bay*, 22.
11. Ibid.
12. Case, "History of the Port of Coos Bay," 104.
13. Quoted in Peterson and Powers, *A Century of Coos and Curry*, 394.
14. Ibid., 397; Case, "History of the Port of Coos Bay," 104.
15. Coos Bay *Harbor*, Oct. 23, 1908; Coos Bay *News*, May 18, 1909.

16. Coos Bay *Times,* Aug. 30 and Oct. 28, 1912.

17. Peterson and Powers, *A Century of Coos and Curry,* 398; *Times,* Aug. 8, 1906, and April 4, 1913.

18. A. G. Walling, *History of Southern Oregon: Comprising Jackson, Josephine, Douglas, Curry and Coos Counties* (Portland: A. G. Walling, 1884), 497–498.

19. *News,* May 13 and June 24, 1874.

20. Walling, *History of Southern Oregon,* 494; *News,* June 10, 1874; Case, "History of the Port of Coos Bay," 13–14.

21. Portland *Oregonian,* Jan. 1, 1884; *News,* April 2, 1884.

22. *News,* April 9, 1890, and March 19, 1901.

23. Ibid., Aug. 5, 1874, and May 12, 1875.

24. Ibid., Dec. 8, 1875, and Nov. 4, 1885.

25. Ibid., April 14, 1886, and Feb. 17, 1897.

26. Interview with Quentin Church, April 3, 1984. All interviews are in Oral History Collection, Southwestern Oregon Community College Library, Coos Bay, Oregon (hereafter SWOCC Library).

27. *News,* May 8, 1889, and April 1, 1891.

28. University of Oregon, Bureau of Municipal Research and Service, *Population of Oregon Cities, Counties and Metropolitan Areas, 1850–1957: A Compilation of Census Counts and Estimates in Oregon,* Information Bulletin No. 106 (Eugene, 1958), 18.

29. Beckham, *Coos Bay,* 40–42; Cox, *Mills and Markets,* 257–259.

30. The sentiments were those of J. H. Upton of the Port Orford *Post.* The editorial was reprinted in the *News,* June 2, 1880; also see *News,* Aug. 24, 1881. Both issues cited in Beckham, *Coos Bay,* 42.

31. *Oregonian,* Sept. 27, 1882; Portland *Telegram,* reprinted in *News,* June 25, 1884.

32. Frank J. Harmon, "Remembering Franklin B. Hough," *American Forests,* 86 (January 1977), 34–37, 52–53; Franklin B. Hough, "On the Duty of Governments in the Preservation of Forests," in *Conservation in the United States: A Documentary History,* ed., Frank E. Smith (New York: Chelsea House, 1971), I:688.

33. Ralph W. Hidy, Frank Ernest Hill, and Allen Nevins, *Timber and Men: The Weyerhaeuser Story* (New York: Macmillan, 1963), 130.

34. Cox, *Mills and Markets,* 227–238; Hidy, Hill, and Nevins, *Timber and Men,* 210–214.

35. Steve Greif, "A Century of Coos County Railroads," manuscript in SWOCC Library.

36. *News,* Sept. 9, 1885; Feb. 15 and 22, and April 25, 1888.

37. *Oregonian,* Dec. 18, 1890.

38. *News,* Aug. 10, 1893.

39. Ibid., Jan. 9 and Sept. 11, 1895; June 24, Sept. 23, and Oct. 21, 1896.

40. Ibid., Feb. 16, 1898.

41. Ibid., July 5, 1898; March 15 and May 16, 1899.

42. Ibid., April 9, 1901.

43. *News,* July 15, 1874, and May 4, 1892.

44. Ibid., Aug. 30, 1893.

45. Ibid., Jan. 2 and Sept. 24, 1884; July 31, 1889; and May 7, 1890.

46. Henry Clepper, *Professional Forestry in the United States* (Baltimore: Johns Hopkins University Press, 1971), 135–136; Jerry A. O'Callaghan, *The Disposition of the Public Domain in Oregon* (Washington, D.C.: Government Printing Office, 1960), 71–96; William G. Robbins, *Land: Its Use and Abuse in Oregon, 1848–1910* (Corvallis: Oregon State University Press, 1974), 15–21.

Chapter 2. An Empire Itself

1. Coos Bay *Harbor,* Dec. 6, 1907.
2. Coos Bay *Times,* July 10 and 26, and Dec. 4, 1906.
3. Donald MacKay, *Empire of Wood: The Macmillan Bloedel Story* (Vancouver, British Columbia: Douglas and McIntyre, 1982), 19–20.
4. Ibid., 15–20. The quote is from p. 20.
5. Robert E. Ficken, "Weyerhaeuser and the Pacific Northwest Timber Industry, 1899–1903," *Pacific Northwest Quarterly,* 70 (1979), 146, 153; Kenneth Erickson, "The Morphology of Lumber Settlements in Western Oregon and Washington" (Ph.D. dissertation, University of California, Berkeley, 1965) 15–16.
6. Erickson, "Morphology of Lumber Settlements," 16.
7. Portland *Oregonian,* Aug. 19, 1902; Coos Bay *News,* April 13, 1898, and May 1, 1900.
8. *News,* Nov. 10, 1898, June 13, 1899, and Sept. 25, 1900; *Oregonian,* Dec. 24, 1902.
9. *Harbor,* Jan. 28 and June 10, 1905.
10. Ibid., March 4, June 10, and Aug. 26, 1905.
11. *Oregonian,* Aug. 19, 1902.
12. *Harbor,* March 17, 1906; *Times,* Aug. 17 and 24, 1906.
13. *Times,* Aug. 18, 1906; Nathan Douthit, *Coos Bay Region, 1890–1944* (Coos Bay: River West Books, 1981), 99.
14. Curt Beckham to the author, May 28, 1984. Mr. Beckham gave the author three photocopy sample pages from the McCarthy diaries.
15. Ibid.; *Times,* June 24, 1911, and Jan. 4, 1913.
16. *Times,* Dec. 4, 1906.
17. *Harbor,* Dec. 22, 1906.
18. Mowry Smith, Jr., and Giles Clark, *One Third Crew, One Third Boat, One Third Luck: The Menasha Corporation Story, 1849–1974* (Neenah, Wis.: The Menasha Wooden-Ware Corporation, 1974), 170–175; *Times,* Aug. 28, Nov. 25, Dec. 22 and 28, 1906; and Feb. 26, 1908; Stephen A. D. Puter, *Looters of the Public Domain* (Portland: Portland Printing House, 1908), 33–34, 186, 295.
19. Puter, *Looters of the Public Domain,* 196, 297, 312.
20. *Oregonian,* Jan. 7, 1907.
21. *American Lumberman* (Nov. 11, 1911), 44–45, 52; *Harbor,* Feb. 16, 1907.
22. Interview with Cliff Thorwald, April 12, 1984; interview with Eleanor Anderson, March 29, 1984.
23. *American Lumberman* (Nov. 11, 1911), 56, 62, 69; interview with Florence Berg, March 14, 1984.
24. *American Lumberman* (Nov. 11, 1911), 69.
25. Interview with Florence Berg, March 14, 1984; *American Lumberman* (Nov. 11, 1911), 62, 69; Emil Peterson and Alfred Powers, *A Century of Coos and Curry* (Portland, Ore: Binfords and Mort, 1952), 528.
26. Interview with Raymond McKeown, 1972; Peterson and Powers, *A Century of Coos and Curry,* 565.
27. *Harbor,* March 30, April 13, and Sept. 27, 1907.
28. Ibid., March 23, 1907.
29. Norman Clark, *Mill Town: A Social History of Everett, Washington* (Seattle: University of Washington Press, 1970), 234; William G. Robbins, *Lumberjacks and Legislators: Political Economy of the U.S. Lumber Industry, 1890–1941* (College Station, Texas: Texas A&M University Press, 1982), 70–75.

30. *News*, May 11, 1898, and Jan. 30, 1900.

31. Ibid., Feb. 6, 1900; interview with Jerry Phillips, April 6, 1984.

32. *Harbor*, Dec. 6, 1907, and June 25, 1909; *News*, Nov. 10, 1909.

33. *Harbor*, June 25, 1909; *Times*, Jan. 22, 1910; Washington Forest Fire Association, *Annual Report* (1908), 10–11, in Office of State and Private Forestry, U.S. Forest Service, Region 6, Portland, Oregon; Robbins, *Lumberjacks and Legislators*, 104.

34. *Times*, Dec. 24, 1907, and June 17, 1911; *Harbor*, Aug. 31, 1907, and Oct. 16, 1908.

35. Douthit, *Coos Bay Region*, 35–36; *Harbor*, Aug. 25, 1906; *News*, July 10, 1906; Coos Bay *Monthly*, May–June, 1907.

36. *Monthly*, December 1906; *Harbor*, Sept. 22, 1910; *News*, Aug. 1, 1911; *Times*, Aug. 1, 1911.

37. Interview with Florence Berg, March 14, 1984; interview with Raymond McKeown, 1972.

38. Douthit, *Coos Bay Region*, 65–67; interview with Raymond McKeown, 1972.

Chapter 3. The "Big Mill" and Its World

1. *American Lumberman* (Nov. 11, 1911), 52.

2. Coos Bay *Times*, Feb. 26 and 29, 1908.

3. Interview with R. J. McCarthy, April 3, 1984; interview with Helen Stack Bower, May 8, 1975; interview with William E. Major, May 22, 1975; interview with Cliff Thorwald, April 12, 1984.

4. *American Lumberman* (Nov. 11, 1911), 76; Coos Bay *News*, Oct. 6 and Dec. 1, 1908, and June 29, 1909.

5. Coos Bay *Harbor*, Sept. 9, 1909; *News*, July 5, 1910.

6. *Times*, April 24 and Nov. 14, 1912.

7. Emil Peterson and Alfred Powers, *A Century of Coos and Curry* (Portland, Ore: Binfords and Mort, 1952), 430.

8. Interview with Florence Berg, March 14, 1984; Henry E. Haefner, "Reminiscences of an Early Forester," *Oregon Historical Quarterly*, 76 (1975), 60.

9. Haefner, "Reminiscences of an Early Forester," 60–61.

10. Ibid., 61; Florence Berg, March 14, 1984.

11. Victor Stevens, *The Powers Story* (North Bend, Ore.: Wegford Publications, 1979), 14: interview with Frank Younker, May, 1975; interview with Henry A. "Bud" Metcalf, May 1, 1975.

12. *News*, Nov. 10, 1908, and Jan 12, 1909.

13. Ibid., Jan. 12, 19, and 26, 1909.

14. Ibid., Dec. 26, 1911.

15. Stevens, *The Powers Story*, 16–17; *Times*, Feb. 20, 1913.

16. *Times*, Feb. 20, 1913; Stevens, *The Powers Story*, 19–20; Peterson and Powers, *A Century of Coos and Curry*, 128.

17. Interview with Clare Lehmonosky, May 13, 1975.

18. Haefner, "Reminiscences of an Early Forester," 61–62.

19. *Times*, July 15, 1912; *Harbor*, July 25, 1912.

20. *Harbor*, Oct. 24, 1912.

21. Nathan Douthit, *Coos Bay Region, 1890–1944* (Coos Bay: River West Books, 1981), 101; *Harbor*, Feb. 20, 1913; Florence Berg, March 14, 1984.

22. George Case, "The History of the Port of Coos Bay" (M.A. thesis, Pan American

University, 1983), 52; *News*, Aug. 27, 1907, Dec. 15, 1908, and March 7, 1911; *Harbor*, Nov. 1, 1909.

23. Case, "History of the Port of Coos Bay," 52–55; *Harbor*, Oct. 20, 1910, and Jan 2, 1913; *Times*, Sept. 9 and Oct. 20, 1912; and Portland *Oregonian*, March 8 and 27, 1912.

24. *American Lumberman* (Nov. 11, 1911), 43–142; *Oregonian*, April 14, 1911.

25. *West Coast Lumberman*, 25 (December 1913), 30, 42; *Timberman*, 16 (February 1915), 36–37; *Timberman*, (March 1916), 14.

26. R. N. Bryon, "Community Stability and Forest Policy in British Columbia," *Canadian Journal of Forest Research*, 8 (1978), 63.

27. Florence Berg, March 14, 1984; Stevens, *The Powers Story*, 110–113; Peterson and Powers, *A Century of Coos and Curry*, 431–432.

28. *Times*, Nov. 4, 1913.

29. Ibid., Aug. 9, 1916.

30. Ibid., Aug. 10, 1916.

31. Ibid., Aug. 19, 1916; Douthit, *Coos Bay Region*, 137–138; *Timberman*, 59 (April 1922), 56.

32. Case, "History of the Port of Coos Bay," 62; *Harbor*, April 30, 1909.

33. Vernon Jensen, *Lumber and Labor* (New York: Farrar and Rinehart, 1945), 125–129; Charlotte Todes, *Labor and Lumber* (New York: International Publishers, 1931), 163–166.

34. Jensen, *Lumber and Labor*, 129–137; Melvyn Dubofsky, *We Shall Be All: A History of the Industrial Workers of the World* (Chicago: Quadrangle, 1969), 413–414; interview with Al E. Martin, May 28, 1975; Stevens, *The Powers Story*, 94.

35. Douthit, *Coos Bay Region*, 134–135; *Harbor*, Dec. 28, 1917, and March 1, 1918.

36. Case, "History of the Port of Coos Bay," 63; Douthit, *Coos Bay Region*, 135–137.

37. Interview with Mary Banks Granger, May 6, 1975; interview with Jack McNab, March 25, 1975; Douthit, *Coos Bay Region*, 14–15.

38. Douthit, *Coos Bay Region*, 137; interview with Mary Banks Granger, May 6, 1975; interview with Jack McNab, March 25, 1975.

39. *Timberman*, 59 (April 1922), 48.

Chapter 4. Logging the Coos Timber

1. Interview with Dow Beckham, March 28, 1984.

2. Barre Toelken, *The Dynamics of Folklore* (Boston: Houghton Mifflin, 1979), 71.

3. Vernon Jensen, *Lumber and Labor* (New York: Farrar and Rinehart, 1945), 3.

4. Ibid., 106; Charlotte Todes, *Labor and Lumber* (New York: International Publishers, 1931), 75.

5. Interview with Orvin C. Stanwood, 1978; interview with George Wittick, Oct. 26, 1976; Stewart Holbrook, *Holy Old Mackinaw* (New York: Macmillan, 1938), 170–173.

6. Interview with Roy Rozell, April 17, 1975; interview with Henry A. "Bud" Metcalf, May 1, 1975.

7. Henry A. "Bud" Metcalf, May 1, 1975.

8. Ibid.

9. Interview with Louis David Root, May 30, 1975.

10. Dow Beckham, March 28, 1984

11. Inteview with Curt Beckham, March 20, 1984.

12. Interview with R. J. McCarthy, April 3, 1984; Dow Beckham, March 28, 1984; Victor Stevens, *The Powers Story* (North Bend, Ore: Wegford Publications, 1979), 69.

13. Dow Beckham, March 28, 1984; Curt Beckham, March 20, 1984. An account of

injury and death in the woods is Andrew Prouty, *More Deadly Than War! Pacific Coast Logging, 1827–1981* (New York: Garland Press, 1986).

14. Dow Beckham, March 28, 1984.

15. Curt Beckham, March 20, 1984.

16. Myrtle Bergren, *Tough Timber: The Loggers of B.C.—Their Story* (Toronto: Progress Books, 1967), 25.

17. Quoted in Todes, *Labor and Lumber,* 70–71.

18. Dow Beckham, March 28, 1984.

19. Interview with Florence Berg, March 14, 1984; Henry E. Haefner, "Reminiscences of an Early Forester," *Oregon Historical Quarterly,* 76 (1975), 65; interview with Clare Lehmonosky, May 13, 1975.

20. Interview with Theolo W. Steckel, June 5, 1975; Curt Beckham, March 20, 1984; Curt Beckham, *Gyppo Logging Days* (Myrtle Point, Ore: Hillside Book Company, 1978), George Wittick, Oct. 26, 1976.

21. Rexford G. Tugwell, "The Casual In The Woods," *Survey,* 43 (July 3, 1920), 473.

22. Theolo W. Steckel, June 5, 1975.

23. Haefner, "Reminiscences of An Early Forester," 65; interview with Bill McKenna, April 11, 1984.

24. Bill McKenna, April 11, 1984; interview with Garnett Johnson, March 7, 1984.

25. Bill McKenna, April 11, 1984.

26. Stevens, *The Powers Story,* 57; Haefner, "Reminiscences of An Early Forester," 65; Garnett Johnson, March 7, 1984; Dow Beckham, March 28, 1984.

27. R. J. McCarthy, April 3, 1984.

28. Curt Beckham, March 20, 1984.

29. Interview with Ivan Laird, May 21, 1975.

30. Interview with William E. Major, May 22, 1975.

31. Dow Beckham, March 28, 1984.

32. Interview with Charles McGeorge, Nov., 1972.

33. R. J. McCarthy, April 3, 1984; Dow Beckham, March 28, 1984.

34. Interview with Richard J. Anderson, May 20, 1975; interview with Bill Brainard, March 13, 1984.

35. Interview with Helen Stack Bower, May 8, 1975; interview with Raymond McKeown, Nov., 1972.

36. Florence Berg, March 14, 1984; interview with Raymond McKeown, Nov., 1972; interview with Jack McNab, March 25, 1975.

Chapter 5. Getting By

1. Interview with Eleanor Anderson, March 29, 1984.

2. *Timberman,* 23 (April 1922), 56–57.

3. Ibid., 59.

4. George Case, "A History of the Port of Coos Bay" (M.A. thesis, Pan American University, 1983), 82–83.

5. Nathan Douthit, *Coos Bay Region, 1890–1944* (Coos Bay: River West Books, 1981), 143; George A. Ulett, "Chips and Sawdust From the Ulett Log," 1972, manuscript in the Southwestern Oregon Community College Library, Coos Bay, Oregon (hereafter SWOCC Library).

6. Eleanor Anderson, March 29, 1984.

7. Coos Bay *Times,* Dec. 15, 1921.

8. Jean S. Monsebroten, "The Swedish-Finn Settlement in Coos Bay," in "History of Southwestern Oregon: Research Papers," compiled by Nathan Douthit, 1974, SWOCC Library.

9. Eleanor Anderson, March 29, 1984.

10. Interview with Cliff Thorwald, April 12, 1984.

11. Monsebroten, "Swedish-Finn Settlement in Coos Bay;" Coos Bay *News*, Sept. 4 and Nov. 20, 1900.

12. Monsebroten, "Swedish-Finn Settlement in Coos Bay."

13. Interview with Roy Rozell, April 10, 1975; Larry Rymon, "A Critical Analysis of Wildlife Conservation in Oregon" (Ph.D. dissertation, Oregon State University, Corvallis, 1969), 117; interview with Rose Younker Liberti, April 10, 1975.

14. Interview with Frank Younker, April 29, 1975; interview with Henry A. "Bud" Metcalf, May 1, 1975; interview with Raymond McKeown, Nov. 1972.

15. Interview with Ruth Marie Wolf, May 1, 1975; Frank Younker, April 29, 1975.

16. Ruth Marie Wolf, May 1, 1975.

17. Douthit, *Coos Bay Region*, 143; interview with Marguerette Therrien Boyd, April 23, 1975.

18. Cliff Thorwald, April 12, 1984.

19. Marguerette Therrien Boyd, April 23, 1975.

20. Interview with Dow Beckham, March 20, 1984.

21. Interview with Curt Beckham, March 28, 1984.

22. Interview with Clare Lehmonosky, May 13, 1975.

23. Interview with Garnett Johnson, March 7, 1984.

24. Interview with Valerie and Forrest Taylor, March 27, 1984.

25. Ibid.

26. Interview with Pete Kromminga, April 13, 1984.

27. Interview with Cal Thompson, June 4, 1975.

28. Interview with Lorance Eickworth, April 25, 1975.

29. Interview with Paula Laurilla, April 12, 1984.

30. Interview with Bill McKenna, April 11, 1984.

31. *Lumber World Review*, 48 (Feb. 10, 1925), 31; Robert E. Ficken, *Lumber and Politics; The Career of Mark Reed* (Seattle: University of Washington Press, 1979), 128–132; F. I. Moravets, *Production of Lumber in Oregon and Washington, 1869–1948*, U.S. Forest Service, Forest Survey Report No. 100, Pacific Northwest Forest and Range Experiment Station (Portland, Ore.: 1949), 3–4.

32. *Timberman*, 30 (July 1929), 20; Case, "History of the Port of Coos Bay," 92.

33. Moravets, *Production of Lumber in Oregon and Washington*, 20; F. I. Moravets, *Forest Statistics for Southwest Oregon Unit*, U.S. Department of Agriculture, Forest Service Report No. 104, Pacific Northwest Forest and Range Experiment Station (Portland, Ore.: 1951), 20.

34. U.S. Department of the Interior, Bonneville Power Administration, *The Economic Base for Power Markets in Coos County, Oregon*, by Frederick Arpke and Carol Colver (Eugene, Ore.: 1943), 9–11.

35. *Times*, Jan. 30 and Nov. 26, 1930.

36. Marguerette Therrien Boyd, April 23, 1975; interview with Bill Brainard, March 13, 1984.

Chapter 6. Surviving the Great Depression

1. Interview with Bill McKenna, April 11, 1984.

2. U.S. Forest Service, *Lumber Production, 1869–1934* (Washington, D.C.: Govern-

ment Printing Office, 1936), 74; John B. Woods, "The Forestry Situation in the U.S. Today and a Simple Workable Remedy," *Journal of Forestry,* 28 (November 1930), 930.

3. William G. Robbins, *Lumberjacks and Legislators: Political Economy of the U.S. Lumber Industry, 1890–1941* (College Station, Texas: Texas A & M University, 1982), 78, 134.

4. Coos Bay *Times,* Jan. 2, 1931.

5. Ibid., Jan. 24, Feb. 2, April 10, July 17, Sept. 14, and Oct. 31, 1931.

6. Ibid., Dec. 10, 1930, Jan. 3, 1931, and Jan. 15, 1932.

7. Ibid., June 2, June 13 and 15, and Aug. 22, 1931.

8. Ibid., Jan. 21, March 23, March 31, April 11, July 30, Aug. 1, Dec. 31, 1932; Jan. 3, Nov. 7, Dec. 1, 4, and 21, 1933.

9. Ibid., September 7 and 19, Oct. 18, and Nov. 7, 1933; May 2 and July 3, 1934; and Robbins, *Lumberjacks and Legislators,* 192.

10. Bill MeKenna, April 11, 1984.

11. *Times,* April 22 and July 13, 1936; Dec. 30, 1937; interview with Victor West, March 15, 1984.

12. Interview with Curt Beckham, March 20, 1984; Curt Beckham, *Gyppo Logging Days* (Myrtle Point, Ore.: Hillside Book Company, 1978), 10.

13. *Times,* Jan. 25 and March 7, 1932; Robbins, *Lumberjacks and Legislators,* 138.

14. *Times,* March 23, April 2, June 13, Sept. 19 and 20, Oct. 23, 1934; Feb. 25 and March 30, 1935; and Dec. 30, 1937.

15. Ibid., June 10, Oct. 11, and Dec. 24, 1931; June 19 and Aug. 22, 1932; and Dec. 23, 1934.

16. Ibid., Feb. 4, March 30, June 6, and July 2, 1932.

17. Ibid., Sept. 20, 1932.

18. Ibid., Aug. 16, 1932.

19. Ibid., May 9, 12, 13 and 15, 1933; for the best general account of the CCC see John R. Salmond, *The Civilian Conservation Corps, 1933–1942: A New Deal Case Study* (Durham, North Carolina: Duke University Press, 1967); Curt Beckham, March 20, 1984.

20. *Times,* March 31, 1938.

21. Ibid., Nov. 27, 1933; and Feb. 14, 1934.

22. Nathan Douthit, *Coos Bay Region, 1890–1944* (Coos Bay: River West Books, 1981), 160–161; *Times,* July 13 and 27, Aug. 30, 1934; and June 1, 1936.

23. Interview with Cliff Thorwald, April 12, 1984; interview with Valerie and Forrest Taylor, March 27, 1984.

24. *Times,* November 23, 1935; and May 8, 1936.

25. Valerie and Forrest Taylor, March 27, 1984; *Times,* Dec. 15, 1939.

26. *Times,* Dec. 2, 1938; June 7, 1939; and Jan. 5, 1940.

27. Jeremy Brecher and Tim Costello, *Common Sense for Hard Times* (Boston: South End Press, 1976), 115.

28. Interview with Eleanor Anderson, March 29, 1984.

29. Interview with Dow Beckham, March 28, 1984.

30. Ibid.

31. Ibid.; Curt Beckham, March 20, 1984.

32. Interview with Harold Walton, April 4, 1984; interview with Garnett Johnson, March 7, 1984.

33. Interview with Quentin Church, April 3, 1984; Dow Beckham, March 28, 1984.

34. Interview with Charles Reigard, March 8, 1984.

35. Bill McKenna, April 11, 1984.

36. Interview with Victor West, March 15, 1984; interview with Everett Richardson, April 3, 1981.

37. Interview with Marguerette Therrien Boyd, April 23, 1975; interview with Bill Brainard, March 13, 1984.

38. Interview with Cliff Thorwald, April 12, 1984.

39. Valerie and Forrest Taylor, March 27, 1984.

40. Interview with Jack Randleman and Harold Morris, 1980; interview with Richard Anderson, May 20, 1975.

41. Interview with Beth Wood, Feb. 14, 1984.

42. Interview with Valerie Taylor and Don Brown, Nov. 1, 1980.

43. *Times*, Jan. 4, June 1, Oct. 30, 1936; Feb. 4 and 23, 1937; University of Oregon, Bureau of Research and Municipal Service, *Coos County: Population Trends, Economic Growth* (Eugene, 1963), 27; George Case, "A History of the Port of Coos Bay" (M.A. thesis, Pan American University, 1983), 107.

44. Interview with George Vaughan, 1972.

45. *Times*, Dec. 28, 1938; interview with Wylie Smith, April 16, 1984.

46. *Times*, Dec. 30, 1939; interview with Wylie Smith, April 16, 1984. The pulp mill opened in 1939 after Germany had cut off Scandinavian pulp shipments to the United States.

47. Interview with Dorotha Richardson, March 26, 1984.

Chapter 7. The Second World War

1. Interview with Everett Richardson, April 3, 1981.

2. University of Oregon, Bureau of Research and Municipal Service, *Population of Oregon Cities, Counties, and Metropolitan Areas, 1850–1957: A Compilation of Census Counts and Estimates in Oregon*, Information Bull. No. 106 (Eugene, 1958), 18; University of Oregon, Bureau of Research and Municipal Service, *1950–1980 Population and Housing Trends, Cities and Counties of Oregon* (Eugene, 1982), 26.

3. *Times*, Sept. 3, 1937; interview with Wylie Smith, April 16, 1984.

4. Wylie Smith, April 16, 1984; *Times*, Jan. 10, 1940.

5. *Times*, March 15, 19, and 25, 1941.

6. Ibid., March 8, 1941.

7. Ibid., March 18, 1941, and April 29, 1942.

8. Ibid., May 26, June 24 and 25, 1941.

9. Ibid., July 17, Aug. 23, Oct. 29; and Dec. 19, 1941; Jan. 13, 1942; interview with Valerie and Forrest Taylor, March 27, 1984.

10. George Case, "A History of the Port of Coos Bay" (M.A. thesis, Pan American University, 1983), 96–97, 107; interview with Beth Wood, Feb. 14, 1984.

11. *Times.*, Feb. 12, March 15, and June 29, 1942; Vernon Jensen, *Lumber and Labor* (New York: Farrar and Rinehart, 1945), 276.

12. *Times*, July 10 and Aug. 18, 1942; Jensen, *Lumber and Labor*, 277.

13. Jensen, *Lumber and Labor*, 278; *Times*, Sept. 11 and 19, 1942.

14. *Times*, Aug. 22 and Nov. 24, 1942, and March 19, 1943.

15. Interview with Garnett Johnson, March 7, 1984; interview with Dow Beckham, March 28, 1984.

16. Interview with Pete Kromminga, April 13, 1984.

17. Dow Beckham, March 28, 1984.

18. Pete Kromminga, April 13, 1984.

19. Ibid.; *Times*, Feb. 12, 1942.

20. *Times*, April 29 and June 4, 1943.

21. Wylie Smith, April 16, 1984.

22. Interview with Cliff Thorwald, April 12, 1984; interview with Lorance Eickworth, April 25, 1975; *Times*, June 12, 1945.

23. Interview with Garnett Johnson, March 7, 1984; interview with Dorotha Richardson, March 26, 1984; Valerie and Forrest Taylor, March 27, 1984.

24. Dorotha Richardson, March 26, 1984.

25. Wylie Smith, April 16, 1984.

26. *Times*, March 9, 1942.

27. Ibid., Jan. 28, 1944.

28. Dow Beckham, March 28, 1984; interview with Victor West, March 15, 1984.

29. Dow Beckham, March 28, 1984.

30. Interview with James Whitty, 1972; interview with Bill McKenna, April 11, 1984; interview with Eugene Wechter, April 16, 1984.

31. *Times*, Feb. 13, 1943.

32. Ibid., Aug. 23, 1945.

33. Bill McKenna, April 11, 1984.

Chapter 8. Lumber Capital of the World

1. University of Oregon, Bureau of Research and Municipal Service, *Population of Oregon Cities, Counties and Metropolitan Areas, 1850–1957: A Compilation of Census Counts and Estimates in Oregon*, Information Bulletin No. 106 (Eugene, 1958), 19; University of Oregon, Bureau of Research and Municipal Service, 1950–1980 *Population and Housing Trends, Cities and Counties of Oregon* (Eugene, 1982), 26.

2. Interview with Bill McKenna, April 11, 1984.

3. Portland *Oregonian*, June 8, 1947; interview with Bill Brainard, March 13, 1984.

4. Bill McKenna, April 11, 1984; Bill Brainard, March 13, 1984.

5. Interview with Ross Youngblood, April 27, 1984.

6. Interview with Jerry Phillips, April 6, 1984; Bill McKenna, April 11, 1984; interview with R. J. McCarthy, April 3, 1984.

7. Ross Youngblood, April 27, 1984; Bill McKenna, April 11, 1984; interview with Wylie Smith, April 16, 1984.

8. *Times*, Oct. 11, 1948; March 25 and June 13, 1950; March 22, 1952; Jan. 15 and Aug. 12, 1953; Feb. 10 and 12, 1954; July 8, 1955; Jan. 14 and Aug. 13, 1957; March 28 and April 12, 1958; and April 15, 1959.

9. Ibid., Oct. 11, 1948, and March 30, 1984.

10. *Oregonian*, July 20, 1946.

11. Interview with Lionel Youst, April 13, 1984.

12. Jerry Phillips, April 6, 1984.

13. Bill McKenna, April 11, 1984; interview with Quentin Church, April 3, 1984.

14. Interview with Charles Reigard, March 8, 1984.

15. Interview with George Vaughan, 1972.

16. William G. Robbins, *Lumberjacks and Legislators: Political Economy of the U. S. Lumber Industry, 1890–1941* (College Station, Texas: Texas A & M University, 1982), 121–126.

17. Interview with Wylie Smith, April 16, 1984; interview with David Mickelson, April 12, 1984.

18. R. J. McCarthy, April 3, 1984.

19. Ross Youngblood, April 27, 1984.

20. Lionel Youst, April 13, 1984.
21. Ibid.
22. Ibid.
23. Ibid.
24. Ibid.
25. Bill McKenna, April 11, 1984; interview with Dow Beckham, March 28, 1984.
26. *Times*, Feb. 10, 1944, and Jan. 21, 1952.
27. Ibid., June 8, 1950; April 14 and May 1, 1951; and Jan. 21, 1952.
28. Ibid., April 14, 1951, and Jan. 21, 1952.
29. Dennis LeMaster, *Mergers among the Largest Forest Products Firms, 1950–1970,* Washington State University, College of Agriculture Research Bulletin 854 (Pullman, 1977), 1.
30. *Oregonian*, Feb. 29, May 27, June 7, and July 11, 1956, and March 25, 1984; *Times*, May 25, June 5 and 7, 1956.
31. Wylie Smith, April 16, 1984.
32. Ibid.; Jerry Phillips, April 6, 1984; Ross Youngblood, April 27, 1984.
33. Interview with Harold Walton, April 4, 1984.
34. *Times*, June 7, 1956.
35. Interview with Cliff Thorwald, April 12, 1984.
36. Ibid; Jerry Phillips, April 6, 1984.
37. Cliff Thorwald, April 12, 1984.
38. *Times*, May 1 and 3, 1958.
39. Ibid., April 8, 1959.
40. Ibid., March 18 and 29, 1950; Jan. 24, 1952; Aug. 20 and Sept. 15, 1953; and Sept. 30, 1959.
41. Ibid., July 10 and Aug. 21, 1957.
42. Ibid., June 17 and 21, 1950; May 1, 1951; Oct. 20, 1952; and May 31, 1956.
43. John Young and Jan Newton, *Capitalism and Human Obsolescence: Corporate Control versus Individual Survival in Rural America* (Montclair, N.J.: Allanheld, Osmun, 1980), 34–36.
44. Interview with Dorotha Richardson, March 26, 1984.
45. *Oregonian*, Jan. 17, 1959.

Chapter 9. Timber Forever

1. Portland *Oregonian*, Aug. 18, 1934.
2. Interview with Frank Younker, April 29, 1975.
3. Interview with Dow Beckham, March 28, 1984; interview with Jack Johnson, March 26, 1984.
4. Interview with Frank J. Fish, May 13, 1975; interview with Stephen J. Spoerl, June 4, 1975.
5. Dow Beckham, March 28, 1984; interview with Curt Beckham, March 20, 1984.
6. Kenneth Erickson, "The Morphology of Lumber Settlements in Western Oregon and Washington" (Ph.D. dissertation, University of California, Berkeley, 1965), 223–228.
7. Richard White, *Land Use, Environment, and Social Change: The Shaping of Island County, Washington* (Seattle: University of Washington, 1980), 131–141.
8. *American Lumberman* (Nov. 11, 1911), 142.
9. Oregon, *Report of the State Forester* (1912), 19–21, and (1919), 33.

10. William B. Greeley, "Washington and Her Forest Industries," undated manuscript, box 16, William B. Greeley Papers, University of Oregon Library, Eugene; Henry Graves, "Federal and State Responsibilities in Forestry," *American Forests*, 31 (November 1925), 677.

11. Thornton Munger, *Timber Growing Practices in the Douglas Fir Region*, U.S. Department of Agriculture Bulletin No.1493 (June 1927), 14; U.S. Forest Service, *Annual Report* (1929), 2, 6; Robert Y. Stuart to Paul Reddington, June 28, 1932, in box 71, National Forest Products Association Records (hereafter NFPA Records), Forest History Society Manuscripts Collection, Durham, North Carolina.

12. Brian Wall, *Log Production in Washington and Oregon, An Historical Perspective*, U.S. Forest Service, Pacific Northwest Forest and Range Experiment Station, Portland, Ore., 1972, Resource Bulletin PNW-42, 5–6.

13. Andrews is quoted in Ibid., 6.

14. I. J. Mason, "Grays Harbor Study," April 4, 1935, in S Plans, Timber Management, Olympic, 1927–1935, Box 54139, Seattle Federal Records Center, Seattle, Washington.

15. Washington State Planning Council, *The Elma Survey* (Olympia, 1941), 1, 35–39.

16. Coos Bay *Times*, Jan. 14, 1931, and Nov. 7, 1933.

17. Ibid., March 5, 1931, and Aug. 18, 1934.

18. Ibid., Dec. 20, 1934.

19. Ibid., Nov. 22, 1935, and July 21, 1936.

20. E. I. Kotok, "Some Economic Problems in Pacific Coast Forestry," *Proceedings of the Seventeenth Annual Conference of the Pacific Coast Economic Association*, 17 (December 1938), 90; U.S. Forest Service, *Annual Report* (1940), 3.

21. Oregon State Planning Board, *Oregon's Forest Problems* (Portland, 1936), 1–2, 4.

22. *Times*, Aug. 12, 1936.

23. Northwest Regional Council, *Forest Depletion in Outline* (Portland, 1940), iii–iv.

24. G. H. Collingwood to Earle Clapp, March 19, and Clapp to Collingwood, Feb. 11, 1942, both in box 54, NFPA Records.

25. U.S. Forest Service, *Annual Report* (1942), 4; *Times*, Jan. 13 and Feb. 1, 1945.

26. Curt Beckham, March 20, 1984.

27. Dow Beckham, March 28, 1984.

28. Interview with Pete Kromminga, April 13, 1984.

29. Interview with Bill Brainard, March 13, 1984.

30. *Times*, August 14, 1945; April 5 and 8, 1946; and April 3, 1947.

31. Ibid., Nov. 2, 1944, and May 1, 1951; *Oregonian*, Dec. 15, 1946.

32. *Times*, July 25, 1949, and March 31, 1956.

33. Ibid., March 31, 1956.

34. Ibid., April 3 and 30, 1956.

35. Interview with Ross Youngblood, April 27, 1984.

36. Interview with Harold Walton, April 4, 1984.

37. Interview with Cliff Thorwald, April 12, 1984; interview with Jerry Lantto, March 15, 1984.

38. *Oregonian*, Aug. 29, 1958.

39. Interview with Jerry Phillips, April 6, 1984.

40. Wall, *Log Production in Washington and Oregon*, 7–8, 29.

41. Alan H. Muir and Richard A. Searle, *A Study of Industrial Development Possibilities for the Coos Bay Port District* (Menlo Park, Calif.: Stanford Research Institute, 1956), 17–20; Stanton's editorial is cited in the *Times*, Aug. 27, 1955.

42. Oregon Coastal Economic Development Commission, *Economic Survey and Analysis of the Oregon Coastal Zone* (Salem, Ore.: 1974), E5, E11; *Oregonian*, Jan. 17, 1959.

43. Jerry Phillips, April 6, 1984.

44. William Greeley to Roderic Olzendam, May 7, 1946, box 7, Greeley Papers.

45. Jerry Phillips, April 6, 1984.

46. John K. Beuter, K. Norman Johnson, and H. Lynn Scheurmann, *Timber for Oregon's Tomorrow*, Forest Research Laboratory, Oregon State University, Research Bulletin 19 (Corvallis, 1976), 1, 18, 43; Russell Sadler, "John Beuter Reckons With Timber," *Willamette Week*, Dec. 26, 1977.

47. *Oregonian*, Nov. 29, 1981.

Chapter 10. Bosses and Workers

1. Interview with Valerie Taylor and Don Brown, Nov. 1, 1980.

2. Coos Bay *News*, Feb. 8, 1888.

3. Quoted in Nathan Douthit, *Coos Bay Region, 1890–1944* (Coos Bay: River West Books, 1981), 107–8.

4. Coos Bay *Times*, July 4 and 17, 1906.

5. Coos Bay *Harbor*, April 23, 1909.

6. Betty V. H. Schneider and Abraham Siegel, *Industrial Relations in the Pacific Coast Longshore Industry* (Berkeley: Institute of Industrial Relations, University of California, 1956), 5–10.

7. *Harbor*, Jan. 27, 1906, and September 28, 1911; *Times*, Oct. 3 and 10, and Nov. 6, 1911.

8. *Times*, April 6, 1912.

9. Ibid., Jan. 8 and May 10, 1913.

10. Ibid., May 12, 13, and 19, 1913.

11. Ibid., June 25, 1913.

12. *Harbor*, June 25, July 17, and Aug. 14, 1913; *Times*, Sept. 3 and Oct. 9, 1913; Douthit, *Coos Bay Region*, 121.

13. Interview with Eleanor Anderson, March 29, 1984.

14. Valerie Taylor and Don Brown, Nov. 1, 1980.

15. Interview with Lewis Barnekoff, Nov. 8, 1980; interview with Alvin Monk, April 4, 1975.

16. Interview with Cliff Thorwald, April 12, 1984; Schneider and Siegel, *Industrial Relations in the Pacific Coast Longshore Industry*, 10.

17. Schneider and Siegel, *Industrial Relations in the Pacific Coast Longshore Industry*, 9–11.

18. Cliff Thorwald, April 12, 1984.

19. *Times*, June 18, July 20 and 24, 1934.

20. Ibid., July 26, 1934; Valerie Taylor and Don Brown, Nov. 1, 1980.

21. Schneider and Siegel, *Industrial Relations in the Pacific Coast Longshore Industry*, 12–15.

22. Alvin Monk, April 4, 1975; Lewis Barnekoff, Nov. 8, 1980.

23. *Times*, July 30, 1934.

24. Ibid., May 6, 13, 29, and 30, and June 20, 1935.

25. Ibid., May 6 and 29, 1935.

26. Ibid., Sept. 4, 5 and 13, 1935; June 23, July 28 and Aug. 15, 1936.

27. Ibid., Oct. 30, 1936, and Feb. 12, 1937; Leaf is quoted in Douthit, *Coos Bay Region*, 153.

28. Interview with Valerie and Forrest Taylor, March 27, 1984; Valerie Taylor and Don Brown, Nov. 1, 1980.

29. Ibid.; *Times*, May 7, 10, and 26, and Sept. 8, 1937; March 11, 18, and 19, 1940.

30. *Times*, June 25, 1938.

31. Ibid., Feb. 6 and 16, 1942; interview with Pete Kromminga, April 13, 1984.

32. *Times*, July 13, 14, and 16, 1934.

33. Pete Kromminga, April 13, 1984.

34. *Times*, Feb. 26, 1946.

35. Myrtle Bergren, *Tough Timber: The Loggers of B.C.—Their Story* (Toronto: Progress Books, 1967), 9; *Times*, April 23, 1946.

36. *Times*, April 23, May 1, 6, and 25, 1946.

37. Interview with Dorotha Richardson, March 26, 1984.

38. *Times*, July 5, 9, 10, 11, and 26, 1946, and Aug. 28, 1948.

39. Ibid., August 28 and 31, 1948.

40. Ibid., Sept. 3, 4, 13, 15, 21, 23, and 24, 1948.

41. Portland *Oregonian*, Sept. 12, 1948; *Times*, Sept. 21 and 30, 1948; Alvin Monk, April 4, 1975.

42. *Times*, Nov. 8, 12, and 29, Dec. 6 and 8, 1948; and April 22, 1949.

43. Dorotha Richardson, March 26, 1984.

44. Interview with Everett Richardson, April 3, 1981; Valerie and Forrest Taylor, March 27, 1984.

45. Valerie and Forrest Taylor, March 27, 1984; interview with Ken Lewis, March 29, 1984.

Chapter 11. Hard Times and Survivors

1. Interview with Jeff Manley, April 12, 1984.

2. Ibid.

3. John Dargavel, "In the Woods," *Australian Society*, (April 1, 1984), 16–19; Jamie Swift, *Cut and Run: The Assault on Canada's Forests* (Toronto: Between The Lines, 1983), 190–230; Con Schallau, "Departures from What? How National Forest Harvesting Policy Has Been Fashioned to Achieve Community Stability," *Western Wildlands* (Winter 1983), 9, 12.

4. State of Oregon, Employment Division, *Economic Survey Analysis*, prepared by John Anderson (Medford, Ore., December 1983), 7.

5. State of Oregon, Employment Division, *Reversion of Occupational Employment Trends in the Governor's Administrative Planning District 7, 1977–1985*, prepared by Research and Statistics Section, 7.

6. Interview with Cal Thompson, June 4, 1975.

7. Interview with Shannon Chamness, April 18, 1984.

8. Interview with Dorotha Richardson, March 26, 1984.

9. Interview with Paul Rudy, April 17, 1984.

10. Ibid.

11. Interview with Don Baldwin, March 12, 1984.

12. Ibid.; interview with Chris Short, April 2, 1984.

13. Interview with Chris Short, April 2, 1984.

14. Coos Bay *World*, July 31, 1979; Portland *Oregonian*, Jan. 26, 1981; Coos County Planning Commission, *A Comparison of Sites for Industrial Development in the Coos Bay Area* (Coos Bay, 1966), 7; Oregon, Department of Economic Development, *Coos Bay: An Oregon Community Profile* (Portland 1977), n.p.

15. Interview with Harold Walton, April 4, 1984; interview with Jerry Lantto, March 15, 1984.

16. *World,* July 31, 1979; Shannon Chamness, April 18, 1984.

17. Shannon Chamness, April 18, 1984.

18. Ibid.

19. Ibid.; Jerry Lantto, March 15, 1984.

20. Eugene *Register-Guard,* Nov. 29, 1981; Corvallis *Gazette-Times,* April 11, 1985.

21. Jeff Manley, April 12, 1984.

22. Ibid.

23. Ibid.

24. Ken Doctor, "Orphans of Recovery," *Oregon Magazine,* 13 (April 1983), 30; interview with David Mickelson, April 12, 1984.

25. David Mickelson, April 12, 1984; Doctor, "Orphans of Recovery," 30.

26. David Mickelson, April 12, 1984.

27. Interview with Eugene Wechter, April 16, 1984.

28. Ibid.

29. Harold Walton, April 4, 1984.

30. Ibid.

31. *Economic Survey Analysis,* 15; interview with Jim Mills, March 19, 1984.

32. Harold Walton, April 4, 1984; Jim Mills, March 19, 1984.

33. Jerry Lantto, March 15, 1984; Jim Mills, March 19, 1984.

34. Don Baldwin, March 12, 1984.

35. Ibid.

36. Ibid.; Jerry Lantto, March 15, 1984; interview with David Willis, March 13, 1984.

37. Don Baldwin, March 12, 1984.

38. Ibid.

39. Interview with Pat Choate Pierce and Carrol Cone, April 27, 1984.

Post Mortem: Reflections on the Present Condition

1. The following sources have informed my argument on this point: Immanuel Wallerstein, *The Capitalist World Economy* (London: Cambridge University Press, 1979); Patricia Marchak, *Green Gold: The Forest Industry in British Columbia* (Vancouver: University of British Columbia, 1983); Jamie Swift, *Cut and Run: The Assault on Canada's Forests* (Toronto: Between The Lines, 1983); John B. Dargavel, "The Development of the Tasmanian Wood Industries: A Radical Analysis" (Ph.D. thesis, Australian National University, 1982); John B. Dargavel, "Radical Analysis of Forest History: A Tasmanian Case," paper presented to International Union of Forest Research Organizations, Portland, Ore., Oct. 18–19, 1983; Thomas R. Cox, "The Social, Economic, and Environmental Impact of the North American-Japanese Lumber Trade—A Preliminary Assessment," manuscript, copy in possession of the author.

2. Seattle *Post-Intelligencer,* April 8, 1984.

3. Portland *Oregonian,* Jan. 30, 1985; Corvallis *Gazette-Times,* Jan. 30, 1985.

4. *Gazette-Times,* Jan. 30, 1985.

5. *Oregonian,* Feb. 20, 1985; *Gazette-Times,* April 11, 1985.

6. *Oregonian,* April 4, 1985.

7. Interview with Charles Reigard, March 8, 1984.

8. Interview with R. J. McCarthy, April 3, 1984.

9. Interview with Dow Beckham, March 28, 1984.

10. Interview with Bill McKenna, April 11, 1984.

11. Interview with Paula Laurilla, April 12, 1984.

Index

Aasen, John, 83
Absentee ownership and management: reaction to, 9
Adelsperger, A. D., 33
Agrarianism: and timber harvesting, 124
Agricultural towns: as anachronisms, 167
Alcoholism: increase in, 161–63
Allen, E. T., 48
Al Peirce Lumber Company, 162
American Association for the Advancement of Science: addressed by Franklin B. Hough, 21
American Federation of Labor (AFL): and south coast organizing, 146
Amsden, Forest W., 119
Anderson, Axel: arrives in Coos Bay, 33; mentioned, 70
Anderson, Eleanor: on Swedish influence, 33; on life in Coos Bay, 70; on marriage, 70; on Finnish societies, 71; on Great Depression, 88; on jobs for Finnish and Swedish women, 142; mentioned, 38
Anderson, Richard, 65
Andrews, H. J.: as chief of Forest Service Region 6, 126
Army Corps of Engineers: dredges Coos Bay bar, 116
Associated Industries of Southwestern Oregon: opposes unions, 148

Baker-Fentress Company, 83
Baldwin, Don: and state employment division, 156–57; on job placement, 164; on older workers, 164
Ball, John, 169
Banks, Robert, 52
Barnekoff, Lewis: on 1934 strike, 145; mentioned, 143
Barter: during Great Depression, 89–90
Beckham, Curt: on logging camp, 58; early life of, 75; on Great Depression, 89; on timber supply, 123; mentioned, 83, 130
Beckham, Dow: on loggers as skilled laborers, 57; on logging bosses, 58; on employment of women, 62; on union influence, 63; on splash dams, 64; early life of, 75; on Great Depression, 88–89;

directs Irwin-Lyons boom system, 103; on old-growth timber supply, 122, 123; on timber industry, 170; mentioned, 59, 83, 99, 100, 130
Beckham, Stephen: on coal mining, 14
Bennett, J. W.: as local editor, 18
Berg, Florence: on Albert Powers, 34; early life of, 38; on C. A. Smith Company, 49; on logging-camp food, 60; mentioned, 43
Big Mill: construction of, 33, 41; production of, 39; and number of employees, 40; destroyed, 40; and West Coast lumber industry, 48; and strike of 1917, 50; and 1920s, 68; and Great Depression, 81
Booming and rafting: dangers of, 63
Bower, Helen Stack, 40
Brainard, Bill: first recollections of, 79; on Great Depression, 91; and new technology, 131; mentioned, 108
Brainard, Henry: on childhood, 74; marriage of, 75; on Great Depression, 91; mentioned, 79
Bridges, Harry: as longshore leader, 145; mentioned, 151
British Columbia: logging camps, 59
Brown, Don: early life of, 92–93; as local longshore leader, 145; as industrial unionist, 147; mentioned, 143
Buck, C. J.: on sustained-yield management, 128
Buehner Lumber Company: purchases Simpson estate, 50; and foreign trade, 68–69
Building boom, 109; and gyppos, 110
Bull-team logging: described, 56
Bunkhouses: described, 60–63
Bureau of Land Management (BLM), 133; and marketing circles, 132–33; and harvest restrictions, 135–36

C. A. Smith Company, 31, 34, 40; and Oregon and California railroad land grant, 32; plans paper mill, 41; and timberland ownership, 31, 36; improves harbor channel, 47; and ocean-going vessels, 47; and seedling nursery,' 48; financial problems of, 48–49; sale of, 50;

Elma, Washington: study of timber depletion in, 127
Emergency Fleet Corporation, 51
Employment: job availability, 28, 35; during World War I, 52; during World War
II, 95, 98, 102; and World War II job
freeze, 100; in post–World War II era,
109; and decline in forest-products
jobs, 120; and turnover, 142; in service
sector, 154; and mill closures, 163–65
Evans Products Company, 102; and Port
Orford cedar, 69; efficiency of, 101; and
plant closure, 121, 135; and union recognition, 147
Everest, Wesley: as martyr for Industrial
Workers of the World, 141

Federal census: and timber employment,
55
Federal Emergency Relief Administration
(FERA), 86
Finnish Brotherhood, 70
Finnish societies, 70–71
Fish, Frank J.: on old-growth timber, 122
Fishing industry, 120
Flanagan, Patrick: and coal mining on
Coos Bay, 14
Forester, J. W.: as Coos Bay Lumber Com-
pany manager, 118
Forest fires: for clearing land, 24
Forest products: and national economy, 3
Fourth of July, 65, 66
Frontier: and far-western timber industry,
55

Georgia-Pacific Corporation: succeeds
C. A. Smith Company, 31; and timberland ownership and "buy out," 116–
17; and timber liquidation, 117–19, 133;
and changes, 119; and concern for image, 119; cutting cycle of, 134; and mill
closures, 157–58, 159; mentioned, 10,
40
Giles, Daniel: as whip-saw operator, 13
Graham, Victor, 101
Granger, Mary Banks, 52
Graves, Henry: and timber depletion, 125
Great Depression, 76; and coal mining,
16; and lumber industry, 78; wages and
subsistence living in; 82–84, 87–90; and
western Washington, 126
Greeley, William: on World War II labor
shortage, 99; on timber dependence,
125; as forestry figure, 136
Green, William: and *Rolando* incident, 150

Gyppos, 148; operations of, 59; in post–
World War II era, 110–15

Haefner, Henry: on Al Powers, 42; as
Powers resident, 46; on logging-camp
food, 60; on employment of women, 62;
mentioned, 43, 61
Hand, Fred, 120
Hand logging, 56; and Coos watershed,
24
Harris, W. L., 87
Hazen, E. B., 48
Hemstrom, Charles, 59
Highball operations, 58–59, 63
High-lead logging, 29
Hill, James J., 16
Hitchcock, Ethan: starts timber-fraud in-
vestigation, 32; as Secretary of Interior,
32
Holden, Dave, 44
Hornish, Harrison: and timber stands,
132
Hough, Franklin B.: and forest-depletion
warnings, 20, 21; address to American
Association for the Advancement of Sci-
ence, 21

Industrial unions, 147
Industrial Workers of the World (IWW), 43,
63, 76; and strike success, 51; Coos Bay
activities of, 141–42
International Longshoremen's and Ware-
housemen's Union (ILWU), 169; forma-
tion of, 145; as CIO affiliate, 147; and
Rolando incident, 150
International Longshoremen's Associa-
tion (ILA), 144, 145; and loss of influ-
ence, 140
International Longshoremen's Union, 139
International Order of Runeberg, 70
International Paper Company: and new
mill, 161; and union concessions, 169
International Woodworkers of America
(IWA), 148, 169; as industrial union, 147;
as focus of antiunionism; 149; and loss
of membership, 159
Investment capital: importance of, 14
Irwin, Howard, 82
Irwin-Lyons Lumber Company, 99; and
increased production in World War II,
102, 104; and *Rolando* incident, 150
Jensen, Vernon, 55, 98
Job actions: as union tactic, 148
Johnson, Garnett: on childhood in log-
ging camps, 62; on early family life, 77–

194   INDEX

University of Oregon Institute of Marine
Biology, 156

Vaughn, George: on log exports, 93; on
gyppos, 112
Voluntary organizations: and Great Depression, 84

Wage Stabilization Act (1942), 101
Wall, Brian: on excessive harvests, 135
Walton, Harold "Cardy": on Georgia-Pa-
cific Corporation, 117, 134, 157; on mill
closures, 162–63; mentioned, 89
War Manpower Commission, 101; and
World War II, 98
War Production Board: on lumber pro-
duction, 103
Washington State Planning Council: Elma
study (1941), 127
Wasson, George B.: and whip-saw opera-
tion, 13
Waterfront Employers' Association: and
CIO, 150–51
Wechter, Eugene: and mill closures, 160–
62; mentioned, 104
West, Oswald: and Industrial Workers of
the World, 142
West, Victor: on Jimmy Lyons, 82, 103; on
subsistence living, 91
West Coast Lumbermen's Association
(WCLA), 81, 97; and grade-marked
lumber, 112
Weyerhaeuser, Frederick: as timberland
investor, 27
Weyerhaeuser Timber Company: and timber purchases, 27, 30; and Oregon and
California railroad land grant, 32; and
fire protection, 35; advantages of, over
gyppos, 115; expansion of, 115–16; and
increase in harvests, 134; and log exports, 135, 167; layoffs in, 159; and

union concessions, 169; and monopoly
on labor market, 169–70; mentioned, 9,
10, 44
Whistle punk: described, 62
Willis, David: on unemployment, 164
Wolfe, Ruth Marie: as moonshiner, 73
Women: and timber industry employment, 55, 74, 142, 143, 163; and logging
camps, 62; and World War II, 95, 98, 99,
102; and ethnic group employment, 142
Wood, Beth: on Great Depression, 92;
mentioned, 98
Woods, John B.: on lumber trade in Great
Depression, 80
Workers' Alliance, 86
Works Progress Administration (WPA), 86,
91
World War I: and lumber industry, 50–51
World War II, 94; and coal mining, 16; and
technological change, 66; labor shortages in, 98; and change to Coos country, 99; and lumber companies, 103;
and union benefits, 148
Wyatt (Taylor), Valerie: and home environment, 76; joins Workers' Alliance,
87; on Great Depression, 92; and World
War II, 98; as industrial union employee, 147; mentioned, 102

"Yarding bonuses," 56
Youngblood, Ross: and postwar era, 108;
on gyppos, 113; and Georgia-Pacific
Corporation timber sales, 177; and liquidation of Georgia-Pacific timber, 133;
mentioned, 109
Younker, Frank: as moonshiner, 73; on
old-growth timber, 122; mentioned, 43
Youst, George: as gyppo operator, 110–11,
113–15; and bankruptcy, 114
Youst, Lionel: on gyppo operations, 111;
on youth, 113